T0303549

Rereading Israel

The Spirit of the Matter

Bonna Devora Haberman

URIM PUBLICATIONS
Jerusalem • New York

Rereading Israel: The Spirit of the Matter
by Bonna Devora Haberman

Copyright © 2012 by Bonna Devora Haberman

Book design by Ariel Walden

Printed in Israel

First Edition

ISBN: 978-965-524-124-2

Urim Publications, P.O. Box 52287, Jerusalem 91521 Israel

Lambda Publishers Inc.
527 Empire Blvd., Brooklyn, New York 11225 U.S.A.
Tel: 718-972-5449 Fax: 718-972-6307

mh@ejudaica.com

www.UrimPublications.com

Table of Contents

Dedication

THE RESEARCH AND writing of this manuscript accompanied my own family's decision to return to Israel after an extended absence. Having been born in our Jerusalem home, Uriel, Bezalel, Amitai, and AdirChai spent many of their growing years away from this land. Together, with our daughter, Tiferet, and Shmuel, my spouse, we chose to leap back onto our Zion Cycle.

I dedicate this work to my family's bold risk-taking, to their readiness to suspend life-as-we-knew-it in order to share in the project of Israel-building, mind, spirit, and body.

1 The Zion Cycle

IN 1992, ISRAEL legislated the Basic Law dealing with human dignity and liberty. This law declares the purpose,

> [T]o establish in a basic law the values of the State of Israel as a *Jewish* and democratic state. [my emphasis][1]

From the founders of the state in the first part of the twentieth century through to recent legislators, the abiding intention of Zionism is to create one society in the world committed to the flourishing of *Jewish civilization*.[2] The Israeli Basic Law does not specify what particular Jewish content it intends. The initial Jewish character of the state was settled pragmatically by dividing jurisdiction over the affairs of society between the religious and secular camps. This schism continues to estrange increasingly stringent religious authorities from increasingly disaffected secularists, and the gamut in between. The Israeli education ministry commits to strengthening engagement with Judaism across

---

1. Passed by the Knesset on the 12th Adar Bet, 5752 (March 17, 1992) and published in *Sefer Ha-Chukkim* No. 1391 of the 20th Adar Bet, 5752 (March 25, 1992).

2. Mordecai Kaplan widened the purview of *Judaism* – it is not a religion, not an ethnicity, not a nation, but a *civilization*. Zionism marks an outstanding opportunity to reformulate Jewish civilization in the context of a full society. *Judaism as a Civilization: Toward a Reconstruction of American-Jewish Life,* (New York: The Macmillan Company, 1934).

the board,[3] yet the prevalent practices of both Judaism and Zionism are not gripping the vast majority of Jewry.[4]

Meanwhile, the tide of anti-Zionism swells among liberals, intellectuals, responsible and thoughtful people in all camps. While twenty-five states acknowledge Islam to be their official religion,[5] and mostly prohibit Israelis, and often Jews even from visiting, the United Nations General Assembly Resolution 3379 determined "that Zionism is a form of racism and racial discrimination."[6] In his response, Israeli UN ambassador Chaim Herzog pointed with pride "to the fact that it is as natural for an Arab to serve in public office in Israel as it is incongruous to think of a Jew serving in any public office in an Arab country, indeed being admitted to many of them. Is that racism? It is not! That . . . is Zionism."[7] Though the UN revoked the resolution unconditionally in 1991, among all nations, the UN uniquely condemns and deplores Israel.[8] Hostile global postures against Israel and her existence detract

---

3. In 2002, the Ministry of Education decreed that biblical studies begin in first grade in all Israeli schools, including the secular state system. "משרד החינוך: לימוד תורה — כבר מכיתה א", ynet, 16.04.02, http://www.ynet.co.il/articles/0,7340,L-1838568,00.html.

4. In April 2007, the Israeli daily *Yediot Ahronot* reported that, ". . . approximately a quarter of the Israeli population was considering emigration" and that "almost half of the country's young people were thinking of leaving the country." http://stlouis.ujcfedweb.org/page.html?ArticleID=144274. "Younger Jews are less pro-Israel than older Jews." Steven M. Cohen, "Israel in the Jewish Identity of American Jews: A Study in Dualities and Contrasts," *Shofar: An Interdisciplinary Journal of Jewish Studies 8*, No. 3 (Spring 1990): 1–15.

5. Afghanistan (Islamic state), Algeria, Bahrain, Bangladesh, Brunei, Comoros, Egypt, Indonesia (recognizes Islam as one of the six recognized religions), Iraq, Jordan, Kuwait, Libya, Malaysia, Maldives, Mauritania, Morocco, Oman, Pakistan (Islamic state), Qatar, Sahrawi Arab Democratic Republic, Saudi Arabia (Islamic kingdom), Somalia, Somaliland, Tunisia, United Arab Emirates, Yemen (Islamic state).

6. Resolution 46/86, December 16, 1991, revoked 3379.

7. Transcript retrieved Apr. 10, 2011, http://www.zionism-israel.com/hdoc/Herzog_Zionism_1975.htm.

8. US President George Bush brought the resolution to the floor with these words, "This body cannot claim to seek peace and at the same time challenge Israel's right to exist. By repealing this resolution unconditionally, the United Nations will enhance its credibility and serve the cause of peace." Address to the 46th Session of the United Nations General Assembly in New York City, retrieved Apr. 10, 2011, http://www.presidency.ucsb.edu/ws/index.php?pid=20012#axzz1J8RFXAg. UN

from a spirited and nuanced conversation. The need for an open, creative, public process to explore the Jewish character of Israel is urgent.

While war and insecurity have been cruel socializers of a young nation, with ingenuity, Israel succeeds to generate ample sustenance from a virtual desert, and to develop vibrant and open democratic institutions of government, economy, education, and culture. From the outset, Israel has been contributing in an unprecedented manner to the human community.[9] Israel innovates in such fields as agriculture, medicine, technology, engineering, communication, energy, conservation and ecology, architecture, business, defense, literature, music, the performance and plastic arts, and social organization. Israel contributes advanced rescue, relief, and development aid – where it is accepted.

During these twilight hours, precisely when Zionism is embattled, this work draws deeply from ancient and evolving Jewish sources to approach the Israel project afresh. *ReReading Israel* sets modern Jewish statecraft in the context of unique perspectives from Jewish textual tradition.

Revival

At the turn of the 19th century, Zionists proposed the revival of Hebrew as the conversational language of Israel.[10] Updating the language for daily speech established the continuity of modern Zionists with the ancient biblical Israelites and all of the generations that proceeded

---

Resolutions can be searched: http://domino.un.org/UNISPAL.NSF/Web%20Search%20Simple2!OpenForm

9. Dan Senor and Saul Singer's *Start-up Nation: The Story of Israel's Economic Miracle* (New York: Twelve, 2009) proposes to explain Israel's technological and economic creativity. *Israel Science Info: The Innovation and International Scientific Performance Magazine Document* is a quarterly popular print magazine documenting the contribution of Israeli research to civil society. The Danish Agency for Science, Technology and Innovation commends Israel as a world leader in its 2010 report, "Innovation index 2010," retrieved Apr. 7, 2011, http://www.ebst.dk/publikationer/ivaerksaettere/ivaerksaetterindeks_2010/ivaerksaetterindeks_2010/kap05.htm.

10. Though it had not been spoken since the Bar Kochba era in the second century, written Hebrew was in continuous use. In addition to liturgy, scholars wrote vast Jewish tracts, poetry, philosophy, politics, science and medicine, and contracts in Hebrew. Hebrew was a shared language of world Jewry.

from them. Hebrew weaves together the threads of the Jewish People throughout our wanderings and centuries; it draws its meaning and expression from rich texts and context.

Even as Israelis communicate in Hebrew, primary Jewish texts are the province of relatively few. When Chaim Nachman Bialik compiled the *Book of Legends* in 1920 to make rabbinic literature available to all, he anticipated dwindling fluency in the Jewish sources. Updating an ancient language for modern life, Zionism effectively lifted Hebrew from its religious, spiritual, literary, legal, and social contexts. The young Zionist narrative of modern Western nation-statehood repressed Jewish sources. With the important exception of prophetic books about the conquest and settlement of ancient Canaan, and the passages that reinforce early Zionist ideas and values, Zionism mainly ignored Jewish textual traditions.

Redacted during thousands of years prior to modern Zionism, Jewish text traditions record conversations that animated generations of Jewry throughout the world. The participants worked with the issues of Jewish society in all of its places and times, but they did not conceive such a national undertaking as modern Zionism. While this generation studies Jewish texts more than ever and in more settings, we have not changed our modes of text study sufficiently to take into account the revolutionary changes in Jewish existence that the State of Israel creates. A full-fledged Jewish society produces a new context for interpretation; Zionism continuously raises new questions, poses new challenges, and demands fresh approaches. Insofar as Israel aspires to be a Jewish state, the literatures of the Jewish People are a formidable resource. Creative engagement with sources enriches current Jewish-Israeli culture and civil discourse, and contributes toward cultivating emotions, values, practices, and purposes of Zionisms – *Zionisms* as a fruitful plurality. *ReReading Israel* turns to an intriguing selection of texts with Israel in mind, interpreting their relevance to inspire the current moment.

Attaining the Unattainable

I pleaded with the Lord at that time, saying, "O Lord God, You who let Your servant see the first works of Your greatness and Your mighty hand, You whose powerful deeds no god in heaven or on earth can equal! Let me, I pray, cross over and see the good land on the other side of the Jordan, that good hill country, and the Lebanon." But the Lord was wrathful with me on your account and would not listen to me. The Lord said to me, "Enough! Never speak to Me of this matter again! Go up to the summit of Pisgah and gaze about, to the west, the north, the south, and the east. Look at it well, for you shall not go across yonder Jordan." (Deuteronomy 3:23–27)

Moses, the greatest Jewish prophet is barred from entry into the Promised Land. He is permitted to see the land, but not touch, feel, smell, hold, turn in his own hands, taste the fruit or be nourished by the produce. The rejection of Moses's final plea formulates the land as unattainable. Moses ends his life in existential and material exile. Concluding its narrative on the far bank of the Jordan River, the Torah authors an enduring condition of longing for Zion.

In 1948, the declaration of the State of Israel inaugurated a paradoxical reality for the Jewish People: The unattainable had been attained. The material fulfillment of Zionism conflicts with the daily conditioning of exile embedded in the Jewish psyche. The new political reality did not instantly transform that consciousness. More than two generations have grown up with the assumption of the existence of Israel. At the same time, the liturgy, texts and traditions of the Jewish People perpetuate the idealization of Zion as an unattainable homeland. Both longing and fulfillment co-exist in the Jewish relationship to Israel. We can activate this creative tension to contribute toward updating the Zionist enterprise for the twenty-first century.

Before world Jewry could adjust to the achievement of freedom from persecution and autonomy to create a Jewish society, the initial euphoria that bore Israel through the first few decades was eroding. The work of refining the practices of Jewish statehood under extremely challenging conditions set in. Since achieving independence, Israel's resolve to secure peace has met with rejection and violent aggression. Egypt and Jordan are notable exceptions – both signed treaties after Israel had vanquished Arab military invasions in 1948, 1967, and 1973. Amidst anti-Israel threats and violence, attaining a peaceful and prosperous Palestine alongside a secure Israel is a supreme challenge. Israel and Zionism are plagued by the unfathomable trials presented by a hostile region and increasingly hostile global community.

During the same post-World War II period and not unrelated to Israel's restoration of the dignity of the Jewish People, Jewish communities throughout the world have been benefiting from the hospitality of their host nations. In the aftermath of the Holocaust, many nations have improved their practice of tolerance and respect for human dignity, and uphold religious freedom. Though these values have long been enshrined in the constitutions of modern nations, they have usually been selectively interpreted. From the late twentieth century onward, in the Americas, in many parts of Europe, East and West, and, more recently, in the Former Soviet Union, Jewish communities are feeling more at home than ever. In view of this liberty, however tenuous it appears during crises, the unlikelihood of the ingathering of the Jewish *diaspora* to Israel is apparent.[11] The Jewish People is diverse, distributed throughout the world, expresses itself through many forms of practice, and is committed to an inestimable variety of lifestyles. Acknowledging this reality, the connections and shared narratives of the Jewish People and Zionism need revision.

This book addresses the convergence of Jewish text with Jewish life at the meeting-point between the Jewish People and our historic homeland. Zionism merges history into contemporary experience. *ReReading Israel* opens texts to the current page of Jewish life, inviting readers from all traditions to participate in exploring an extraordinary human endeavor. The following points clarify the framework of this current work.

BOOKS

Often the Jewish People are called "the People of the Book." Narrowly defined, "the Book" is the Hebrew Bible, the *Tanakh*: the Five Books of Moses, the prophetic chapters, and the sacred writings. Jewish sages compiled these texts to form what became a foundational sacred canon for Jews, Christians, and Muslims. At the onset of the first millennium of the Common Era, when Rome transformed into a Christian Empire and Christianity was over-riding the *Old* Testament of the

---

11. The spate of Anti-Semitic incidents in France during the early 2000s and the racist shooting at a Jewish institution in Seattle, Washington in 2006 are examples of growing twenty-first century anti-Semitism. See Pierre-André Taguieff, *Rising from the Muck: The New Anti-Semitism in Europe* (Novelle judéophobie, trans.: Patrick Camiller, Chicago: Ivan R. Dee, 2004).

Jews with the *New* Testament of Jesus, the Jewish People was forging the biblical tradition into rabbinic Judaism. At no point has Jewish occupation with the canon atrophied or ceased to evolve. For Jews, the Hebrew Bible never became *old*. Throughout thousands of years, Jewish communities have been interpreting layers of the Torah – its simple, complex, and secret meanings. While "the Book" is a singular word, the Torah of the Jewish People comprises a plethora of evolving systems of interpretation. The Talmud, midrash and subsequent compendia of law and literature document Jewish study and life in vibrant communities throughout many dispersions and in Israel. The Jewish People continues to reformulate the Written Torah in the many forms and streams of the Oral Torah. The Torah continues to be a source of values, inspiration, and nurture, and the ground for passionate contention and dispute. Ongoing connection with the ancient texts has helped to sustain a sense of collectivity and shared identity among Jews, even under the most trying conditions. In this sense, the Jewish People are People of *Books* – multiple, dynamic textual traditions.

In the current renaissance of Jewish learning, more and varied institutions than ever offer opportunities to study Jewish texts. Far beyond the orbit of the religious faithful, the Torah and diverse Jewish literatures are taking their place on the bookshelves of human culture, connecting this present moment with ongoing streams of interpretation. Texts and literatures record the constant striving of the Jewish People to relate the Torah to our lives with an enduring expectation that it is relevant and important.

The conversation that proceeds from the biblical period toward the future welcomes participation. With the onset of the digital era, many of the resources of Jewish scholarship have migrated to computer technology. Sophisticated new tools make the cumulative textual resources of the Jewish People more accessible than ever. The internet and databases enable storage, organization, access, searching, and interaction. Textual productivity is one important way that the Jewish People has and continues to transmit, debate, and fulfill its destiny.

LIVING

The Torah is not an object or a detached ideal, inert, lifeless on the shelf or enclosed in the holy ark of the synagogue sanctuary.[12] Its meaningfulness depends upon whether and how people relate to it. One relationship is study – engaging the Torah with our minds. Another connection with the Torah is living in relation to it. People express the potency of their texts by means of their actions in society, with their bodies and souls. In the most extreme cases, the text even makes claims on life and limb.[13] Jewish tradition focuses on the sacredness of the study of text in living contexts, where study influences and improves behavior. Ultimately, each community and individual is responsible to choose how to live and behave. The text can inform choices, but does not determine them; it is not definitive, but an input into a life process. Each new situation requires human deliberation which gives rise to new texts and interpretations.[14] The vigor of the Torah transpires in the human interplay between text and life.

ACTIVE

Living in relation to the Torah does not necessitate performing a text or behaving faithfully according to its teachings. Probing, challenging, revising, reformulating, even rejecting are all relationships with the Torah. Reinterpreting the meaning of a text through the prisms of each generation keeps it active and relevant. Sometimes texts affirm positions that are already accepted; sometimes they challenge, contradict, or confront. Studying Torah, therefore, actively raises questions that bear on the values and practices of life. There is no presupposition of agreement or concurrence. What is necessary is seriousness and respect, willingness to struggle openly, and to expect life consequences.[15]

---

12. "The study of Torah is greater (than good action) because it brings forth good action" *Kiddushin* 40b.

13. The Talmud requires a person to die first rather than commit three grave prohibitions: murder, idolatry, and forbidden sexual relations, *Yoma* 72a.

14. "She (the Torah) is not in heaven!" *Eruvin* 55a.

15. See Bonna Devora Haberman, "Difficult Texts," *Shma*, April 2001, http://www.shma.com/apr01/haberman.htm.

ZION CYCLE

Sigmund Freud persuaded modern culture about the deep unconscious layers of the human mind. Through analysis of unconscious experience, people can achieve greater self-understanding and capability to choose our life paths willfully. The psychoanalytic tradition encourages people to probe their early family histories and relationships, and to interpret effects on their lives. Interactions with parents and siblings form the dynamic and backdrop of personal biography. Understanding early experiences, patterns, unresolved connections, dreams and desires frees people to live more intentionally.

Similarly to the way each individual belongs to his or her personal family context, every person also belongs to a cultural context, to a people or peoples. Just as primary family relationships are significant even at unconscious levels, so also are the ties of peoplehood and culture. Theodore Herzl, parent of modern Zionism, lived and studied in Vienna from 1878, at the same time as Freud was developing his theories. In many respects, Herzl's modern dream of the homeland for the Jewish People is a national version of the individual unconscious that Freud suggested.

From the biblical narrative onward, throughout the better part of five millennia, the Jewish People has been exceedingly attentive to the land of Israel. The term, "Zion Cycle" describes a biography of the Jewish People that unfolds in history and imagination, conscious and unconscious. Movement toward, incursion into, settling, conflict and destruction, exile, dwelling in the Diaspora, yearning, and returning to the land of Israel form a complex and cyclical narrative. The flow toward and away from Israel beats at the heart of Jewish experience, pulsing life-blood into Jewish identity and agency. Both historically and in the modern Zionist period, motions to and from Israel transpire on the geographic territory of the earth.[16] Even more, they have been transpiring in the Jewish psyche. Though a large proportion of world Jewry has not literally made the journey to Israel, Jews have been experiencing the journey to and from Zion in the realms of spirit and

---

16. For an analysis of literary and political constructions of Zionism, see Eric Zakim, "To build and be built: landscape, literature, and the construction of Zionist identity" (Philadelphia: Penn UP, 2006).

imagination. Patterns of immigration and war, mystic fantasy, prayers, anguish, and desperate longing all infuse the Zion Cycle with archetypal significance.

Each member of the Jewish People is on the Zion Cycle, whether coming or going, yearning, ignoring, resisting or condemning. For some, the relationship to Zion is one of endearment and mutual sustenance, for others, an undiscovered passion or a critical tension, for yet others, denial, repression, or (self)hatred. Whatever the posture, the Jewish connection to Israel is as undeniable as one's personal family, lineage, and roots. Zion organizes a Jewish national biography, a meta-narrative of world Jewry.

Proposing the Zion Cycle as a foundation of Jewish experience is highly contentious. For people who have lived most of their lives without considering a relationship with Israel, or that Israel is significant to them, the Zion Cycle is foreign and even objectionable. Interrupting the flow of life in order to be present – intellectually, emotionally, physically – in a relationship with Israel marks one's personal biography on the itinerary of the Zion Cycle. The relatively recent attainment of Israeli statehood affords each Jew the possibility to investigate and delve into her/his motion on the Zion Cycle. This is an achievement for which Jews have longed during extended periods of exile, a precious gift for which we must continue to earn and demonstrate worthiness, and take responsibility. The quality of our presence depends upon our intentions.

It is undoubtedly possible and fashionable to be impervious or inimical, to shun Israel. Resisting the Zion Cycle is a posture of least resistance, particularly in these times. John Lennon popularized the dream of peace built on universal, undifferentiated one-ness – by erasing or overcoming outmoded religious and national ideas.[17] However, acknowledging, refining, and expressing our cultures neither limits our humanity nor condemns us to strife. Just as our specific personal biography contributes to our identity and enriches our membership in society, so also our cultural, national, ethnic, religious, spiritual, and linguistic identities can contribute to the richness of human life. This precious richness gives meaning to pluralism and diversity. This book aims for open, meaningful, ethical, and creative engagement with Zion.

---

17. John Lennon's song *Imagine*.

EMBODIED

While there is some accuracy to the characterization of Jews as a "People of the Book(s)," the emphasis on the *book* renders Judaism somewhat ethereal and abstract, if not a relic of an ancient and defunct era. Books, while they contain ideas, are printed with ink on paper and bound with glue – they partake of the material realm. In the Torah, God chooses to become manifest by creating the world, a world that we explore by means of our bodily senses. To a remarkable extent, Jewish tradition guides us toward the material world to encounter, learn about and serve the divine. In the sense that Jews are a people whose books beckon to physical experience with spiritual intention, Jews are also "People of the Body." Whereas many religions yearn for transcendence of the body and the material world, the practice of Judaism takes root in corporeality. This *embodied* aspect of Jewish life has important implications and complications. The inextricable and precarious connection between the soul/mind and the body is a metaphor for the connection between the Jewish People and the land of Israel.

BLAZE is the acronym for these five points, Books, Living, Active, Zion Cycle, and Embodied – these ideas fuel the ensuing explorations. Embarking on this BLAZE process demands willingness to eschew ingrained postures, to inspect life and experience. BLAZE seeks to illumine a journey in deep recesses of heart and mind, ancient and modern.

The following chapters contextualize Israel and Zionism at vital intersections of ideas with action. Each chapter invites exploration of a different theme, cumulatively composing a perspective of what might be termed *spiritual materialism*, hence the subtitle, *The Spirit of the Matter*. Beginning with the problematic dualism and opposition of mind and body, the second chapter proposes a more integrated foundation. Formal education, religious practice and ritual are too often oblivious to and even repress the body. Interpreting exemplary figures, I elaborate an embodied spirituality. Hannah brazenly accosts the divine about her breasts; Hillel bathes himself according to the example of idol worshippers; and human and divine bodies mutually bind themselves to one other.

The third chapter overlays the spiritual body onto the Jewish historical narrative of exile and homecoming. We appraise the health of the body of the Jewish People. Strengthening the proposal of sacred materiality, this chapter offers a model for a sublime collaborative national project. Society expresses mortal meaning and yearnings through intricate service, mobilizing the power of symbolic and ritual action. Zionism experiments with Jewish society-building. The desire for "normalcy" is sincere – a society that functions at a tolerable level of stress, where the unhampered pursuit of daily good living is secure. However, in the current era of global instabilities, non-governmental actors, extreme and violent ethnic and class tensions that impinge on most every nation, normalcy is an elusive goal.

No national pattern is applicable for Israel. Israel needs continuously to form and reform itself, and its Jewishness. Among the many nations, ethnic, linguistic and religious groups, the singular Jewish state is inescapably unique. Particularly as the one pluralistic democratic society in the region, at a convergence point of East and West, of Judaism and Islam, Israel is a conscionable contributor to the emerging twenty-first century. The homogenizing force of globalization erodes discreet and precious cultures. Meaningful human diversity depends upon nurturing specific cultural languages. Chapter four investigates an erotic metaphor of Jewish literatures and its application to Israel: the garden. Growing from lush texts, tending the garden relates to prayer, ecology, and poverty with imminent, aroused passion.

Jewish yearning for the land as a sacred place is glorious and inspiring. Living out the dream is much more difficult. The pioneers built a sustaining country and bequeathed to us complex challenges of coexistence with Palestinians and among Arab neighbors. The question of our relationship with the land arises anew. Sanctity is one of the attributes that has informed Jewish connection to Israel. Competing territorial claims, disputes about boundaries and the relative values of life and land beg for new interpretations of the meaning of sacred land. Sacredness is not only about geography, ancient cities, temples or graves. Close readings of biblical and rabbinic passages undergird alternative perspectives on Jewish territorial sovereignty and the sacredness of the land in chapter five.

The Israeli Defense Force is one way that Israel has reframed Jewish identity. With the entrenchment of the Israeli occupation in

Judaea and Samaria – the West Bank – Palestinian resistance grows, posing mortal and moral danger to civilians and to soldiers. This danger threatens Zionism profoundly. Israel's spirit and ethical fiber, her sense of justice and humanity depend upon tough choices about how to conduct herself and instruct her young people to wield power. Negotiating the appropriate use of force for security is a constant Israeli occupation. Not the first occasion that the Jewish People has exercised power, the case of Hasmonean sovereignty illumines contemporary Israeli struggles to accommodate the values of land, life, and self-determination. Immersed in the imperialism of Hellenistic culture, the Jewish community faced similar threats of assimilation to those posed in the current period. Chapter six examines, interprets, and critiques material and spiritual power.

The concluding chapter draws implications of this interrogation of sources and proposals about Zionism. We progress in the narrative beyond the glossy surfaces of Israel toward living on the Zion Cycle. Taking on the dissonances and difficulties of the Zionist process is more thrilling and rewarding than facile support or rejection. The study guided by the ensuing chapters presents an opportunity to apply our finest resources to grapple creatively with land and people, history, text, and spirit.

Imagine that you could take a pill that would make it seem true to you that you have been to Israel, encountered the land and peoples, and returned safely to your home. With that experience neatly behind you, you can get on with your life.

One of the proposals of Zionism is that it is not only about our personal life as individuals, though that is very important. It is also about what happens to the Jewish People and to Israel through our involvement. So much depends upon our willful participation. This journey is *in*ward bound; it touches the meaning of our life as well as our relationship with Jewish civilization. Engaging with Israel is about how *we* make a difference. The need for our contribution is tremendous. So, forget the pill and (un)pack your bag.

2 Body and Mind

THIS CHAPTER EXCAVATES our complex and troubled mind-body connection – one of the foundations of Zionism and of our relationship with the land of Israel altogether. We become more aware of our assumptions, more capable to choose our views and to act intentionally.

Education mostly addresses the minds of students, separating the physical body from study. Schools mainly focus on *immaterial* activities – speech, reading, memory and thought, reasoning, and sometimes, imagining. Bodily exertion happens in different places from mental work – outside the classroom, in the gym or on the playing field. Custodians work after-hours, mainly out of sight. In *play*, young people apply powerful, raw energy to exciting and intense interactions. Muscles glisten with sweat; mind and body coordinate together in motion. Rarely do students express comparable enthusiasm in class – those who do are often labeled hyperactive, often diagnosed with Attention Deficit Disorder and given medications to calm them down. Even though the same students do both, rarely are mind and body activities integrated for the sake of learning.

What has come to be known as *mind-body dualism* divides human pursuits into separate *mind* and *body* categories. In general, *mental* occupations are rewarded with more prestige, power, and resources than *physical* ones. White-collar professions – law, medicine, accounting, finance, academics, and management are clean, respectable, and highly compensated. Blue-collar jobs in farming, manufacturing, construction, maintenance, services, *et cetera* are manual, from the Latin root, "*manus,*" hand. They are *dirty*, less-well paid and bear lower status. Mind-body dualism privileges the work that represents the *mind* of society over the physical labor that represents the *body* of society, stratifying the professions along with the people who perform them. Exercise and play are *recreational* and healthy for privileged classes, but physical labor is menial. The social definitions of laborers as lower class than professionals frequently align with race, and often with gender. Under the Western regime, elite strata of government, professions, and business are dominated by white males. Menial work tends to be relegated to people of color; domestic laborers are mostly poor women of color.

Western media exposes the human body as a consumable material, a for-profit commodity. (Porno)graphic images confront us everywhere: Seductively-poised, scantily-clothed models, performers, and actors ply our computer, television, and movie screens, billboards, magazines, and papers. According to theologian Grace Janzen, the current obsession with sexuality derives from the long-standing Christian fixation and is really "the same preoccupation, turned inside out."[1] Centuries of religious repression focused negative attention on the body and its functions. Today's marketing exploits the seductions of sex to sell almost everything. We substitute shopping and consuming for healthy, active, and satisfying lives that integrate body, mind, emotions, and spirit. These unhealthy and wasteful behaviors develop from a cultural tradition that relates to our body as an unruly, even corrupt object.

Greek and Christian Roots

Mind-body dualism dates back to the ancient Greek roots of Western culture. During the fifth century before the Common Era, Plato taught that the soul and body are two different, separate substances. For the ancient Greeks, the realm of spirit, mind, and the transcendent divine is the ultimate reality; the body is but an abode and servant of the soul.

Christianity inherited mind-body dualism from the Greeks and

---

1. *Good Sex: Feminist Perspectives from the World's Religions*, ed., Patricia Beattie Jung, Mary E. Hung, Radhika Balakrishnan (New Brunswick, N.J.: Rutgers University Press, 2001), 3.

their Roman successors. Among the church fathers, Saint Augustine
(354–430 CE) saw sexual passion as the conduit of original sin. So
heinous and infectious is the lust of parents that leads to conception
that it befouls the souls of newborns. Saint Ambrose (340–397 CE)
taught that in the Kingdom of Heaven there is complete abstention
from all fleshly pursuits, eating and sex. Repressing the corruption of
the sexual body, in the Catholic Church, only male celibate hands can
administer the sacraments. Thomas Aquinas (ca. 1227–1274) considers marriage to be the least of the sacraments.

From the early moments of the creation narrative in the Hebrew
Bible, many Christian interpreters draw connections between primal
sin, the body and sexuality – the common causes of evil, suffering,
and death. Monumental renaissance paintings of the Garden of Eden
scene concretize the fall of humanity from grace into sin.[2] Images of
the original seduction in the Garden are etched in our consciousness.
They inform our gendered identities and experience.[3]

Mind-body dualism handicaps the unfolding of Zionism. Revisiting
the creation narrative(s) in Genesis-*Bereishit*, we begin to reconceive
the relationship of mind and body.

Dual-ing Geneses

Genesis narrates two versions of the creation of humanity. The first
chapter tells of Adam, an androgynous being – male and female. I
translate the verses to convey the double identity of both the Creator
and the new creature.

> God said, "Let us make human in Our image, after Our likeness.
> . . ." And God created human in Her/His image, in the image of
> God S/He created him/her; male and female S/He created them.
> (Genesis 1:26–7)

The repeated statement that God created Adam *in the divine image*
poses the question about the meaning of human resemblance to the
divine – in what aspect(s) is Adam *like* God? Though we often focus

---

2. Michelangelo and Rubens, for example.

3. See the first chapter of Lori Hope Lefkovitz's *In Scripture: The First Stories
of Jewish Sexual Identities* (Lanham, MD: Rowman & Littlefield Publishers, 2010).

on *appearance*, the text does not specify in what way human resembles God. Some interpret the first chapter of Genesis accounting for the *immaterial* aspect of humanness – the *soul*, consciousness, or intelligence, while the second chapter relates the *physical* creation of humans. Philo of Alexandria (20 BCE–50 CE), who seams together Jewish and Greek cultures during the early years of Christianity, views Greek philosophy as a natural development of the Torah. According to Philo, Adam's likeness to the divine is the mind – the most refined aspect of the soul.

> Moses [in the Torah] says that human was made in the image and likeness of God. And he says well; for nothing that is born on the earth is more resembling God than human. And let no one think that he is able to judge of this likeness from the characters of the body: for neither is God a being with the form of a man, nor is the human body like the form of God; but the resemblance is spoken of with reference to the most important part of the soul, namely, the mind: for the mind which exists in each individual has been created after the likeness of that one mind which is in the universe as its primitive model, being in some sort the God of that body which carries it about and bears its image within it.[4]

For Philo, the mind is sovereign of the body as God is sovereign of the universe. The mind is the aspect of humanity that resembles the divine. Most resembling the divine, the mind desires to know the infinite. This desire is the root of human curiosity, motivating inquiry, investigation, and innovation.

Two thousand years after Philo, a major Jewish theologian of the twentieth century, Joseph B. Soleveitchik (known simply as "the Rav") suggests that the aspect of humanity that resembles the divine is creativity. Soleveitchik includes scientific exploration, medicine, art, literature, music as human expressions of the divine image.[5] Beyond the work of perfecting the creation, Soleveitchik envisions a more sublime meaning. "Herein is embodied the entire task of creation and the obligation to participate in the renewal of the cosmos. The most fundamental principle of all is that [hu]man must create [her/]himself."[6]

---

4. Philo of Alexandria, *On the Creation of the Cosmos According to Moses*, 69–72.

5. *The Lonely Man of Faith* (New York: Doubleday, 1992), 9–20.

6. *Halakhic Man* (Philadelphia: Jewish Publication Society, 1983), 109.

Following Soleveitchik's reading, creation is not an historic event that happened once in the ancient or mythic past, but an ongoing process. Similarly, living in the divine image is a progressive activity. Uniquely human self-consciousness opens the possibility to *create* – ourselves and in our world, as individuals, as communities, as nations, and as a species. Human civilization is the collective labor of human minds and bodies.

Traditional monotheisms read the utterance, "Let there be light," as creation from nothing, *ex nihilo* – by means of speech, perhaps with letters. Yet the opening verses of Genesis do mention matter – formless mass, chaos, darkness, void, and water, over which divine presence hovers.[7] These descriptions suggest *somethingness* rather than *nothingness* before Genesis. In a textual elaboration, a *midrash*, Rabban Gamliel, the president of the religious council in Babylon, refutes the seeming inconsistency between the material of Genesis and the theory of creation from nothing, *ex nihilo*. He cites verses from the prophets asserting that God created the chaos and the void, the darkness, the wind/spirit, and the *tehom*, the abyss.[8] Rabban Gamliel counters the evidence that material pre-exists the divine creation.[9] Though the text suggests a more complex relationship between mind and matter than creation by means of divine speech, the creation-from-nothing interpretation mainly succeeds to squelch controversy about the very first verses of the Torah.[10]

The second chapter of Genesis specifies that God creates Adam from *earth* and *breath* – "The Lord God formed human from the dust of the earth. S/He blew into his/her nostrils the breath of life, and human became a living being" (Genesis 2:7), whereas the initial biblical account does not specify any material – "And God created human in

7. Catherine Keller has written a compelling account of the construction of creation from pre-existing matter. *Face of the Deep: A Theology of Being* (London: Routledge, 2003).

8. Genesis Rabbah 1:12.

9. Rashi comments on another talmudic passage that God creates as many as 974 generations before Adam. Rashi on BT *Hagigah* 14a. A verse from Psalms – 105:8 – is the prooftext.

10. The ancient Babylonian *Enûma Eliš* tells a tumultuous and disturbing creation myth, parallel in many respects to *Bereishit*, but filled with the intrigue and violence of divine characters. Ultimately, Marduk triumphs over Tiamat, a supreme male god dismembers the unruly divine abyss.

His/Her image, in the image of God S/He created him/her; male and female S/He created them" (1:27). This text specifies an important human trait – Adam is created both male and female – an androgyne. The text does not define *male* and *female*, only that they are different. This difference in humans, created in the divine image derives from the divine Creator: "This is the genealogy of Adam, S/He made him/ her in the likeness of God; male and female S/He created them" (5:1). Difference is contained within the One and consequently manifest in the creation.

Before the creation of Adam, the first chapter of Genesis deals in differentiation – God separates between light and darkness, between upper and lower waters, between heaven and earth, between day and night. Under the influence of the dualism in Greek thought, these separations become opposites. One is often held to be morally superior to the other, mind over body and light over darkness, for example. Rather than conflict, it is possible to conceive *difference* differently – separation generates productive and erotic tension and desire for reunion, for oneness. Heaven and earth, day and night, female and male long for one another. Longing arouses energy and passion. Difference installs a dynamic flow in creation, an ongoing process of drawing near, the climax of union, separation and renewed longing. Desire to unite and create fills the world with life energy – fertility and productivity. When and how *difference* takes material form is one of the main themes of the second rendition of the biblical creation story.

The creation of Adam in the second chapter of Genesis diverges from the first. The second Adam does not contain the two sexes – he is gendered male. In this version, God creates Eve, a woman, from Adam's side *after* Adam.[11] Like the other differentiated elements of creation, these two human aspects – male and female – long for union.

Human Purpose

The second chapter of Genesis specifies a reason for creating humanity: There is no-one to tend the creation. *Adam* associates closely with *adama*-earth from which he is made. He is to be a laborer, a steward of the earth. This job description amounts to partnership in creation.

---

11. Gen. 3:22.

The text depicts God creating and working with matter; God is a maker, a sculptor, a gardener. At this moment in the text, there are no separations of mind from body or divisions of labor or class that stigmatize the human body or its material.

When Jewish sages later fantasize the ideal Garden of Eden state, some conceive a *beit midrash,* a house of Torah study where the righteous will sit at a table and study the sacred writ. This disembodied version of heaven – more like school without gym or recess than utopia –ignores one of the original purposes of humanity – to steward the garden. *Tending the garden* is a metaphor for working with our hands and bodies to earn a living. Ultimately, the first human pair is cursed and driven out of the Garden of Eden.

> The earth is cursed on your account, by labor shall you eat of it. Thorns and thistles it shall grow for you ... By the sweat of your brow shall you eat bread ... (Genesis 3:17–19) ... The Lord God sent Adam from the Garden of Eden to work the earth from which he was taken. (3:23)

These verses certainly indicate the hardship of sustenance.

Sweat of the Brow – Blessing or Curse

In a Talmudic passage, two sages debate the relative value of physical labor and Torah study. Interpreting a verse from the text of the *Shema,* the central credo of Jewish liturgy, "You shall gather in your new grain and wine and oil,"[12] the sages suggest that reaping the harvest of the land depends upon the words of Torah abiding on our lips, literally, *in our mouth.* Study and sustenance are inter-connected. They cite a verse from the biblical Book of Joshua to support their position, "Do not let this book of the Torah (Teaching) cease from your lips, but recite it day and night, so that you may observe faithfully all that is written in it. Only then will you prosper in your undertakings and only then will you be successful" (Joshua 1:8).

> Our sages taught [about the verse]: "You shall gather in your grain" (Deuteronomy 11:14). What is to be learnt from these words? Since it

---

12. Deut. 11:14.

says, "This book of the law shall not depart *from your mouth*" (Joshua 1:8), I might think that this injunction is to be taken literally. Therefore it says, "You shall gather in your grain," which implies that you are to combine the study of the Torah with a worldly occupation. This is the view of R. Ishmael.

R. Shimon bar Yochai says: Is it possible for a person to plough at the time of plowing, sow at the time of sowing, harvest in the season of harvesting, thresh at the time of threshing, and winnow in the time of the wind? What would become of Torah for such a person?! [He therefore concludes,] at the time when Israel is behaving according to the divine will, then their labors are performed/done by others, as Isaiah says, "Strangers shall stand and pasture your flocks, the children of strangers shall plough your fields and tend your vines" (Isaiah 61:5). At the time when Israel is not doing the divine will, then they will perform their own labor, as it says, "You shall gather in your new grain and wine and oil" (Deuteronomy 11:14). Not only that, but they will perform the labor of others, as it says, "You shall serve your enemy" (28:48). (*Berakhot* 35b)

These two sages take very different positions about our roles on this earth. Rabbi Yishmael understands that one ought to pursue one's labor of working and harvesting, "according to the way of the land," respecting all concerned. Rashbi – Rabbi Shimon bar Yochai – contradicts Rabbi Yishmael. He argues that the effort of sustenance is too demanding – in every season, at every moment, there is work to do. Rashbi enumerates the various labors of living off the land: plowing, sowing, harvesting, threshing, and winnowing. Rabbi Yishmael sees these acts as harmonious with a life guided by Torah study. Like the observance of the festivals of the seasons and ritual commandments, each act must be done at its appropriate time, in the proper sequence, according to the life-cycle. The demands of the earth are similar to and compatible with the obligations of the Torah. We cannot grind, knead and bake the page upon which our texts are printed. We need to work for our living. By contrast, in Rashbi's view, agricultural obligations rival the demands of Torah. Work and study are an incompatible zero sum. Physical labor distracts from the higher priority of Torah study and commandments. Based on the attitude that work for sustenance is a waste of time that could be spent studying, Rashbi concludes that

Torah study is the optimal pursuit – everything else is *bitul Torah*, a negation of Torah.[13]

The opinions of these sages are irreconcilable. For Rashbi, manual labor contradicts the Torah life-style; it is undesirable and degrading. Rabbi Yishmael teaches that the study of Torah and productive work fulfill one another.

Early Zionists romanticized returning to the earth as redemptive. In the first generations of immigration, the kibbutz movement fulfilled the dream of a new society based on shared settlement and work in the fields. Rav Avraham Yitzchak HaCohen Kook, (1864–1935), the first Ashkenazi Chief Rabbi of Israel, taught that the agricultural work of the land *is* sacred service.[14] Torah and Labor, *Torah veAvoda*, is the motto for the modern Orthodox Zionist youth movement – B'nai Akiva, and for an Israeli national social movement that,

> seeks to return Religious Zionism to its roots, works to create a think-ing religious culture that is open and self-critical, and encourages a courageous halakhic [religious legal] discourse that deals with the challenges of contemporary times. Its orientation aims to promote the values of tolerance, equality, and justice in religious society and to have a real influence on the Jewish-democratic character of Israeli society.[15]

The founders criticize a trend among Orthodox Jews toward religious narrow-mindedness, and affirm their responsibility for livelihood, state, and society. The youth movement strives to socialize young people into the co-existing values of Torah and service. The motto relates to an ancient utterance in the *Mishna* – the Oral Torah. Shimon the Righteous states that the world stands on three things: on the

---

13. Desisting from the physical labor of making a livelihood has consequences for the body. Contemporary researchers investigating health in ultra-Orthodox communities correlate religiously prescribed behaviors such as studying texts in unhealthy postures for prolonged periods with low bone mineral density. Taha, W., Chin, D., Silverberg, A. L., Lashiker, L., Khateeb, N., & Anhalt, H. (2001), "Reduced spinal bone mineral density in adolescents of an ultra-Orthodox Jewish community in Brooklyn." *Pediatrics*, I07(5), e79. Retrieved Aug. 12, 2005, from http://www.pediatrics.aappublications.org/content/full/107/5/e79.

14. *Ma'amarei HaR'Iyah*, I, 179–181.

15. *Ne'emanei Torah veAvoda*: http://toravoda.org.il/en.

[study of] Torah, on service, and on acts of kindness.[16] Some interpret *service* to indicate the work of sustenance by which humanity takes part in the creation.[17]

Throughout the ages, Jewish scholars earned a respectable livelihood, often with their hands.

> Hillel was a woodchopper before he became the president of the Sanhedrin; Shammai the Elder was a builder; Abba Chilkiyah was a field laborer; Rabbi Yochanan ben Zakkai was a businessman for forty years; Abba Shaul was a gravedigger; Abba Oshiya was a launderer; Rabbi Shimon P'kuli was a cotton dealer; Rabbi Shmuel child of Shilas was a school teacher, Rabbi Meir and Rabi Chananel were scribes; Rabbi Yosi child of Chalafta was a tanner; Rabbi Yochanan Hasandlar was a shoemaker; Rabbi Yehoshua child of Chananiah was a blacksmith; Rabbi Safra and Rabbi Dimi of Nehardea were merchants; Rabbi Abba child of Zavina was a tailor; Rabbi Yosef child of Chiya and Rabbi Yannai owned vineyards; Rabbi Huna was a farmer and raised cattle; Rabbi Chisda and Rabbi Papa were beer brewers; Karna was a wine smeller who determined which wine could be stored and which had to be sold immediately; Rabbi Chiya child of Yosef was in the salt business; Abba Bar Abba, father of Mar Shmuel was a silk merchant; and (Mar) Shmuel was a doctor.[18]

By contrast with Talmudic sages whose teachings they venerate, many ultra-Orthodox Jews consider Torah study to be the *only* worthwhile pursuit. For the purpose of wooing ultra-Orthodox parties into the government, Israeli coalition agreements exempt a growing ultra-Orthodox population from the *mandatory* core Israeli curriculum and from *compulsory* army service. As a result, many ultra-Orthodox young people mature into adulthood without sharing the responsibilities of national defense, and lacking the tools to earn a living. The relation-

---

16. *Avot* 1:2.

17. Solomon ben Isaac Levi, *Sefer Hameor, Lev Avot* (Thessaloniki, 1565), on *Avot* 1:2.

18. Hershey H. Friedman, "Ideal Occupations: The Talmudic Perspective," retrieved July 29, 2010, http://www.jlaw.com/Articles/idealoccupa.html. See also Mordechai Judovits, *Sages of the Talmud: The Lives, Sayings and Stories of 400 Rabbinic Masters* (Jerusalem: Urim Publications, 2009).

ship between the obligations of work, study, and national service are pressing issues for Israeli society today.

Soul and Substance

The debate about dualism, the relationship between mind and body raged throughout the Middle Ages. In his defense of Judaism, Yehuda HaLevi (ca. 1070–1141) praises the pure state of Adam.

> Adam was perfection itself, because no flaw could be found in a work of a wise and Almighty Creator, wrought from a substance chosen by Him[/Her], and fashioned according to His[/Her] own design. There was no restraining influence, no fear of atavism [the reappearance of a characteristic from a previous generation], no question of [poor] nutrition or education during the years of childhood and growth; neither was there the influence of climate, water, or soil to consider. For S/He created him in the form of an adolescent, perfect in body and mind. The soul with which he was endowed was perfect; his intellect was the loftiest which it is possible for a human being to possess, and beyond this he was gifted with the divine power of such high rank, that it brought him into connexion with beings divine and spiritual, and enabled him, with slight reflection, to comprehend the great truths without instruction. We call him God's son, and we call all those who were like him also children of God. (*The Kuzari* 1.95)

According to Yehuda HaLevi, the original Adam, is created an untainted adolescent. HaLevi claims that the material conditions of life unavoidably degrade the fine quality of the human being and gradually erode innate knowledge. All aspects of physical living – genes, weather, food, and water – corrupt the original pure divine *substance* from which s/he is created. HaLevi does not believe that the body and mind are separate or opposite. In his view, there is divine material – spiritual material. His approach is a less extreme version of Rashbi's. Both see physical experience detracting from the highest potential inherent in each human who is created in the divine image. Whereas HaLevi considers the influence of physicality on the mind and soul to be negative, Rabbi Yishmael integrates material labor with study, proposing that both components contribute to and fortify the other. HaLevi holds the mind to be more pristine than the body, and corruptible. Both perspectives play out in the formative, early chapters of Genesis. Food and desire bring human consciousness into relation with creation and drive the biblical narrative forward.

The Rise of the Fall

In the continuation of the second story of human creation, Eve disobeys the first divine prohibition – she eats and shares fruit from the forbidden tree. Mortality, curses, and opposition between Adam and Eve ensues. More than the fall of humanity, these verses signal a fall in biblical interpretation.

One of the problems with mind-body dualism is that it conceives the body as an opponent to intellectual, moral, and spiritual life. Accordingly, the body has its own desires, needs, *instincts*, affiliated more with the animal, even bestial than with the creative, refined provinces of the human mind and soul. Bodily hunger for food, sex, gluttonies and indulgences of all kinds lead to sin. Most interpreters of the Garden of Eden story see Eve as the embodiment of such bodily traits. Not only does she disobey the divine rule of law, but she seduces Adam into her debauchery. In a double dualist model, mind aligns with male, and body aligns with female. From this story, Western culture deduces and installs the roles of woman as dangerous temptress, seductress – the inferior and less disciplined of the sexes. We are so often taught that humanity is driven from immortality, from the *perfect* Garden state into *exile* on her account. We may read this original episode alternately – opening the historic project of human choice and responsibility.

Disobedience, Freedom and Responsibility

The commandment to refrain from eating from the Tree of Knowledge of good and evil poses a question about intentions. If the divine intention in creating Adam and Eve is obedience to God's own will, then the creature is an extension of the Creator, not differentiated from the Creator. If people behave in perfect correspondence with God's will, then it is difficult to attribute to them free choice; they do not exercise their own will – they fulfill God's will. While a possible meaning of the text, this is surely not the exclusive one. The Talmudic expression, "everything is in God's hands except for awe of God" suggests that there is no meaning to awe of God if God causes the awe.[19] Every prohibition implicitly contains the potential of its inverse. Every prohibition proposes the possibility of transgression.

At the moment of Eve's choice, the text uses the word, "desire," תַאֲוָה for the first time. Eve's desire for the fruit arises in her whole being; her senses enliven at the prospect of acquiring divine knowledge. Yearning for knowledge blends with excited feelings. There is no separation of body from mind in Eve's act. When Eve eats the forbidden fruit, she exercises her divinely-intended will to be, to create herself, to use Soleveitchik's expression. At that instant, she establishes independent action. For the first time, creature differentiates from her Creator. Eve initiates a new attribute into creation – a human, willful, risk-taking, adventurous spunk.

Where both Eve and Adam fail utterly in their garden debut is not in their disobedience, but in their unwillingness to accept the consequences of their choice and action.

> And they heard the voice of the Lord God walking in the garden toward the cool of the day; and the man and his woman hid themselves from the presence of the Lord God amongst the trees of the garden. And the Lord God called to the man, and said to him: "Where are you?" And he said: "I heard Your voice in the garden, and I was afraid, because I was naked; and I hid myself." And S/He said: "Who told you that you are naked? Have you eaten from the tree from which I commanded you not to eat?" And the man said: "The woman whom You gave to be with me, she gave me from the tree, and I did eat." And the Lord God said to the woman: "What is this you have done?" And the woman said: "The serpent beguiled me, and I did eat." (Genesis 3:8–13)

Hiding rather than standing tall to deal with the outcomes of their disobedience signals their immaturity. During the interrogation, each of the participants blames the next. Irresponsibility is their sin – one important meaning of exile from paradise. Unwillingness to present oneself, to engage with others, to work through consequences, to rebound creatively – all of these evasions generate exile. Exile of the mind and soul from the body is one form. The ensuing curses create

19. *Megilla* 25a.

opposition between Eve and Adam, and institute a hierarchy of domination. God subordinates Eve to Adam, "he will rule over you."

One way to read this text is as an etiological myth – explaining existing social arrangements and reinforcing the dualism of male and female roles as we find them in so many cultures. However, the text does not state or even suggest that it intends the roles of Adam and Eve for anyone beyond their characters in the story. The text does not indicate that Eve and Adam are meant to be the male and female archetypes for all of humanity. The text does not even hint that the behaviors of Adam and Eve are related to sexuality or gender. With the possibility of many readings of this ancient source, dualism does not contribute positive value either to individuals or to society. It aligns mind-body opposition with male-female opposition. These oppositions separate people into categories of rank and privilege that exclude and even lead to abuse and suffering. Rachel Adler, a contemporary theologian, counters the domination in male-female dualism.

> We can invent ways of coexisting without dominating one another.
> The urge to oppose and conquer the other may ultimately be more deadly to our kind than any of its earlier hardships. Dorothy Sayers once asked, "If women are the opposite sex, then what is the neighboring sex?" When woman is defined as derivative, אשה – isha from איש – ish, or invaded נקבה – neqeva, a shared reality is denied. We all live deeply within one another's boundaries. The question is whether we can do so in justice.[20]

Rachel Adler states one facet of difference – defining people as *other* renders us all vulnerable to oppression, as perpetrators and as victims. Seeing difference as negative is a problem that stems from dualism. Difference does not in itself mean that the *other* is less, bad, or wrong. Our challenge is to protect the integrity of difference as a positive value, a dynamic tension that generates creative growth and initiative, and most of all, responsibility. Living "within each other's boundaries in justice" is an antidote to exile. It is one of the challenges of homecoming for all peoples.

---

20. *Engendering Judaism* (Philadelphia, Jerusalem: JPS, 1998), 125.

Human function

Having explored roots of dualism, the following examples from biblical and rabbinic sources demonstrate alternative models for integrating mind/soul and body in daily life contexts. These are non-dualist approaches to human predicaments.

On Hannah's Heart

The biblical book of Samuel begins with a tale of childlessness. Like the foremother Sarah, Hannah feels dejected by God because of her unfulfilled yearning to bring forth new life. The two stories of resolving the unbearable barrenness are read together on Rosh HaShanah, the Days of Awe. Mortals humbled by the limits of their procreative power face their omnipotent Creator. Both stories portray exceptional human challenges arising in the life-cycle. Though each of the characters is materially prosperous, each has a desperate desire for fulfillment that she cannot attain. Hannah bargains with God for the privilege to conceive a child. The original version of the narrative is in the first biblical chapter of the first book of Samuel.

People tend to put more faith in God when they are desperate, and less when they are prosperous. The desperation of Hannah's situation accentuates her faith. Her desire to participate in creation consumes her. Giving birth, a person transcends the limits of her own life, of her mortality. Longing for what is beyond her control opens her heart and soul, and makes her emotionally vulnerable. The second spouse, Peninnah, her cruelty and the misunderstanding priest, Eli – who interprets her as a drunkard – aggravate Hannah's pain. She vows to bring the child for whom she prays to serve in the temple, a promise that she later fulfills. The child, Samuel, whose life Hannah dedicates in gratitude, becomes a great prophet among the Jewish People, a visionary social, political, and ethical critic. Samuel grows to strive with his people and their leaders, arbitrating their inclinations to power and excess.

Rather than as mundane physical reproduction, the Hannah story conceives pregnancy, birth, and nurturing an infant as sublime labor bound up with the sacred realm, with ultimate meaning. She turns to God from the depths of desperation. Awareness of mortality peels away the veneer of control and masks of pretense. Hannah's desperate prayer reveals her material body to be inseparable from her mind and soul – her whole self unites as an integrated, purposeful authentic being. Hannah summons all aspects of herself toward her purpose, contracting an agreement with her Creator for the power to give life.

The Jewish sages derive from Hannah the model for prayer. The Talmud presents a midrash that fills in details missing from the text of Hannah's story. In this passage, they intuit the content of her mumbled prayer from the verse in the biblical chapter, "Hannah was praying *upon her heart.*"

> HANNAH SPOKE UPON HER HEART (I Samuel 1:13).
> Rabi Elazar in the name of Rabi Yossi ben Zimra said, "Concerning the work of her heart/chest/breast." She said,
> "Sovereign of the Universe, everything that You created in woman, you have created nothing in vain.
> Eyes for seeing, ears for hearing, noses for smelling, mouths for speaking, hands for working, legs to walk with, breasts to suckle with. These breasts that you have put on my heart/chest, why are they not for suckling?
> Give me a child and I shall use them to suckle!" (*Berakhot* 31b)

The sages suggest that the biblical phrase, "upon her heart," refers literally to her breasts. From this connection, the midrash derives the idea of Hannah's prayer relating to the proper function of her body. Hannah believes that God can be convinced to fulfill every potential of her body –none of the creation should be wasted. Hannah argues that humans are entitled to fulfill the gift of having been created in the divine image, as a co-creator. The greatness of the human form is diminished, she claims, if we do not fulfill every aspect of its intended purpose. For one special aspect she holds God specially accountable: (pro)creation. Frustrated with her inactive womb, she expresses her desire in relation to her breasts, a more outward feature of her physique. She will put her breasts to use – suckling a child. This midrash interprets each new life to be a collaborative reenactment of creation.

While concern with fertility occupies the biblical *mothers* considerably, the rabbinic readings frame barrenness as an ultimate mortal concern. The fact that the sages model personal prayer after Hannah indicates their perception of the totality of desire that fills a human being who longs for a child. This mortal yearning is not gendered female – it belongs to every creature; it is an underpinning of human virtue. The desire for intimacy, the capacity for caring and empathy affiliate with the will to procreate. Hannah's example asserts that the qualities and activities of procreation – nurturing, feeding, attending to the tender and weak – are important endeavors for the sake of men's and women's humanity. They are a source of the ethical impulse altogether. One crucial element of worthy personhood is living according to our responsibility for the next generation.

Idol-izing Hillel's Holy Body

A midrash tells of how Hillel the Elder's students question him about his frequent visits to the bathhouse. He responds with a remarkable comparison between his body and a heathen statue.

> Hillel the Elder was once leaving his disciples when they said to him, "Master, where are you going?"
> He replied, "To perform a religious duty."
> They said, "And what may that be?"
> He said, "To wash in the bath-house."
> They said, "Is that a religious duty?!"
> He said, "Yes, for if the person who is appointed to scrub and wash the statues (icons) of sovereigns which are set up in theaters and circuses, receives rations for doing so, and is often publicly honored, I, who am created in the divine image of God, as it says, 'In the divine image S/He made the Adam' (Genesis 9:6), how much more incumbent is it upon me to scrub and wash my own body!"[21]

While many Jewish sources and attitudes emphasize the uniqueness and even superiority of Jewish practices and reinforce a deep sense of the otherness of non-Jews, this midrash implicitly critiques the distinction between Jew and heathen. The first of the Ten Commandments declares the Oneness of God, and the second commandment prohibits sculpted images.[22] Though there is no necessary connection between these two commandments, polytheism is often thought to

---

21. Leviticus Rabbah, Behar 34:3
22. Ex. 20:2–4; Deut. 5:6–8.

infringe both simultaneously. Cultures that worship many deities usually represent them in sculpted forms. These forms often depict the gods closely resembling the human body. Throughout thousands of years of observing the biblical restrictions, Jews have carefully avoided representing human and divine forms. This is one of the principles that differentiates monotheism from polytheism. While the aesthetic of the body developed in the ancient Near Eastern cults and in the civilizations of Hinduism, Buddhism, Greece, Rome, and Christianity, Jewish culture has largely excluded sculpture. Sometimes, appreciating the body is even spurned and disdained. This midrash about Hillel the Elder is a notable alternative.

Hillel the Elder exemplifies a respectful rabbinic attitude toward an idolatrous culture's enthusiasm about bodily beauty. He learns the obligation to care for the human body, created in the divine image, from the practices of idolators. If heathen sovereigns ensure that scrupulous care is taken of their human-made stone effigies, then so much more ought we to care for our own bodies that are created by and resemble God, argues Hillel the Elder. In view of the close association of the bath-house with the Roman lifestyle and values, Hillel's openness to teach their example is remarkable. The reactions of his students testify to their amazement at his attitude. The midrash continues with another story.

> Once when Hillel the Elder had concluded his studies with his students, he walked along with them. His students asked him, "Master, where are you gong?"
> He replied, "To bestow kindness upon a guest in the house."
> They said to him, "Every day you have a guest?"
> He replied, "Is not the soul a poor guest in the body? Today it is here and tomorrow no longer?"[23]

Hillel the Elder does not state what precise kindness he intends to bestow upon his guest, his soul. The text interprets a verse from Proverbs that praises a person, "who performs an act of kindness to her/himself."[24] This midrash represents the inter-dependence between the body and soul as a metaphor for complex relationships among various

---

23. Leviticus Rabbah, Behar 34:3
24. Prov. 11:17.

parts of society. The guest in the house, perhaps a poor member of the community he is hosting, symbolizes the soul in the body. Taking this metaphor farther, *neediness* represents the soul housed in the body of the community. By this analogy, each member of a community is potentially vulnerable and needy; each member is worthy of lovingkindness; each member infuses the whole body of society with life. Hillel the Elder seems to make these suggestions without concern about the danger of idolatry that the statuary and adoration of the body suggest to many. The way that Hillel the Elder chooses to describe the kindness one bestows on the guest reinforces the view expressed in the previous story about his respect for and commitment to an integrated approach to his body and soul.

In this midrash, Hillel the Elder asserts that careful attention to the material body is significant to meaningful living. It is even divinely willed – a commandment. This midrash constructs a fearless aesthetic. According to this model, kind and respectful attention to the human body, created by God in the divine image, is a model for personal and social life. Attention to physicality is not only desirable, but inseparable from knowledge and service of the divine, who is, after all, manifest to humanity as the Creator of the material world.[25] This midrash elegantly integrates caring for our bodies and physical well-being with intellectual and spiritual work.

Binding with Glory

The preceding examples make evident the intimate connection between the Torah and the human body. The Torah is often explicit and unabashed in its treatment of physical matters – sex, ejaculation, menstruation, and defecation. Not symptoms of fallen-ness and corruption, all of these topics bear on the sacred realm. In Judaism, the body is a spiritual and intellectual concern. Making this connection

---

25. A similar idea is expressed in the following Talmudic passage:
One day Rabbi Huna asked his son Rabbah why he did not go to study with Rabbi Hisda whose teaching lessons were said to be superlative. The son replied, "When I go to him, he speaks mundane matters. He tells me about certain natural functions of the digestive organs, and how one should behave in regard to them." His father replied, "He occupies himself with the human body, God's special creation, and you call that a mundane matter! All the more should you go to him." (*Shabbat* 82a)

literal, the Torah refers to affixing its own words, its text to the body. Twice in Deuteronomy the Torah states a commandment to attach signs and symbols to the body.[26]

> Tie them as a letter/ sign on your arm, and they will be a symbol between your eyes. (Deuteronomy 6:8)

> Therefore impress these My words upon your own heart: Bind them as a sign on your hand and let them serve as a symbol on your forehead. (11:18)

The sages interpret the meaning of this opaque commandment. Rabbinic authorities pass along the tradition of *tefillin,* phylacteries – small black boxes tied with long leather straps used to bind the box to the head, the seat of consciousness, and wrap around the arm, a limb of action, and facing the heart, the place associated with thought and feeling. These boxes contain the hand-scribed verses of the Torah that command their observance. By this act, a Jew binds his/her body with and to the sacred text. The parchment, enclosed within its skin encasement is held in contact with human skin during prayer; the scrolls encircle the body. According to a Talmudic passage, they encompass one's being with the divine presence.

> Israel is dear because the Holy One, Blessed Be S/he, surrounds/ encompasses them with ritual observances: phylacteries upon their heads, phylacteries upon their arms, fringes upon their garments and *mezuzot* [scriptures] upon their openings [doorposts]. (*Menachot* 43b)

The divine presence, according to this text, becomes manifest in the performance of commandments that literally bind the Torah to the body. Rabbinic tradition associates the *tefillin* with פאר, *pe'er*, glory.[27] While in the prophet Ezekiel's vision this term, *pe'er*, seems to refer to a head wrapping or turban, the sages emphasize the meaning of *pe'er* as glorification. "There are those who say that, 'Wear your *pe'er*, glory, on you(r head)' refers to the *tefillin.*"[28] The Talmud discusses how a person who is in the turmoil of burial arrangements for a dead loved

---

26. See also Ex. 13:9 where the *tefillin* are also mentioned as a sign and reminder.
27. Ez. 24:17.
28. JT *Moed Katan*, 15, 1; ch. 3:5.

one is exempt from the commandment of *tefillin*, for the experience of the divine glory is diminished by the imminence of mortality, death.[29] While not wearing *tefillin* is associated with the trauma of death, wearing *tefillin* is associated with the *en-souled* body, a body infused with life and will. Another Talmudic passage expresses how the *tefillin* are a medium for human-divine reciprocity.

Divine Tefillin

R. Abin son of R. Ada in the name of R. Yitzchak says [further]: How do you know that the Holy One, Blessed Be S/He, puts on *tefillin*? For it is said: 'The Lord has sworn by Her/His right hand, and by the arm of His/Her strength' (Isaiah 62:8). 'By His/Her right hand,' this is the Torah; for it is said: 'At His/Her right hand was a fiery law to them' (Deuteronomy 33:2). 'And by the arm of His/Her strength': This is the *tefillin*; as it says: 'The Lord will give strength to His/Her people' (Psalms 29:11). And how do you know that the *tefillin* are a strength to Israel? For it is written: 'And all the peoples of the earth shall see that the name of the Lord is called upon you, and they shall be afraid of you' (Deuteronomy 27:20), and it has been taught. R. Eliezer the Great says, This refers to the *tefillin* of the head.

R. Nahman child of Isaac said to R. Hiyya child of Abin: What is written in the *tefillin* of the Sovereign of the Universe? – He replied to him: Who is like the Jewish People, a unique nation in the land (I Chronicles 17:21)." (*Berakhot* 6a)

While Maimonides (1135–1204) toiled to explain away biblical images that seem to imply that God has a body (anthropomorphism) in his treatise, *Guide for the Perplexed*, this rabbinic passage explicitly envisions God wearing *tefillin* on the divine head and arm. Figuring God in a human form, when God is not meant to have a physical form at all, the sages provoke us to question in what sense God has a body.

There are many passages that allude to the divine body. In a moment of longing, Moses asks God an unusual request, "Please show me Your Glory,"[30] as if it is possible to *see* God. God replies that human beings cannot apprehend the divine presence and continue to live. This

---

29. BT *Berakhot* 16b.
30. Ex. 33:18.

response does not eschew the existence of the divine body, but rather substantiates it. God agrees to place Moses in a crevice in a rock, protecting the prophet from the dangerous presence until God *passes by*.

> See, there is a place near Me. Station yourself on the rock and, as My Presence passes by, I will put you in a cleft of the rock and shield you with My hand until I have passed by. Then I will take My hand away and you will see My back; but My face must not be seen. (Exodus 33:22)

The terms *back* and *face* allude to a divine body that resembles the human. The sages explain the meaning creatively. "Rabbi Shimon Hasida explains that God showed Moses the knot (*kesher*) of the divine *tefillin*."[31] This text about *tefillin* fantasizes the divine resembling a human being – inverting, or perhaps reciprocating the creation narrative according to which human resembles the divine. Even more extraordinary, the sages envision God's body bound with inscriptions that commit God to People – human and divine function inter-dependently. The sages figure the Creator and created as a dyad of connection and commitment. In this relationship, the dualist categories soften into a reciprocity of divine material and human spirit.

Interfusion

Rather than opposites, these sources propose that human physicality is continuous with an intelligent soul; mind and body interfuse with one another. The texts demand respect for the body as a formidable element of human spiritual and intellectual qualities; mind/soul and body derive from and are continuously sustained by creative force.

The Jewish People innovated abstract monotheism, belief in an immaterial deity. Maimonides and other great thinkers who follow an Aristotelean tradition idealize transcendence of the material world into the realms of pure thought. Nonetheless, there is a great deal of emphasis in Jewish life on material action as the daily medium for sanctifying life. Jewish observances sanctify the Shabbat with candles and wine, wrap body and soul in prayer shawls and bind arms and heads with sacred texts, immerse in natural water for purification,

---

31. *Berakhot* 7a.

separate milk and meat, shake palm and willow branches and fondle citron fruit and wave palm branches to express the joy of the harvest during the Festival of Tabernacles, Sukkot. We scour our kitchens to remove leaven before Passover, *et cetera*. Intentional action enables human beings to experience the imminent divine, make spirit more accessible, more knowable. According to Jewish practice, our physical body is not an albatross that prevents us from soaring into the sublime realms of intellect and spirit – the body participates in mindful spiritual action. The goal is not transcendence of the body and its corruptions, but experience of our bodies in this material world, where spirit and mind participate fully in the meaning-making of daily ritual and life.

Deeply rooted in Western culture, mind-body dualism alienates people from important dimensions of ourselves and one other. Alternative models in Jewish texts and practice conjoin mind, spirit, and body in a more coherent approach to life. These models have important implications for the relationship of the Jewish People to the land of Israel. They help conceive one of the driving purposes of Zionism: to better integrate the dualism of Jewish mind and body on a personal and national scale. One of the great innovations of Zionism is reconnecting the mind, soul, and body of the Jewish People.

3 Home-Building Project

EXILE IS THE CONDITION of dislocation from *home*.

More than a place to live, home implies attachment and belonging. Sometimes home has to do with familiarity, with ancestry, with ancient memory, or with a sense of holiness. Though we might spend most of our life away from home after fire and destruction, the desire for home does not necessarily abate – sometimes it grows more acute. The Jewish People has long been questing for home.

During the middle of the twentieth century, European Jewry suffered terribly as a direct result of homelessness. Today, Jewish organizations often try to arouse the emotions of belonging, rallying to defy Hitler's *Final Solution* to render the Jewish People extinct. Yet, *continuity* of an ancient people for its own sake and guilt do not motivate vibrant Jewish life. Many Jews in this generation find the Zionist achievement of homecoming irrelevant or even burdensome. Rather than resisting the rebelliousness of young people defensively, we can channel doubts, disaffection, and criticism toward renewing Zionism(s).

Throughout the unfolding Jewish relationship to space, one of the abiding themes is Beit Hamikdash-Temple – sacred home. The life-cycle of the Jerusalem Temples marks Jewish historical periods – building, service, destruction, exile and return. The Babylonian destruction of the First Temple in 586 BCE moved prophets to visions of just society and sublime spirit, sent Jews into captivity, and inaugurated the Diaspora. In 537 BCE, exiles returned to the land, rebuilt the Jerusalem Temple, and ushered in a turbulent period. The Second

Temple era ended with the brutal Roman conquest that ravaged Judaea in 70 CE and banished the Jewish People. During two millennia, most of the Jewish People lived away from home, dispersed throughout the world. According to legend, the *Shekhina* – the female divine presence left her dwelling when the Jerusalem Temple was destroyed, and wandered with the exiles.[1]

More than geographic absence, exile transpires in Jewish consciousness. Exile describes the alienation of the mind from the body. While the Jewish body often experienced pain –crusades, inquisitions, pogroms, and expulsions – Jews displaced material discomfort and disempowerment, and lit on desire for Israel, *home*. The greatest biblical prophet, Moses himself, bequeathed the tradition of dying with longing; his final supplication is to enter the Promised Land.[2] Every generation of the Jewish People has been reliving Moses's desire. "Gather us from our dispersion and lead us upright to our land," pleads the traditional daily liturgy. Though remote and unrealistic, the hope to dwell at home in Zion abides throughout millennia of exile.

While many immigrants look favorably upon the absorption of their descendants into host cultures, Jews have usually resisted assimilation and persisted to cultivate distinct ways of life – languages, food, clothing, cultural habits and beliefs. Detaching from the often inhospitable Diaspora and its oppressions, Jews developed a demeanor of not belonging. Because we regarded ourselves as temporary sojourners, we resisted investing fully in our surroundings. A form of dualism – disengagement of the mind and soul from the body –coalesced around *homelessness*. Jews came to dissociate the sacred ideal of Israel from the profane realm of exile. The possibility of rebuilding a fully functional Jewish society lay dormant until the modern period while the fantasy of home grew. The material unattainability of the *Promised Land* became indispensable to the Diaspora desire for transcendence, for the sacred. Yearning moved the Jewish soul to channel effort into intellectual and spiritual pursuits. Jews insulated and protected their mind and spirit from the difficult experience of the body. This antidote to powerlessness helps to account for the tremendous spiritual, intel-

---

1. *Avoda Zara* 29a.
2. *Devarim* 3:23–25.

lectual, and musical productivity of Jews during nearly two thousand years in exile.

Sent from their land by the Roman destruction in 70 CE, Jews established prosperous academies in Babylon. There, sages composed and redacted a core rabbinic corpus – the Babylonian Talmud. Jewish life-styles and literatures flowed forth from the communities of the Oral Torah. New approaches and practices replaced the Temple service that had once been the center of Jewish life, and made it possible for Jews and Judaism to thrive away from home. In the twelfth and thirteenth centuries, the bold innovations of Kabbala grew in southern France and Spain. Hasidism took root in the impoverished hamlets of Eastern Europe during the eighteenth century. Jews in Turkey, Syria, Iraq, North Africa and Yemen elaborated sublime mystical, musical, literary, and legal traditions. Jewish communities negotiated their survival, adapting and evolving Jewish life in their cultural milieu. Enduring adverse conditions with creativity and hope became one of the hallmarks of Jewish Peoplehood.[3] Jews cultivated a sublime desire for home in poetry, prayer, and song. During the first Crusade in the eleventh century, while Christians conquer distant Jerusalem, Yehuda HaLevi (ca. 1070–1141) sings of the pain of exile and longing in odes to Zion.

My heart is in the east, and I in the uttermost West –	לִבִּי בְמִזְרָח וְאָנֹכִי בְּסוֹף מַעֲרָב
How can I find savor in food? How shall it delight me?	אֵיךְ אֶטְעֲמָה אֵת אֲשֶׁר אֹכַל וְאֵיךְ יֶעֱרָב
How shall I pay my vows and my bonds, while yet	אֵיכָה אֲשַׁלֵּם נְדָרַי וַאֱסָרַי, בְּעוֹד
Zion lies beneath the fetter of Rome, and I in Arab chains?	צִיּוֹן בְּחֶבֶל אֱדוֹם וַאֲנִי בְּכֶבֶל עֲרָב
In my eyes, abandoning all the good things of Spain is as easy as	יֵקַל בְּעֵינַי עֲזֹב כָּל טוֹב סְפָרַד, כְּמוֹ
Seeing how precious in my eyes it is to behold the dust of the destroyed Holy of Holies.[4]	יֵקַר בְּעֵינַי רְאוֹת עַפְרוֹת דְּבִיר נֶחֱרָב.

---

3. The Tibetan leader, the Dalai Lama looks to the Jewish People as a model for survival during oppression and exile.

4. Slightly modified translation by Nina Salaman, 1924, published in 1924 by

The poet idealizes Zion as the ultimate destination because its meaning exceeds material. The dust of the destroyed Temple is more precious than the luxuries of Spain during the Golden Age. The spiritual torment of exile traumatizes his daily life. Eating, pleasure, and fortune all betray the urgency of returning to Zion. For HaLevi, in exile, the body is unredeemed, its delight unjustified. Yehuda HaLevi began his life in Muslim Spain, in Toledo, the capital of Castile. During the constant Muslim-Christian contests, he moved to Cordoba, under Christian control, the cultural capital of Spanish Jewry. He died either on his journey, or shortly after he arrived in the land of Israel.

Yehuda HaLevi's poetry suggests how the privation of exile is unabated even during prosperity such as in his native Spain. The vagaries of competing empires, religious powers, inimical popular sentiments, and national ideologies breed uncertainty and fear. Moreover, long stints of normalization are punctuated by anti-Semitic disturbances that often lead to homelessness, destruction, and migration. In this generation, record numbers of French Jews are coming to Israel as they feel anti-Semitism rising.[5]

To whatever extent uniqueness feeds persecution, Jews have been subjected to cruel policies and violence. The demeanor of aloofness might have contributed to the vulnerability of the Jewish People to persecution. Even embracing Western European culture, Jews were selected for extermination. At the hours of most extreme need, the world virtually sealed its borders to Jews – before, during, and after the Second World War. The effect of the suffering and loss that the Jewish People has endured is inestimable. The Holocaust of European Jewry, and the destruction and mass exodus of major Jewish communities from North Africa and the Arab states inform Jewish attitudes and life choices, consciously and unconsciously. Pain and fear, distrust and sadness are deeply etched – like numbers branded into the Jewish soul. When the divine image was torn from human life, the coming into existence of the State of Israel verges on the miraculous. One of Israel's founding purposes – articulated in the Law of Return – is to welcome

---

Jewish Publication Society of America. Original Hebrew publication: 1141.

5. 3,300 French Jews immigrated to Israel in 2005. "Record number of French olim arriving," *Jerusalem Post*, 07/25/2006, retrieved Oct. 4, 2011, http://www.jpost.com/CafeOleh/CafeTalk/Article.aspx?id=29317.

every Jew at every moment.[6] While a small number of Israelis holds dual citizenship, for the vast majority, Israel is the one and only home. The healing work of homebuilding is sacred and incremental. Israel has continuously rescued and absorbed survivors and refugees, giving tremendous solace to world Jewry, nurture for a broken body.

Arab inhabitants of southern Ottoman Syria – which later became British Mandate Palestine – did not favor the influx of Jews in the late nineteenth and twentieth century to the land they also considered *home*. The resulting conflict displaced hundreds of thousands of Arabs and Jews.[7] Twenty-two Arab nations refused to absorb the 711,000 Arab refugees of the 1948 war as immigrants. Together with the United Nations, they perpetuate Palestinian refugee status.[8] During the same period from 1948, the new Jewish state received 800,000–1,000,000 Jews who left, fled, or were expelled from their homes in Arab and Muslim countries, and approximately 200,000 Jewish survivors and refugees from post-Holocaust Europe as full citizens of an open democratic society.[9]

---

6. The Law of Return was passed by the Knesset on the 20th Tammuz, 5710 (July 5, 1950) and published in *Sefer HaChukkim* No. 51 of the 21st Tammuz, 5710 (July 5, 1950), 159.

7. The 1948 war period is hotly debated among historians. In the 1980s an Israeli academic school of "New Historians" arose who criticize the "Old Historians'" interpretations, paving a road for post-Zionism. Among the protagonists are Benny Morris, Ilan Pappé, Avi Shlaim, Tom Segev, and Hillel Cohen.

8. UNRWA estimates for 1948. The United Nations Relief and Works Agency for Palestine Refugees is the sole UN Agency dedicated to one refugee group, the only refugee status conferred generation-to-generation. The current estimate is 4.8 million. "General Progress Report and Supplementary Report of the United Nations Conciliation Commission for Palestine, Covering the Period from 11 December 1949 to 23 October 1950," United Nations Conciliation Commission for Palestine, 1950, retrieved May 5, 2011, http://domino.un.org/unispal.nsf/9a798adbf322aff3852561 7b006d88d7/93037e3b939746de8525610200567883.

In a 1957 resolution, "The Arab League has instructed that Palestinians living in Arab countries should not be given citizenship to avoid dissolution of their identity and protect their right to return to their homeland." P.K. Abdul Ghafour, "A Million Expatriates to Benefit From New Citizenship Law," *Arab News*, retrieved May 12, 2011, http://archive.arabnews.com/?page=1&section=0&article=53213&d=21&m =10&y=2004.

9. See Malka Hillel Shulewitz (ed.), *The Forgotten Millions: The Modern Jewish Exodus from Arab Lands* (London; New York: Cassell, 1999).

More than a place of refuge, the State of Israel reunites the Jewish body, mind, and soul, and enables Jewry to rejoice in a new wholeness. Zionism resurrects the dignity of world Jewry from grotesque abuse and humiliation, from the ashes of Auschwitz. Resembling a prophetic vision, Israel gives flesh to dry bones.[10] At home at last, Zionism aims to unbridle expression of thousands of years of Jewish creativity in all aspects of human endeavor. From the founding of the State, Israel succeeds to overcome threats to her existence, to generate viable sustenance – pioneering agriculture that "makes the desert bloom" – and to contribute innovations to human society, science, and culture. During her early decades, Israel renewed the grandeur of Jewish destiny.

In the June 1967 war, Israel defeated the combined Egyptian, Jordanian, and Syrian armies in six days. Driving enemy forces out of the Sinai Peninsula, Gaza Strip, the West Bank, and the Golan Heights, Israel became a reluctant administrator of a sizable Arab population. Israel repelled the incursions of the 1973 surprise Yom Kippur attack by a Syrian and Egyptian-led coalition that profoundly threatened her existence. After this series of military defeats, first Egypt – in 1979, then Jordan – in 1994, made peace with Israel. As part of the agreement with Egypt, Israel dismantled its settlements and military installations and withdrew fully from the Sinai Peninsula. Meanwhile, Israel's Arab enemies shifted strategy away from conventional warfare to execute a terror offensive and launch an economic campaign. From 1968, pro-Palestinian groups carried out international attacks on civilians, killing Israelis and other nationals in airports and at the Olympics, at school, and on buses. Flight hijackings held Western states ransom.[11] In 1973, the Organization of Arab Petroleum Exporting Countries mobilized oil power to undermine support for Israel throughout the world. This concerted campaign gradually morphed the Western concept of the "Arab-Israeli" conflict – powerful, wealthy, autocratic, and populous

---

10. See Ez. 37.

11. On July 4, 1976, the Israel Defense Forces carried out *Operation Jonathan* at Entebbe Airport in Uganda, rescuing 103 Jewish hostages. The other 145 non-Jewish hostages of the 248 taken captive on the Air France Athens to Paris Airbus A300 had been released. On October 13, 1977 four members of the Popular Front for the Liberation of Palestine hijacked Lufthansa Flight 181. West German counter-terrorism group GSG 9 stormed the airplane in Mogadishu, Somalia, and rescued all 86 passengers.

Arab nations lined up against a small, lone, isolated, democratic Israel
– into the "Palestinian liberation struggle" against Israel. Portraying
Israeli military rule over unwilling Palestinians, stone-throwing Palestinian youths appropriate the image of a small, lone David facing a
Goliath-like Israeli armed force. The dispute about the Palestinian-
populated West Bank – known as biblical Judaea and Samaria to Jews
who have made their homes in ancient Jewish sites – poses serious
political and ethical challenges to Israel and serves as ground for
condemnation. In this new millennium, many are losing perspective
on the Zionist enterprise. Once a young and bold adventurer, Israel
has reached middle age and appears to many to have become part of a
sordid establishment. Disillusionment sets in.

Israeli Jews feel little of the control and security that would accompany the strength attributed to Israel. Palestinian uprisings – *Intifadas*
with their suicide bombers traumatize Israelis.[12] The wars in Lebanon
against Hezbollah and in Gaza against Hamas seem nearly futile while
wealthy enemy Arab regimes arm and train their terrorist proxies. The
danger, threat, and injury to the Jewish body persists, even intensifies.
Rejection and aggression from neighbors mutes the joy of accomplish-
ing the long-desired return to Zion.

Israel unilaterally withdrew from the Gaza Strip in 2005 – without
securing an agreement with the Palestinians. The national turmoil
about forcing the Israeli Gush Katif inhabitants out of their homes in
Gaza rent Israeli society.

> But since the withdrawal, the terms of debate have changed. There is
> not only an argument over land and the occupation but also a cultural
> war between two parts of Israeli society: Israelis who believe that the
> Jewish state cannot exist without a strong connection to the Jewish
> religion, and Israelis who think that Israel must become a secular
> society.[13]

The debate during 2005 indicates the struggle for the identity of
Israel as homeland. Whether for or against the Gaza disengagement,
the rise to power of Hamas in the aftermath is as demoralizing as it

---

12. Suicide attacks on Israel, retrieved June 1, 2011, http://en.wikipedia.org/wiki/
List_of_Palestinian_suicide_attacks.

13. Meyrav Wurmser, "Zionism in Crisis," *Middle East Quarterly*, Winter 2006,
39–47.

was unforeseen. Hamas – the Islamist Palestinian-Gaza regime – vows commitment to the destruction of Israel, barraging Israeli civilian targets in the south with rockets. In the winter of 2008–9, Israel conducted Operation Cast Lead to restrain the attacks.

Despite the complete lack of evidence, the Goldstone Report condemned Israel for intentionally targeting civilians during the Gaza military operation. Judge Richard Goldstone himself later retracted this central claim. At the same time, he maintains, "the crimes allegedly committed by Hamas were intentional goes without saying – its rockets were purposefully and indiscriminately aimed at civilian targets."[14] The Report remarks about Hamas strategy,

> In July 2009, Hamas declared that it was entering a period of "cultural resistance," stating that it was suspending its use of rockets and shifting its focus to winning support at home and abroad through cultural initiatives and public relations.[15]

In spite of the declaration, rocket attacks against Israelis have continued while the cultural campaign is in full force.[16] The Egyptian-Israeli blockade of Gaza feeds rather than weakens Hamas's anti-Israel policies. Meanwhile, during the Arab Spring of 2011, Egypt opened the Rafah border to human movement. Surrounded by revolutions and unknowable prospects in the region, Israel persists with the desire for stability and cooperation while forced to maintain constant vigilance and preparedness against aggression.

Uncertainty about how to relate to the burgeoning national will of the Palestinians in a responsible way that also achieves security and peaceful coexistence gnaws at the Jewish psyche, in Israel and abroad. Though the intense hostile atmosphere tends to push Israeli politics

14. "Reconsidering the Goldstone Report on Israel and war crimes," *Washington Post,* April 2, 2011, retrieved May 3, 2011, http://www.washingtonpost.com/opinions/reconsidering-the-goldstone-report-on-israel-and-war-crimes/2011/04/01/AFg111JC_story.html.

15. The Goldstone Report, of the United Nations Fact Finding Mission on the Gaza Conflict, headed by Richard Goldstone, p. 523, para. 1680. The US House of Representatives overwhelmingly passed a resolution denouncing the report as "irredeemably biased and unworthy of further consideration or legitimacy" on November 3, 2009.

16. On April 7, 2011, Hamas fired a laser-guided anti-tank missile at an Israeli school bus near Kibbutz Nahal Oz.

toward more defensiveness, most Israelis accept the inevitability of Palestinian autonomy. The consensus in Israel favors a two-state solution – with secure, defensible borders.[17] The 2011 pact between Hamas and Fatah – whose policies held promise of peaceful side-by-side statehood – discombobulates. Zionism is at the nexus of a global struggle between Islam and the West.

Constant public delegitimizing of Israel mitigates against a constructive and nuanced relationship; supporting Israel is becoming passé. Non-Orthodox Jews contest the Israeli ultra-Orthodox religious establishment.[18] The Diaspora and Israel are increasingly estranged, worsening Israel's sense of isolation.[19] Recent Israeli administrations appeal to few among the young generation who were raised with liberal politics, "a belief in open debate, a skepticism about military force, a commitment to human rights."[20] Ironically, unlike any other country in the Middle East, Israel upholds and implements these values.

At this point, positions about the conflict are exceedingly polarized. American Jewish lobbies – AIPAC and the youthful J Street – are pitted against one another. Literary scholar, Michael Gluzman, remarks about the differences between earlier and current conversations,

> When you read Brenner [a prominent Zionist intellectual from the second aliya period, 1904–1914], for example, you see that his criticism of Zionism is far more acute than that of a lot of post-Zionists today, *but he perceived himself as part of the Zionist discourse*. I am very critical of many Zionist phenomena, but I still see myself as part of the camp. I think that Jews are also entitled to self-definition."[21] [my emphasis]

---

17. "Israel Accepts Unarmed Palestinian State," CBS News, June 14, 2009, retrieved May 24, 2011, http://www.cbsnews.com/stories/2009/06/14/world/main5087808.shtml.

18. The most numerous denominations outside of Israel – Reform and Conservative – dissent from the Israeli Chief Rabbinate's control of conversion, marriage, divorce, and burial, and criteria for who counts as a Jew.

19. By contrast, many Orthodox communities and conservative Christians offer unconditional support of Israel.

20. Peter Beinart, "The Failure of the American Jewish Establishment," *NYT Book Review*, retrieved June 10, 2010, http://www.nybooks.com/articles/archives/2010/jun/10/failure-american-jewish-establishment/.

21. Michael Gluzman, author of *The Zionist Body: Nationalism, Gender and*

History has dealt cruelly with both Israelis and Palestinians; each feels afflicted by the other. Many fan the flames and reap ideological, political, and economic gains from the enmity. We need to move beyond the narratives of condemnation and fear. Those directly suffering the conflict will benefit more if people resist self-righteousness and self-justifying postures. We ought to evaluate our interventions, words and deeds, and aim for understanding, caring, and commitment to resolution, to achieving security and peace.

In spite of criticism, leaders among all of the Jewish denominations continue to hold Israel to be significant to Jewish identity. Institutions invest in Israel experience – Birthright and MASA, and study programs for educators and rabbis. Most of the organizers see Israel as an immersion in Judaism and Jewish Peoplehood: Israel is a purveyor of Hebrew language, Jewish content, social and religious experience, Jewish books and products, and Jewish identity. Here, we explore spiritual dimensions of the Jewish *home-exile* narrative with the aim to contribute depth and perspective. We turn to the wandering biblical Israelites and the model of sacred *home*.

Revealing Scenes

Escaping from slavery in Egypt en route to the Promised Land, the Israelites journey into an expansive desert. They camp at the foot of Mount Sinai, exhilarated and anxious, filled with anticipation. The young nation of Israel encounters the *sacred* for the first time.

The revelation at Mount Sinai and the birth of the State of Israel are both spectacular collective events in the Jewish meta-narrative. The question is how to keep their freshness from fading and infuse their significance into the everyday life of a people. Immediately after receiving the Torah at Mount Sinai, the Torah prescribes the building of the Tabernacle, the Mishkan. The first national project of the Jewish People is constructing a public sanctuary. God speaks to Moses, "They will make me a sanctuary-Tabernacle that I may dwell in/

Sexuality in Modern Hebrew Literature (Tel Aviv: Hakibbutz Hameuchad, 2007), *Haaretz*, May 24, 2011, retrieved May 24, 2011, http://www.haaretz.com/weekend/week-s-end/the-gay-man-s-guide-to-zionist-literature-1.222013.

among them."²² Rather than a verbal, unearthly covenant, the Mishkan embeds the revelation in an intricate material-spiritual system – retaining the liveliness of the sacred revelation, protecting and making it accessible. Physicality is at the heart of Jewish sanctification.

From the introduction of the Mishkan onward, the biblical books of Exodus and much of Leviticus are preoccupied with its construction and function. With the settlement of the Jewish People in the land of Israel, the roving Mishkan transfers permanently to Jerusalem. The Jewish People twice built a Temple, a sacred home in Jerusalem – in the tenth century BCE and again in the late sixth century BCE. The Mishkan-Temple model institutes community service during the ancient periods of Jewish sovereignty in the land of Israel. After the destruction, Mishkan-Temple ideas mobilize the energy and organize the social, civil, and spiritual life of the Jewish nation for thousands of years away from home. The structure, function, purposes, and controversies involving the Mishkan-Temple are relevant to Zionism – comparable national projects of the Jewish People.

What Matters?

The Tabernacle-Mishkan constructs a home for the divine in the midst of the community. The raw materials for the project are to be collected from each person whose heart moves him/her to give. The people are instructed to offer contributions, *terumah*.

> These are the offerings that you shall take from them: gold, silver, and copper; azure blue, purple, and crimson, fine linen, goats' hair; tanned ram skins, *tachash* [dolphin?] skins, and acacia wood; oil for lighting, spices for the anointing oil and for the aromatic incense; lapis lazuli and other stones for setting, for the ephod [vest] and for the breast-piece. (Exodus 25:2–7)

This list draws from the diverse creation – metals from the veins of the earth, vivid colors exuded by sea creatures, skins from animals, wood, oil and spices from the plant world, and stones from the earth's crust. The Mishkan combines diverse human endeavors and encourages participation without separating manual from mental work. People

---

22. Exodus 25:8.

combine their skillful craft and art with raw material, infusing material with spirit and intellect to produce sacred forms and service. Bezalel coordinates the project. The Torah states his qualifications and his job description,

> God has filled him with a divine spirit, ability and knowledge in every kind of craft. And to conceive designs to make in gold, silver and copper, to cut stones for setting and to carve wood – to work in every thoughtful craft. And to teach – S/He put in his heart. (35:31–34)

The Mishkan project puts the community to work beyond the purposes of sustenance. Rabbinic discourses elaborate the spiritual-material national project. A debate about the Mishkan between two famous medieval commentators, Rashi (1040–1105 CE) and Nachmanides/ Ramban (1194–1270) is relevant to modern Zionism.

Rashi argues that the Torah does not initially intend for the Jewish People to build a physical dwelling for the divine presence. Commenting about the Mishkan commandment, Rashi states his often-cited theory that the Torah text is not chronological.[23] Rashi claims that the commandment to build the Tabernacle comes only *after* the sin of the golden calf – as a concession to implacable human desire for tangible ritual.

When Moses delays for a few extra hours communing with God on the summit of Mount Sinai, the people grow anxious. Though only a few verses earlier they had made a binding covenant with a formless God, they long for corroboration of the Exodus and the revelation. Moses's brother Aaron steps in as leader. He collects contributions of gold, fashions a calf and plans a festival complete with sacrifices, feasting, and dancing.

Meanwhile, Moses is receiving the stone tablets etched by God's hand. The material of the tablets is the subject of creative speculation in a midrash.

> Rabi Pinchas in the name of Rabi Shimon ben Lakish [taught], "The Torah that the Holy One gave to him was white fire etched with black fire, fire intermingled with fire, incised with fire, and given from fire, as it says, 'At His/Her right hand was a fiery law to them'" (Deuteronomy 33:2). (JT *Shekalim* 25, 2, 6, i)

23. Rashi on Ex. 31:18.

Whereas stone and black ink letters are cold and fixed, the Talmud conceives the letters as fire – hot and live. Faced with idolatrous revelry, the holy letters break free and send the empty stone tablets crashing to the ground. The broken tablets illustrate an aim for Zionism – reassembling scattered broken shards to create a vessel capable of sustaining the inspiration and covenant of the Jewish People.

God's threat to destroy the entire unfaithful nation jolts Moses into leading the Israelites in repentance. His supplications elicit from God the thirteen divine attributes of compassion that form the core of the Yom Kippur prayers – the most sacred day of the Jewish year.[24] After easing the crisis, Moses and God co-produce a second set of tablets – Moses hews the stone and engraves the Ten Commandments, etching them into the foundation of Western social and religious ethics.

According to Rashi, on account of the sin of the golden calf, God commands the Mishkan to focus Israelite materialism on the covenant with God. Having proven that they stray so easily from the intangible divine One, the people need a permissible channel for their idolatrous inclinations.[25] The Mishkan is an acceptable accommodation to human folly.

Ramban rejects Rashi's view outright. Ramban argues that the order of the text *is* chronological – the instruction to build the Mishkan comes *before* the golden calf. Just as human relationships sometimes suffer setbacks, in the enduring love affair between the Jewish People and the Creator, the golden calf incident is a brief fling. The divine intention had all along been to instruct the building of the Mishkan – to put physical materials to sacred use. According to Ramban's theory, the Jewish People comes to know and love God more fully through artistic creation and spiritually-informed material ritual. The Jewish People comes to know and love God more fully also, we impute, by sometimes straying. In Ramban's view, the Mishkan is not a compromise, but a desirable way to merge body, soul, and mind in the created world, and to connect with the Creator.[26]

The golden calf incident and the inauguration of the Mishkan are

---

24. Ex. 34.
25. Midrash Tanchuma, *Truma*, 8.
26. Ramban on Ex. 35:1.

strikingly similar – a very thin line separates *holy* from *foreign* worship.[27] Both services use physical objects made from precious material contributed by the people. They are both auspicious public festive gatherings with similar animal sacrifices. At both, the people are emotionally aroused – in one case rising to dance, in the other case, rejoicing and falling on their faces. Subtle preparation and initiation into intricate service, diversity of materials and extensive artistic labor, blessing of the people, and the divine epiphany – distinguish the Mishkan from idolatry.

These two different views also apply to Zionism. According to Rashi, desire for material is reprehensible, whereas for Ramban, it is beyond reproach. Ramban believes that physical service is not only legitimate, but desirable – it is one of the purposes for the creation of the world. Ramban's approach embraces Zionism, while Rashi's is reticent. Rashi might have considered the Jewish state an expedient necessity due to the historical need that anti-Semitism generated – the Jewish *problem*; Ramban might have endorsed the project as intrinsically worthwhile. Ramban's view supports the legitimacy and value of collaborative material service. Ramban affirms the sincerity of the people's desire to engage in and with Creation and aim for the sacred, beckoning each individual to contribute to a national purpose. These attitudes help explain divine leniency in respect to Aaron's role with the golden calf and selection as High Priest. God seems to tolerate sincere attempts even when they sometimes err.[28] The idolatry and the Mishkan share the same underlying yearning – collective service using the full array of human senses and vitality. This yearning is a relevant purpose for Zionism. Ramban respects the value of the project along with Israel's mistakes, affirming capability to grow and improve through loving commitment and the will to give and serve.

Giving Freely

The Mishkan poses a conundrum – the Torah *commands* each person whose heart moves her or him to offer a gift *voluntarily*. The text

---

27. Ex. 32:1–5 and Lev. 9:22–24.

28. The civil war described in the text as part of the atonement is nonetheless problematic. See Ex. 32:25–29.

presumes that obligation to contribute to society coexists with free choice to give. The biblical Israelites respond with overwhelming generosity. When the warehouse is bursting with gifts from the people, the craftspeople need to declare, "enough."[29]

The initial Zionist inspiration is to build a new society – a collective expression of the contributions of the Jewish People, past, present, and future. Lamentably, within and outside Israel, the disposition to contribute erodes. Israelis are wearying from the stress of defending for survival, and from the resulting traumas of war, terror, and loss. The 2005 Lebanon War that jeopardized the residents of the north and their livelihood did not elicit the same public outpouring as previous national emergencies. Afterwards, the Winograd Report indicted the government for its reckless management of the war, prompting public outcry for the resignation of the Prime Minister. The effort proved ineffectual – the government outlived the protest. Disillusionment with institutions of society neutralizes much public involvement. At the same time, the fierce winds of individualism from the West and the profit motive of today's market economy blow, eroding the collective national focus of Zionism. The goals need to be refreshed. Where once the Zionist priority was to establish and secure the state, today, improving civic engagement, political responsibility, education, health, resource distribution, ecology, religious pluralism are items for the Zionist agenda. These purposes require renewed social values and an ethos of contributing toward a shared project. The summer of 2011 public outcry for social justice needs to channel into strategic and productive effort. The Mishkan model is instructive for individuals and society.

The Mishkan model values every person's capacity to give. It also presumes mutual respect and the dignity of all. Giving well requires a balance between self-confidence and humility, belief in and appreciating one's own gift at the same time as knowing that it is not definitive. *Terumah*-contribution is a complex personal and collective process. One task is for each person to discern and prepare her or his own offering – talent and capability – and to integrate one's gift coherently with others. Another task is for the community and its leaders to welcome and value the gifts.

---

29. Ex. 36:4–7.

Among the offerings, the Torah specifically notes women, spinning and weaving,[30] and contributing copper. Midrashic traditions record controversy about the copper. Moses's inventory of the Mishkan materials does not mention the copper for the water basin used by the priests' to purify their hands.[31] An earlier verse explains the source of the copper, "He made the basin from copper and its stand from copper, from the mirrors of the [legions of] women who served at the entrance to the Tent of Meeting."[32] Midrash Tanchuma, a ninth century collection, elaborates about the women.

The women find that God has provided small fish in the basins of water they draw from the Nile. They sell a percentage of the fish – buying wine with their proceeds – and cook what remains. With fish and wine they greet their spouses in the fields.[33]

Rashi summarizes the midrash,

When their spouses would be exhausted from the grueling labor imposed upon them by the Egyptians, [the women] would go and take them food and drink, and feed them. Then they would take the mirrors, and each one would view herself with her spouse in the mirror, and seduce him with words, saying, "I am more handsome than you." In this way, they would arouse their spouses, and would have sexual relations with them. God would bestow Her/His countenance upon them and they would conceive and give birth there . . . ."

Moses rejects the women's offer of the mirrors for the basin. God overrules Moses,

The Holy One, Blessed is S/He, said, "Accept them, because these are the dearest to Me of all, for by means of them, the women established many legions of offspring in Egypt."[34]

According to this midrash, Moses considers copper used for erotic purposes – to arouse intimacy between men and women – unfit for a

30. Ibid., 35:25.

31. Ibid.38:29–31.

32. Ibid.38:8.

33. Tanchuma, *Pekudai*, 9.

34. Rashi on Ex. 38:8.

sacred function. God asserts that these very mirrors are specially fit for the basin, for the sacred service.

The dispute about women's contributions to public society continues long after the Mishkan. Rabbi Avraham Yitzchak HaCohen Kook, an eloquent early proponent of religious Zionism, argues forcefully against women's suffrage in the new State of Israel.

> Do not touch the foundation of foundations of the rights of our mothers, sisters and daughters. The original firm rights, that are founded upon the beautification of the special internal moral and natural power, and on the sacred, refined and noble value of the woman of Israel, which make deep roots in life, and bring it a lasting happiness.
>
> The Israelite woman bases her rights on the refined content of her unique psychic value, not on measured and limited laws, formed in a mechanical cast, which are for her iron horns, which do not suit at all her psychic refinement.[35]

Rav Kook argues against women's suffrage on the basis of women's *psyche* which he considers unsuited to matters of state. Like Moses, he rejects women's contribution to the Jewish public project of his day. Zionism overcame Kook's objection. However, the work of enabling women's full public participation and leadership among the Jewish People is incomplete. Though Golda Meir served as Prime Minister, and Dorit Beinisch president of the Supreme Court, in 2011, only seventeen of one hundred and twenty Knesset members are women. At fourteen percent women in government, Israel ranks between the Arab world and developing countries, slightly behind the USA.[36] Our medieval midrash conveys divine instruction to welcome the offerings of all those who seek to contribute constructively – an inspiration for Israel and all communities.

---

35. "General Responsum," *Maamrei Haraaya* (Jerusalem: Avner Publishing, 1984 (1920)), 192.

36. 40 percent of Scandinavian legislators are women. "Only 5 percent of the leadership of Jewish organizations in the United States is headed by women." California State Senator Jackie Speier, "Women on Top," May 9, 2002, Marin JCC, San Rafael, http://www.jewishsf.com/content/2-0-/module/displaystory/story_id/18241/ edition_id/365/format/html/displaystory.html.

The Temple Body

The Mishkan-Temple facilitates interactions – among personal and public life, and heaven and earth, and joins them together in an ongoing cyclical narrative. Its materials, structure, and ritual create a shared language for society.

Apart from its portability for travel with the Israelite camp during desert wanderings, the Mishkan is the model for the architecture and function of the later Jerusalem Temple. The Mishkan is an oblong structure. The wooden frame, its posts and planks joined by silver sockets and tenon joints, dissembles for each journey of the camp and reassembles at the new encampment. An embroidered linen screen defines the entrance to the Mishkan. The walls are embroidered linen and wool curtains that loop into clasps held on the wooden beams. Animal skins and goat-hair fabric cover the inner domain, a tent within the courtyard. Curtains separate successive enclosures. Altars for burnt offerings and incense, and the table are inside. The altar for burnt offerings has copper utensils – pans, shovels, bowls, forks, and fire-pans. The show bread is laid on the table. The *menorah*-candelabra is made from pure beaten gold with bulbs and flowers on its seven branches. The incense altar and implements are made from acacia wood overlaid with pure gold. This altar stands in front of the inner veil before the Ark of Testimony. The Mishkan furniture is transported by gold-overlaid acacia-wood poles. Separating the innermost Holy of Holies from the inner court area there is a veil, *parochet*, of azure blue, purple and scarlet with the *keruvim* – winged divine beings as an embroidered motif. Within this sanctum is the Holy Ark, *aron kodesh*, topped by two sculpted golden *keruvim*-cherubs. According to the Talmud, the Ark houses the broken shards of the first set of stone tablets together with the intact second set.[37] These stones bear witness to the complex divine covenant with the Jewish People.

When the Mishkan is completed, the Torah describes the divine presence filling the enclosure as the breath/soul fills the body.[38]

---

37. *Bava Batra* 14b.
38. Ex. 40:33–6. See Benjamin D. Sommer, *The Bodies of God and the World of Ancient Israel* (Cambridge, New York: Cambridge University Press, 2009).

	Human	Mishkan-Temple	Creation
Coverings			
	flesh	gold leaf overlay	earth/sand/vegetation/grass/ moss
	skin	outer skins/hanging curtains	heavens covering earth
Skeletal frame			
	ribs, spine and bones/ limbs	wooden beams and boards	mountains and trees
	set in joints with sinew/ muscle	tenons fitted in sockets	fixed in earth
Life fluids			
	sweat, blood, urine, semen, menstrual flux, bile	sacrificial blood and water libations	rain, dew, rivers, sea, lava
Flesh			
	flesh, food/nurture	offerings on wooden altar/show bread	animal world/harvest, fruit
	eyes	*Menorah* (candelabra)	celestial lights
	brain/ mind/ soul	*Keruvim* (cherubs)	angels, birds, God, *Shekhina*
	heart/womb	Holy of Holies	Israel/Jerusalem/ Temple/Holy of Holies
Divisions			
	internal organs separated by membranes	Priestly & Israelite Courts separated by curtains	geographic/political
	diaphragm dividing heart from stomach	veil, *parochet* between enclosure and Holy of Holies	firmament dividing upper from lower waters
Processes			
	digestion, birth-life-death cycle	altar service/ sacrifices/ fire	cycle of year, seasons/destruction-regeneration
	bodily odors, perfumes	"sweet savor," incense	aromas, fragrances
	firing of synapses	*ner tamid* – burning menorah	sun

The table suggests analogies in the symbolic system of the Mishkan-Temple – paralleling both the human being and Creation.[39]

This table compares physical elements and functions with the Mishkan-Temple. Each of the body, Mishkan and Creation have a skeletal frame, skin covering, fluids, and innards. All three also process life materials, consuming, digesting, and producing aromas. Beyond symbolically mirroring the Creation and the human form, the Mishkan ritual is also meant to influence each of the other two domains, to activate life processes.

One of the passions of the Mishkan service is ritual purity. Meticulous treatment of personal materials of life and death expresses this theme – purification from contact with a corpse and genital discharges, for example. Nearly all of the purity codes become obsolete when the Temple is destroyed except those related to sexual intimacy.[40] Talmudic sages obligate Jews to sanctify sexual intimacy and fertility by observing purification rituals similar to those prescribed for the Mishkan.[41]

---

39. Flavius Josephus attributes symbolism to every detail of the *Mishkan*. *Jewish Antiquities*, III, 6.

See Raphael Patai's anthropological study of Jewish sources concerned with the Temple, *Man and Temple in Ancient Jewish Myth and Ritual* (London, New York: T. Nelson, 1947). In his commentary on Ex. 26.1, 12th century Spanish commentator Ibn Ezra cites the 10th century Babylonian Saadia Gaon's view of the Mishkan as a microcosm of the universe and macrocosm of the human being. Saadia lays out eighteen parallels between the Mishkan, the Creation and the human being. For example, the Mishkan curtains partitioning its spaces parallels the sky dividing the earth from the heavens; in the human being the diaphragm separates the 'higher' organs of respiration from the 'lower' organs of digestion. In Creation, angels parallel the cherubs on the Ark of the Mishkan, parallel to human thought. See also Daniel Sperber, *A Commentary on Derech Erez Zuta,* 3rd edition (Ramat-Gan, Israel: Bar-Ilan University Press, 1990 [Hebrew]), 157.

40. Charlotte Elisheva Fonrobert, *Menstrual Purity: Rabbinic and Christian Reconstructions of Biblical Gender* (Stanford, CA: Stanford University Press, 2000).

41. The period when couples desist from sex is the same as the period during which *halakha* restricts women's access to the *Mishkan*-Temple. Like the ritual for re-entry into the Temple, the couple re-unites after purification. During recent years, some women and men, medical experts, and halakhic authorities debate the sexual purity rituals. Avram Israel Reisner, "Observing Niddah in Our Day," Committee on Jewish Law and Standards Conservative Movement, Rabbinical Assembly. September 13, 2006. In Hebrew, see, (1) דניאל רוזנק, ההלכה והלכות נידה — מצוי ורצוי, (2) בנימין ונועה לאו, "תגובה למאמר על חומרת http://www.toravoda.org.il/he/node/9;

They appoint women responsible for the ritual purity of regeneration.[42]

The Mishkan-Temple is occupied with the fertile cycle – fruitfulness, potency, and life-bearing; much of the service connects with the rhythms of the land and the livelihood of its inhabitants. The purpose is to elicit the Creator's generosity, to stimulate the flow of nurture and blessing. The Yom Kippur ritual, for example, aspires to effect spiritual and moral atonement, to bring yearly forgiveness and joy. Drawing water from the Gichon Spring and pouring it on the altar during the festival of Tabernacles, Sukkot, is meant to stimulate the rain and produce a bountiful harvest.[43] The Temple service functions to alleviate angst about mortality – illness, suffering, and death – and to enable sustenance and well-being. These are essential public functions that foster shared confidence in the meaning and value of life, and a sense of purpose and hope.

(Re)Placing Sacredness

The end of central public sacred ritual in Jerusalem might have signaled the demise of Jewish life. In the first centuries of the Common Era, sages were arguing about how to respond to the destruction.

From the time of the destruction of the Temple, the Pharisees multiplied in Israel, and they neither ate meat nor drank wine.

R. Yehoshua said to them, "My children, why do you not eat meat?"

The Pharisees replied, "We will eat meat when every day it is offered on the altar, but now it is annulled."

R. Yehoshua said, "Why do you not drink wine?"

Pharisees, "We will drink wine from which libations are poured onto the altar, but now it is annulled."

R. Yehoshua: "Also figs and grapes we will not eat because from them they used to take first-fruit offerings on the festival of Sukkot/

רבי זירא — החשיבה המחודשת", מדור ספרות של חיותה דויטש בצופה
www.kolech.org/show.asp?id=15937=, http://, 10/11/2006

42. Much of tractates *Niddah, Sotah* address the issues of women's role in maintaining family ritual purity.

43. *Sukkah* 48a–b.

Atzeret. Bread we will not eat because we used to lay the Showbreads out in the Temple. Water we will not drink because from it they used to pour libations on the Festival (Sukkot)."

The Pharisees fell silent.

R. Yehoshua, "Do not mourn excessively, the edict has already been passed, and more mourning is too much. Therefore the sages said, 'Plaster your house, and leave off one small area in memory of Jerusalem. Prepare a meal, and leave a small piece in memory of Jerusalem. Adorn yourself with jewelry, and leave off a small element in memory of Jerusalem . . .'

Every person who mourns for Jerusalem remembers and sees/witnesses her joy, as it says, "'Rejoice in Jerusalem and celebrate in her all those who love her, celebrate her joyously all who mourn (Isaiah 66:10)."'[44]

While the Pharisees in this passage wallow in the destruction and perpetuate mourning, Rabbi Yehoshua moves on. He clarifies that the Temple symbolizes life, but is not equivalent to life. His optimism prevails. Memorializing appropriately, and educating with hope toward a better future is the strategy the sages prefer. Celebrate! instructs the text, for Zion is committed to peace.

In the modern period, the Jewish People rebound from unfathomable destruction by founding the State of Israel. Today, Israel is mired in a mid-life crisis. Cumulative loss and suffering from war and terror compound with the bitterness of the occupation. The rabbinic sages long ago established the priority of life in peace and with joy. When Jewry is utterly vanquished, the sages overcome their fear, search their souls for the strength to remake Judaism for the new reality of exile. The contemporary task is similar – to remake Zionism for the new reality of Israel in the twenty-first century, fulfilling the Zion priorities of peace and joy.

During the end of the Mishnaic period until 200 CE, the sages substitute for the Temple service with creativity and responsibility. Pointing to the disconnection between the Temple service and urgent issues in society, the prophet Hoshea had long ago advocated the replacement of sacrifice with prayer, "We will serve the offerings of

---

44. *Tosefta Sotah* 15:11–15.

our lips in place of bullocks [sacrifices]."⁴⁵ From the conclusion of the
Mishnaic period onward, the sages establish prayer and study as the
pillars to support their renovated system of sacred service. Their vision
preserves the symbolic structure of the past service while responding
to the needs of dispersed communities. Household versions of former
Temple rituals come to address the same profound human themes as
the rituals of the Mishkan-Temple. The private home and personal
body became ritual centers in exile. Replacing the priestly privileged
class who operated a centralized Judaism, the sages obligate all Jews to
pray and study. Exempting women from most of the public obligations
that bestow power and prestige created inequality that Jewish patriar-
chy only began to acknowledge in the mid-twentieth century. Today,
Jewish women are gaining unprecedented access to and mastery of
texts and ritual. As the Talmudic academies rendered Judaism relevant
and accountable in their time, new women's and co-ed academies are
responding to the exigencies of our time.

The rabbinic sages made another substitution for Temple service,

> Rav Yehuda taught: Three things lengthen a person's days and years.
> Extending one's time at prayer, extending one's time at the table, and
> extending one's time in the bathroom . . .
>
> [Why is] extending one's time at the table [worthy of reward]?
> Perhaps a poor person will come, and you will be able to give him/
> her [something to eat].
>
> [How do we know that a table has the power to lengthen one's
> life?] Since it says in Scripture: . . . *in front of the Shrine was something
> resembling a wooden altar three cubits high and two cubits long, with
> inner corners. Its length and its walls were made of wood. And he said to
> me, "This is the table that stands before God."* (Ezekiel 41:21–22)
>
> The Torah first called it an "altar" and then called it a "table"
> [thus equating the two: our table is like an altar, and altars serve to
> lengthen a person›s life]. [Noting this similarity between tables and
> the altar] Rabbi Yohanan and Rabbi Eleazar both taught: "During
> the time that the Temple stood, the altar atoned for Israel. And now,
> a person's table atones for him/her." (*Berakhot* 54b–55a)

---

45. *Hoshea* 14:3. See also *Berakhot* 26b; Maimonides, *Sefer Ahava, Hilkhot
Tfilla*, 1:7.

This Talmudic passage suggests an equivalence between the altar in the sanctuary and the dining table at home; both can atone. However, the value of the table is not ritualistic. The merit and reward for lengthening time at the table is based upon helping poor people and welcoming guests. While in the Mishkan-Temple, people prayed to God for food, the sages hold each person responsible for the needy in her/his community. In this way, sustaining a compassionate community substitutes for Temple ritual. Like many rabbinic texts, this passage challenges Israel to instill the obligations of social justice among individuals and communities, and to better ensure the wellbeing of all. The separation of ritual from human welfare has created rifts in Israeli society, and between denominations of Jews, secular and religious. Whereas Orthodox denominations emphasize ritual practice, the Reform Movement views social justice as sacred service.[46]

Food Fitness

Another topic on the table is Jewish adherence to the dietary demands of *kashrut* – an embodied practice that sanctifies the functions of the home and body. Fastidious food preparation, including ritual slaughter, reminds of the daily ritual sacrifices of the Mishkan. While once the sacrificial rituals were performed as a public enactment in the Temple, Jewish dietary rules instruct in the observance of similar acts with similar implements in the kitchen. Restricting food to the ritually fit-*kasher*, blessing the source of nurture when eating – these practices aim to recreate the sacred intentions of the sanctuary.[47] The *challah*, a portion taken from bread dough as a gift to the priests is obligatory throughout the Jewish world after the destruction – in memory of the Temple. This dough is burned separately, symbolizing the destroyed

---

46. "We reaffirm social action and social justice as a central prophetic focus of traditional Reform Jewish belief and practice. Reform Movement Statement of Principles, http://www.ccarnet.org/platforms/principles.html.

47. In our day, the formal kashrut institutions of Israel are not succeeding to overcome cruelties of industrial food production. Raphael Ahren, "Despite rabbinate's promises, meat from inhumane slaughterhouses still being marked as kosher," *Haaretz*, 12.6.2011, retrieved Feb. 12, 2012, http://www.haaretz.com/weekend/anglo-file/despite-rabbinate-s-promises-meat-from-inhumane-slaughterhouses-still-being-marked-as-kosher-1.366882.

Temple and defunct priestly rituals. The rabbinic sages encode new ways to embody Jewish spiritual values in everyday life.

Throughout extended absence from the land of Israel, even during persecution, or, perhaps in defiance, the Jewish People has persisted to observe its beliefs and rituals, even at high risk. Temple-like practices connect homes with Jewish sacred time and space. Like the wide-scale engagement of the collectivity of the Jewish People that the Mishkan project envisions, Israel needs dedicated, active participation.

While the implicit public cultural background in the West is Christianity, Israel is the one society where Judaism informs the public sphere. Israel sets a sacred calendar – according to Shabbat, the cycle of the land and Jewish festivals. Jewish texts beckon Israel to develop thousands of years of endeavor beyond the current forms, to continue the rabbinic agenda, enabling a fuller and more compelling plurality of live Jewish interpretation.

A Virtual Temple

The sages construct Jerusalem as an abstraction of sacred life. Jacob Neusner describes the Mishna's approach to the displacement of the Temple cult,

> What Mishnah does, by representing this cult, laying out its measurements, describing its rite, and specifying its rules, is to permit Israel in the words of the Mishnah to experience anywhere and anytime that cosmic center of the world described by Mishnah: Cosmic center in words is made utopia. Mishnah permits the people, Israel, to carry that world along through time, until the center once more will be re-gained.[48]

Neusner voices the rabbinic intention that the Temple service will one time be restored. Nonetheless, the rabbinic literatures enable a new form of sacred living away from the Temple and land of Israel. Talmudic imagination animates the seasons and agriculture work. On the pages of the text, Jews carry baskets laden with their first-fruits, tithes and offerings, sacrificial gifts and atonements. They pour liba-

---

48. Jacob Neusner, "Map Without Territory: Mishnah's System of Sacrifice and Sanctuary," *History of Religions* 19 (1979), 110.

tions, wave offerings, contribute donations, bathe their bodies, circle with their dead and bury them outside their walled cities. The sages idealize the Temple as the locus for family and communal connection, auspicious gathering, supplication, and celebration. The fertile process of the distant, inaccessible land and its harvest orchestrates the fantasized journeys of the Jewish People from the periphery to the core. In constant relation to an unearthly Jerusalem, the Jewish People expresses its shared identity and experiences collective union with its Creator. All of these activities transpire in the virtual reality constructed by the *beit midrash*, the rabbinic study and prayer halls. Studying and interpreting the Mishkan-Temple rituals and all the refined details of an intricate symbolic system become equivalent to doing them.[49]

Study and prayer are both verbal activities, entirely built of letters; they keep our hands clean. Replacing the materials and functions of the Temple with words relieves the Jewish People of manual service. However palpable, both study and prayer are abstractions of the embodied Mishkan-Temple ritual. In the *beit midrash*-house of study, there is no blood, no incense, no fragrant anointing oil, no burning savor of sacrifices, no elaborate garments, no instrumental music, no wooden structure to transport, assemble and dissemble, and no central sacred space that houses the divine presence among the people. The uniquely Israeli materials of offering and sacrifice, earth, spices and fruit, the daily agricultural, social, and political life nearly vanished from our sacred repertoire during the long exile. In the post-Temple era, private homes and community houses of worship and study become the ritual centers, the sanctuaries of a dispersed nation. Prayer and study, wings for escape from the material constrictions of exile, romanticize the sacred work of the Promised Land. Verbal performances also alienate the Jewish People from the public embodied ritual of the Mishkan.

Rebelling against the disembodiment of Jewish life, early Zionists idealized Jewish labor. They reformulated Jewish sacred life and spiritual service as working and settling the land.

> Manual labor was seen as a regenerative process whose task was to change the Jew's essential nature: to transform the alienated city dweller, typically a middleman, into a productive individual, living

---

49. Midrash Tanhuma, *Tzav*, 14.

off the fruits of his own labor. It was intended to bring him closer to nature, to the soil, to primordial forces. This was to be the moral revolution which would accompany the national revolution: The new Jew would arise from his immediate contact with the land of Palestine. He would signify the end of the dichotomy between matter and spirit, the personal and the national.[50]

A. D. Gordon conceives a fruitful blend of manual and intellectual pursuits. In support of the establishment of Hebrew University in Jerusalem, Gordon argues, "So long as we hold on to the banal view that labor and learning are in conflict, that one who works cannot have higher education and one who learns cannot work, the entire idea of labor becomes meaningless. What value is there in an idea which does not permit the spirit to ascend, but instead forces it to descend!"[51] Against Rashbi, Gordon affirms Rabbi Yishmael's position – in Israel, Jewish mind, sprit, and body can live at home together.[52]

The idealism of the connection between labor and spirit has all but faded in Israel. Whereas the principles of self-sustenance and building the land motivated collective agriculture, "The kibbutz and moshav farming communities of today's Israel rely almost entirely on foreign labor, a far cry from the days when working on the kibbutz was part of the Jewish pioneering spirit and kibbutzniks were considered members of the elite."[53] Recent estimates of the number of foreign workers in Israel range between 200–300,000, some of them without proper work permits and human services. They hail from an array of poorer countries including Romania, Philippines, Thailand, Nepal, Ghana, Nigeria, Colombia and Jordan.[54] Today, a few idealists live according to the dream of Jews laboring on the land. The global technological economy and mobile and inexpensive migrant labor affect Israeli identity and relationship to the land and manual work, concepts that we need to reevaluate and reconfigure.

---

50. Anita Shapira, "The Zionist labor movement and the Hebrew University," *Judaism: A Quarterly Journal of Jewish Life and Thought*, 45(2) Spring1996.

51. A. D. Gordon, *"Universita Ivrit"* ("A Hebrew University"), *Ha-Uma ve-ha-Avoda* (Labor and the Nation) (Israel, 1957), 168, cited by Anita Shapira.

52. *Berakhot* 35b, discussed in the previous chapter.

53. "Growing Non-Jewish Population Concerns Some Israelis," *Chicago Tribune*, July 19, 2005.

54. "Foreign workers: Israel's migrant underclass," *Haaretz*, January 27, 2005.

A Palace in Time

Abraham Joshua Heschel's 1951 essay, "The Sabbath," one of the great theological works of the twentieth century, affirms the relevance of the Mishkan-Temple to modern Jewry, with a twist. In that essay, Heschel conceives Jewish religious experience as quintessentially temporal rather than spatial. "The Seventh day is a *palace in time* which we build. It is made of soul, of joy and reticence."[55] Heschel claims that by sanctifying the Sabbath, Jews attain a non-spatial territory, an escape from space to abide in the infinitely expansive divine. Heschel contrasts time with space – the domain of power and control, acquisition, and labor. During the week, our focus on material pursuits blinds us from grasping that which is first sanctified, time. For Heschel, time is not the fearsome opponent that heralds triumphant death, but the abode of the infinite spiritual presence of the divine who dwells in, or perhaps more aptly, *during* Shabbat.

Heschel's view epitomizes a Western tradition immortalized by the eighteenth century German philosopher, Immanuel Kant. Kant asserts that time is a supreme independent condition of existence. Heschel's sublime message about Shabbat celebrates the grandeur of time. Heschel cites another text about Rabbi Shimon bar Yochai (Rashbi), the second century Palestinian sage.

Rashbi emerges from a cave after twelve years of hiding from the Romans during the Bar Kochba revolt of 132–135 CE. Having been immersed for so long in hidden meanings of the Torah, Rashbi expresses loathing for the material world. Observing an old person walking to greet the Shabbat queen with fragrant myrtle, he finds consolation. The old person, claims Heschel, represents the Jewish People ever uplifted by observing Shabbat. According to the story, Shabbat justifies materiality and sustains hope and purpose when history defies both.

From Heschel's point of view, Shabbat concretizes the absent Temple – time stands for space. Accessible weekly, Shabbat resists restrictions on Jewish life, and fuels the fervent hope for redemption from the sufferings of this world. Shabbat makes it possible to infuse space with the sacredness of time. Homes and synagogues replace the

---

55. *The Sabbath: Its Meaning for Modern Man* (New York: Farrar, Straus and Young, 1951), 3. Page numbers in parentheses.

Jerusalem Temple; fields become the intimate dwelling spaces of holy presence, the divine bride and queen. Shabbat is a gateway between Diaspora sanctuaries and otherworldly realms to which Judaism aspires, beyond both space and time. Shabbat is at the cusp of the material world and eternity.

Heschel's Shabbat masterpiece lifts off from the Jewish People's difficult relationship to space. Rabbinic sages acknowledge and take full responsibility for the failure of Jewish autonomy over sacred space preceding the destruction and exile in 70 CE Talmudic passages attribute the destructions to moral, political, and religious corruption, and to "senseless hatred" among Jews.[56] From the destruction onward, the Jewish dream of return to the ancient homeland seemed utterly impossible. Heschel's escape from an inhospitable place into the sacredness of time is a superb theological adaptation to exile. In Shabbat, Jews have the possibility to experience a form of redemption every single week that is relatively impervious to persecution. Heschel also affirms the profound spiritual attainment of the Jews in their dispersed communities. "Zion is in ruins, Jerusalem lies in the dust. All week there is only hope of redemption. But when the Sabbath is entering the world, [hu]man is touched by a moment of actual redemption. . ." (68). For Heschel, we achieve "actual redemption" by withdrawing from space into the sanctuary of time. We make a "pilgrimage to the seventh day" (90). Substituting Shabbat for Jerusalem, Heschel's metaphoric palace sustains and justifies a disembodied Jewish identity. "We usually think that the earth is our mother," writes Heschel, "that time is money and profit our mate. The seventh day is a reminder that God is our father, that time is life and the spirit our mate" (76). According to Heschel in 1951, time partakes of the holy. "We share time, we own space" (99). Whereas God sanctifies the holiness of Shabbat – it is eternal and independent, the holiness of the land of Israel is unstable – it depends upon the holiness of the people of Israel, the unreliable actions of humans.

---

56. Why was the First Temple destroyed? Because of the three elements which existed in it: idolatry, immorality, and bloodshed . . . But why was the Second Temple destroyed, since at that time people were involved with study, *mitzvot*, and deeds of kindness? Because at that time there was senseless hatred among the people. This teaches that senseless hatred is as powerful and evil as idolatry, immorality, and bloodshed! *Yoma* 9b.

Interrogating Heschel's concepts, the opposition between time and place suits the pre-Zionist period when Israel was inconceivable.[57] The pair of binaries – space-time and mother-father – privileges an unearthly "father," time, over a corporeal, corruptible "mother," place. When the modern State of Israel was at a foundling stage, Heschel constructs the land as mother, susceptible to the seductions of power and material whereas the father, time, is immune.

More than sixty years of Israeli national independence leave little room for doubt that the earthly state is indeed corruptible. Moshe Katsav's unceremonious resignation from the presidency in 2007 and conviction for rape and sexual harassment of employees, breach of trust, and obstruction of justice indicates the decay. The power of statehood corrupts; no nation is immune. The vital question is how to address the challenges rather than how to escape from them. The claim that time is more pure and immune from moral decay encourages detachment. This position is at odds with Heschel's own life work as an outstanding proponent of Judaism's commitment to improving society and redressing the problems of power. A visionary activist, he marched alongside Martin Luther King, Jr. during the tumultuous civil rights struggles of the 1950s and 1960s, and organized the religious campaign against the Vietnam war, on behalf of the *people* of Vietnam.[58]

Zionism inverts Heschel's maneuver in his *Palace in Time*. Using Heschel's terminology, Israel aspires to be a Palace *in Space*. The Zionist project of creating a homeland for the Jewish People in Israel propels Jewish tradition another step – taking on the toughest demands of the material world and tackling the seductions of power. Drawing nurture from a hopeful commitment to space-the-mother, in Heschel's terms, Zionism seeks to render the sacred in space as well as time. Zionism holds sacred space, while wholly corruptible, to be also a realm for potentially redemptive change, rebirth.

---

57. Scholar of Jewish mysticism, Gershom Scholem fervently critiqued Heschel's exile consciousness in the *Palace*. See Moshe Idel's analysis of their theological differences, *Old Worlds, New Mirrors: On Jewish Mysticism and Twentieth-Century Thought* (Philadelphia: University of Pennsylvania Press, 2010), 230–3.

58. See Reuven Kimelman, "Abraham Joshua Heschel: Our Generation's Teacher," *Melton Journal* issue entitled "Leadership: Portraits of Challenge, Vision and Responsibility," No. 15, Winter 1983.

Rabbi Kook uses the metaphor of the Mishkan-Temple to convey his ideal of spiritual Zionism.

> Within the inner heart, in its chambers of purity and holiness, the Jewish flame strengthens itself. It fervently seeks the mighty and constant connection of life with all of the commandments of God. Through this connection, it seeks to solidify the full Jewish spirit that fills the entire volume of the soul, and to express the full Jewish expression with a total gesture, action and ideal. . . . Holy fire kindled in the heart of all people of the nation, burns since ancient days, "a fire burning on the altar, never to be extinguished." . . . And all the yearning of life, all hope for redemption, flow only from this source, in order to bring Jewish vibrancy to life in its fullness, without contradiction, without limit. This is the aroused desire for Eretz Yisrael, the holy land, the land of God.[59]

Rav Kook formulates the activity of Zionism as reigniting the aspiration to the Infinite, like the fire that burned constantly on the altar of the Mishkan-Temple. According to Kook, Israel affords an opportunity to fulfill Jewish life in space and soul; Israel combines the spatial and eternal realms in a uniquely Jewish expression. Israel is a vessel capable of resuming and innovating the sacred service that is the work of the Jewish People.

In many respects, the Mishkan is an inspiring model, a paradigm for Jewish private and community life. Participation and collaboration, focus and shared purpose are desirable qualities for the State of Israel. The symbolism and aesthetic, the ritual framework for addressing sustenance and mortality, these are compelling. But there is no point to misappropriating the metaphor. There are some who believe that bringing redemption is rebuilding the *Third* Temple in Jerusalem; they plan and train.[60] The Temple Institute has begun to make the sacred vessels to be used in the Third Temple,[61] displacing responsibility for human affairs onto fantasy. Beyond the political dangers, the idea that the third temple will be identical to the first two lacks humility. Surely

---

59. HaRav Kook, *Orot* (Lights), Eretz Yisrael 8, 1920 (my translation).

60. *The Jerusalem Temple Foundation, To the Mountain of the Lord,* and *The Faithful of the Temple Mount.*

61. See http://www.templemount.org/tempprep.html.

the ritual of the Jewish People must reflect the growth and refinements of two thousand years.

Homeward Bound

The Jewish People adjusts dramatically to changes throughout a long history. Incorporating the broken tablets, remnant of the first national crisis, the Mishkan channels failure toward material and spiritual service. After the destruction of the Jerusalem Temple, the rabbinic sages utterly reformulate Judaism and the Mishkan-Temple system. The work demanded by the current period is comparable to the period following the destruction of the Temple in the first century – both in urgency and scale. The multiple challenges facing the Jewish People in modernity require similar ingenuity. Particularly during the 1950s and 1960s, many believed in the State of Israel as deliverance from suffering. Time has revealed far more complications than could have been anticipated by the early Zionists. Building a state is not a solution but a process. Unfortunately, the initial pioneering fervor flags while the need for creativity and innovation persists. In the twenty-first century, mainly among West Bank settlers, and the evacuees from Gush Katif, the spirited sense of the collaborative Zionist endeavor lives on. In those camps, the messianic ideology approaches a religious faith that contravenes values and institutions of Israeli democracy.[62] The heated and sometimes physical contest between Israeli soldiers and West Bank settlers who defied the government building freeze in 2009–10 and, ultra-Orthodox communities' defiance of civil law, particularly in their repression of women, are symptomatic of fissures in civil society.[63]

Two thousand years ago, the Jewish People survived destruction

---

62. The cultic behavior of the supporters of Yigal Amir, the jailed assassin of former Prime Minister Yitzchak Rabin, is evidence of this disturbing phenomenon. Amir has a large following among right-wing factions in Israel. The circumcision of his son, on the twelfth anniversary of his assassination of Israeli Prime Minister Yitzchak Rabin, was a highly publicized media event. Dan Izenberg, "Yigal Amir's son circumcised inside prison," *Jerusalem Post*, Nov 4, 2007, http://www.jpost.com/servlet/Satellite?pagename=JPost%2FJPArticle%2FShowFull&cid=1192380726062.

63. Dina Kraft, "Growing gender segregation among Israeli haredim seen as repressing women," JTA, November 13, 2011, retrieved Jan. 11, 2012, http://www.jta.org/news/article/2011/11/13/3090256/growing-gender-segregation-among-israeli-haredim-seen-as-repressing-women.

by redistributing privileges and responsibilities. From the inherited priestly cast who once performed the service in Jerusalem, the sages shift the obligations to the general population. The "democratization" of Jewish life that began in the first century of this era opened the gates to contributions that produced multiple theologies and denominations, and diverse creativity. Jews formulate mystical, poetic, literary, musical, ethical, philosophic, comical, historic, academic, and legal expressions of Judaism, extreme and moderate, faithful and atheist, traditional and radical. Most of these dwell only in books, in minds and souls, but not yet in the body. Few have been rendered in the full dimensions of society.

Even entering and living in the physical territory of Israel, it is nonetheless possible to remain in the consciousness and practices of exile – fearful, constricted, detached, protective. Zionism proposes to fulfill Jewish life beyond exile. The Mishkan-Temple suggests development goals for Zionism: cultivating the dispositions of giving generously with pride and dignity, receiving with respect and humility, and collaborating fruitfully. Israel challenges us to envision and work to refine embodied public Jewish life – with joy and responsibility.[64] In many respects, the State of Israel *is* the Mishkan-Temple project of our time.

---

64. David Hartman used the term as the title for *Joy and Responsibility: Israel, Modernity and the Renewal of Judaism* (Jerusalem: Ben-Zvi-Posner with the Shalom Hartman Institute, 1997).

4 (Re)Entering the Garden

ONE EVENING DURING the mid-1970s, well-known Canadian scientist and activist, David Suzuki, explained to a packed lecture hall at the University of Ottawa that geneticists are able to make every baby born white. The audience was exercised by the announcement. While many were pondering how well this innovation will solve racism, a black woman stood up. She declared how proud she is to be black and that she hopes that her children and grandchildren will be black like her. Suzuki provoked his audience by pointing to ethical issues on the agenda of science. His example from genetics shows how well-meaning zeal for universalism endangers precious human experience.

Most groups draw nourishment and grow from the well-tilled ground of their traditions. In Sweden, for example, every household used to eat a national menu each night of the week, varying according to the festivals and seasons. Some continue to serve the traditional Thursday night supper of hearty *artsoppa* (pea soup) and *plättar* (pancakes). Until recently, nationality referred to a coherent lifestyle and values – of which local food customs are one facet. Members were versed in their common practices; they shared a canon, history, and destiny. In our time, cultural homogeneity is becoming rare as mobility increases. Some states minimize exposure to what they consider to be corrupting external influences by restricting the entry and behavior of "foreigners."[1] Many Asian, African, and Middle Eastern

---

1. For example, other than the two types of visas which are only available to

states enforce religious and cultural behavior among their citizens by means of laws; transgressions of some codes, such as modest dress and sexual mores even bear corporal punishments, particularly for women. By contrast, the borders of Europe and North America are more permeable. During the post-colonial and post-World Wars era, they have been absorbing immigrants from many religious, ethnic, and national backgrounds. Migrations westward and northward are amalgamating cultures and confounding previous concepts of nationality. A state flag no longer necessarily signals common bonds to a past, the present, or the future.

Many populations are a kaleidoscope of minority cultures. The United States census recognizes the following categories: White – including Hispanic or Latino; American Indian and Alaska Native; Asian; Black or African American; Native Hawaiian and Other Pacific Islander; and people of two or more races.[2] There are 87 distinct "peoples of Europe," of which 33 are the majority population in at least one sovereign state, while the remaining 54 are ethnic minorities.[3] Modern Israel has absorbed Jews from as many as 103 countries who speak more than 70 different languages.[4]

There is no straightforward optimal approach to the complex demographics of the West. Societies embrace diversity to varying degrees and according to different world-views; *de facto*, many segregate. The once-popular melting pot boiled away immigrants' traditions; they adopted or submitted to a dominant national ethos. American playwright Israel Zangwill describes the process in his turn-of-the-twentieth century play,

Muslims, Saudi Arabia does not issue visitors' visas, residence visas or transit visas. In all cases, a person entering the Kingdom must have a Saudi sponsor, which means an individual or a company to vouch for the individual's conduct while in the country. "Saudi Arabia Visas, Permits and Immigration," retrieved July 27, 2010, http://www.expatforum.com/articles/visas-permits-and-immigration/saudi-arabia-visas-permits-and-immigration.html.

2. "Detailed Tables – American FactFinder; T3-2008. Race [7]." 2008 Population Estimates. U.S. Census Bureau, retrieved Feb. 28, 2010.

3. Christoph Pan, Beate Sibylle Pfeil, *Minderheitenrechte in Europa. Handbuch der europäischen Volksgruppen* (2002). Living-diversity.eu, English translation 2004.

4. Helen Chapin Metz, ed. *Israel: A Country Study* (Washington: GPO for the Library of Congress, 1988).

America is God's Crucible, the great Melting-Pot where all the races
of Europe are melting and reforming . . . Germans and Frenchmen,
Irishmen and Englishmen, Jews and Russians – into the Crucible
with you all! God is making the American.[5]

More recently, the hot forge of cultural uniformity has cooled into a
mixed salad of ethnic, religious, and national multiculturalism. The
contemporary cultural smorgasbord often simplifies and sentimental-
izes traditions. Among Jewish young people, falafel in flat pita bread
with chopped tomato and cucumber salad accompanying Idan Reichel
– a popular Israeli music band – are codes for Israel. Corn chips with
salsa and the Buena Vista Social Club are codes for Latino culture;
sushi, karate and thick, black Kanji letters are codes for Japan. Cultural
codes satisfy the palette with a wide range of delicacies – food, fashion,
and goods from distant lands. But meaningful pluralism depends on
more than an appetite for exciting cuisine, "political correctness,"
and even tolerance of difference. Codes barely give a taste of refined,
deep traditions; they neither express nor nurture growth. In the era
of globalization, both within nations and among them, it is becoming
increasingly difficult for minority groups to maintain, pass on, let alone
evolve their unique traditions. Community structures, education, arts,
languages, literatures, beliefs, and practices at the heart of many precious cultures are in peril.

On the Diversity of Cultures

Vital diversity depends upon conditions that foster the intricate
interdependence of life. Similar to biological and botanical species,
human cultures take a long time to evolve their complex and refined
forms. Without adequate resources and protection, and in the presence of predators, cultures are threatened with extinction. As the
bluebuck antelope and the atlas bear, they can disappear from the
earth. Many cultural groups struggle to survive inundation by a vast
tide of assimilation forces. At the same time as promoting tolerance
and respect for difference, cultural diversity requires careful policies to
nurture the subtle mechanisms that enable traditions to continue and

---

5. From the play, *The Melting Pot* by Israel Zangwill, first produced in 1908,
quoted in Gary Gerstle, *American Crucible; Race and Nation in the Twentieth Century*
(Princeton: Princeton University Press, 2001), 51.

develop.[6] The same global market and industrial cycle of production, consumption, and waste that pollutes the delicate biological environment, destroys habitats, and leads to the extinction of species also endangers the diversity and quality of human society. The ecological environment and local cultures and practices – the bulwarks of quality human life – are similarly vulnerable. The entertainment industry is one example of the unprecedented control over cultural resources. Since the turn of the millennium, six corporations sell eighty percent of all recorded music worldwide.[7]

Against the global tide of assimilation, some nations sponsor programs to keep their culture alive and pass it on to their youth. The South Korean government sponsors programs for young people of Korean descent who have grown up abroad to visit their "mother-land," learn about their roots, and become initiated into the traditions and values of their ancestors. The largely disinterested teenagers reluctantly partake of the sights and lectures. Many participants regard the programs as brainwashing and propaganda; they whine during the day, party, drink, and "hook up" during the night. In spite of their resistance, many marry Koreans they meet on the trip.[8] This Korean program is similar to programs that invest in taking Jewish young people to Israel. Both programs grapple with eroding identity in a Diaspora, and try to perpetuate their special human language.[9] Holding on to the past does not guarantee meaningful continuity into the future. Often, delivering a straightforward message – telling young people to love, honor and commit to their birth traditions – evokes resistance. People acquire cultural values and practices by subtle processes, often by story, symbol, image, and metaphor, through participation, mentoring, immersion, and by example. These fragile mechanisms are bound up with repetition and ritual, with caring for past generations and their

6. Concerning the case of Latino culture, see, García Canclini, Nestor, *Hybrid Cultures: Strategies for Entering and Leaving Modernity* (Minneapolis: University of Minnesota Press 1995).

7. Medard Gabel & Henry Bruner, *Globalinc: An Atlas of The Multinational Corporation* (New York: The New Press, 2003), 130.

8. Phuong Ly, "A Cultural Connection: Parents' Homelands Seek Lasting Link With Thoroughly American Teenagers," *Washington Post,* July 30, 2004. Retrieved Feb. 21, 2012, http://www.globalpolicy.org/globaliz/cultural/2004/0730exchang eprograms.html.

9. Bonna Devora Haberman, "What is the Content of Education in Democratic Society?," *Journal of Philosophy of Education,* vol. 28:2, 1994, 183–190.

wisdom, with seasons and festivals, customs, and delicacies, subtle messages passed through spoken and unspoken experience.

Universal and Particular

The previous chapter explores one of the narratives that carries people aloft – their story of home. Most cultures define a relationship between people and homeland, expressing values, world-views, and aesthetic sensibilities, and, often, a destiny. Islam, is relatively aloof from geography. Though the Haj, the pilgrimage to Mecca, is one of the Five Pillars of Islam, observance of the cycle of the Muslim calendar, the festivals and teachings is independent of any location, season, or place. This universality opens Islam to widespread global adherence.

By contrast, Tibetan culture has a deep connection with the Tibetan homeland. Particular geography, seasons, and climate, and the historical junction of the Indian subcontinent and China have influenced and refined Tibetan spiritual expressions, values, and lifestyle. The Dalai Lama deems his nation's destiny to be bound up with that specific place. Owing to their connection to a particular land, some groups face more fearsome threats of assimilation than others. The Tibetan people endure difficult trials under Chinese occupation and in exile. The Dalai Lama persists in an inspiring path of non-violence. He teaches that seeking control, or aspiring to the infinite in the realm of material things is a cause of suffering. "We can serve a tremendous quantity of food, but we have only one stomach; we can own as many rings as we want, but we have only ten fingers." Because material is necessarily finite, it is not an appropriate medium to seek human fulfillment, the Dalai Lama instructs. However, there are no limits to the realms of the intellect and spirit.[10] However much he disavows the pursuit of material and attachment, the Dalai Lama yearns for the Tibetan people to return to their homeland. His Holiness believes that the uniqueness of Tibetan Buddhism, its faith, language, and culture are rooted in the particular Tibetan Himalayan mountain ranges. Furthermore, he proposes that the role of the Tibetan people is connected with the location of Tibet at a strategic Asian crossroads of peoples, cultures and religions. The destiny of Tibet as a contributor to humanity

---

10. Lecture at Brandeis University, Waltham MA, May, 1998.

is inextricable from its homeland at the summit of planet earth.

Like the Tibetans' love for Tibet, the Jewish People has a complex and riveting love affair with the land of Israel. Throughout Jewish texts, a recurring theme expresses the three-way partnership among the Jewish People, the land of Israel, and the Creator: the *garden*. The garden is deeply rooted in the Zionist imagination from which experiments in collective settlement grew – the kibbutz and the moshav. In the early Zionist period and throughout the first decades of the state, the collective settlements and their gardens provided both material and spiritual sustenance for the Jewish community in Israel, and strategic defense. The kibbutz and the moshav modeled a lifestyle of collaboration and responsibility through shared labor and direct, participatory democracy. During the 1960s and 1970s, volunteering on kibbutz was a popular activity for young people from all over the world who looked to Israel as a bold and pioneering society. Appreciation for Israeli innovations has faded for a number of reasons. In the 1967 Six-Day War, Israel occupied the West Bank of the Jordan River, the Sinai Peninsula, Golan Heights, and the Gaza Strip. The difficulties of the occupation take a toll on Israeli society. Constant international scrutiny and anti-Israel rhetoric tarnish her image. Internal changes have also caused the old garden ideal to recede as Israel developed a dense urban center, advances commerce, manufacturing, and high-technology. Meanwhile, Israel returned the Sinai in exchange for peace with Egypt, and withdrew from Gaza unilaterally, leaving the Golan and the West Bank – a romanticized biblical landscape, in Israeli hands. Beginning in 1977, the election of the Likud and subsequent right-of-center political parties shifted the national agenda away from former visions of shared sustenance. The religious settlement movement took literal and figurative possession of the remaining *garden* ideal. Settlers who dot the mainly Palestinian-populated areas make their homes in the West Bank, ancient territories of Judaea and Samaria near the holy sites where the biblical matriarchs and patriarchs, prophets, sovereigns, and tribes of Israel lived and were buried. Hostility among Israeli settlers and Palestinians who live side-by-side contradicts the pastoral ideal of gardening.

While the steam-roller of globalization flattens much of the humanity, flora, and fauna in its path, the importance of cultivating unique, and varied cultural expressions grows. The previous two chapters aspire to a fuller Jewish integration of the material realm and body with the mind and soul. Building on the Mishkan-Temple model, this chapter seeks to inspire Zionism with the desire and passion of the garden. This garden discourse is particular to Jewish culture. It arouses the Jewish People toward some of the core elements of national meaning – the garden labors of nurture, community-building, social responsibility, poetry, and song.

Garden of Songs

The biblical corpus abounds with sensual descriptions of the land.

> I have come down to rescue them from the Egyptians and to bring them out of that land to a good and spacious land, a land flowing with milk and honey. (Exodus 3:8)

The dryness of Egypt alludes to barrenness, the privation of lovers from one another – in Jewish narratives, Egypt is a symbol for exile. By contrast, the beloved divine leads the people to the land coursing with abundant water – source of livelihood and symbol of fertility.

> For your God is bringing you into a good land, a land of streams, springs and fountains flowing out from the valley and the mountain. (Deuteronomy 8:7)

At the same time as signaling material prosperity, according to the prophet Isaiah, abundant water in the land refers to pervasive knowledge of the divine and the end of corruption.

> No evil or vile act shall be done in all My sacred mountain, for the land shall be filled with knowledge of God as water covers the sea. (Isaiah 11:9)

Entering the land of Israel is the physical culmination of a connection between lovers who have been separated for thousands of years and miles. These wandering lovers have unrelentingly anticipated their reunion, longing to return *home* to each other. The land is the place to give each other fitting attention, to cohabit together and to delight in each other's presence. In the land, as they explore and reveal themselves to one another, they also become more aware of the divine presence among them. With this awareness, each inspires and elicits from the other her and his finest spirit, values, and behavior. The land is also an object and medium for their love.

Song of Songs

The biblical Song of Songs and the mystical literatures that flow from it celebrate the intersecting imagery of material land and the body of Israel. Abounding with the lushness and fruitfulness of the land of Israel, the garden of the Songs is the setting for erotic passion.

> [You are] a garden spring, a well of fresh/living water, pouring forth from Lebanon. (Song of Songs 4:15)

Every aspect of the garden and all of its elements participate in the intimacy of love.

> Awake North Wind, come South Wind,
> Blow upon my garden, its ambrosia will spread forth;
> Let my beloved come to his garden and consume its luscious fruits!
> (4:16)

The male lover speaks his experience in metaphoric terms of the garden.

> I have come to my garden, my sister, my bride . . .
> I have eaten my honeycomb with my honey, I have drunk my wine and milk. (5:1)

The eight chapters, a series of poems, exquisitely express uninhibited female erotic desire.

> Let him give me the kisses of his mouth for your love is more delightful than wine.
> The aroma of your fragrant oils is excellent, like fine oil is your name.
> (1:2–3)

These verses allude to the intoxicating power of love to alter awareness. The woman imbibes her lover; she inhales him like fragrant oil. He is like a sensuous field, the delectable produce of the land; he is like and better than wine from the vineyard and oil pressed from the orchard, infused with incense.

I will go up into the date palm, I will grasp its boughs; and your breasts will be like clusters of the grape vine, your scent like apples. (7:9)

Man and woman both sing their fantasy openly. Unlike any other biblical source, reciprocity between partners pervades the poetry.

I am my beloved's and he is mine, who grazes among the lilies. (6:3)

Ignoring the explicit eroticism, traditional interpretations view the text as a parable of the relationship between God and the people of Israel. Accordingly, the series of poems is a drama of God and the Jewish People yearning to be present with one another. Even with this orientation, the intimacy between lovers, land, and people is unavoidable. Lover and the fertile earth awaken to desire; they are interchangeable symbols of each other. The following poem identifies an unmediated connection between human being and the zones of the land of Israel.

> Pulse of fresh water at the sources of the Jordan,
> > blood surging in my veins;
> skeletal ridges of the Carmel,
> > cage of my ribs;
> rolling contours of the Galil,
> > my shoulders and hips;
> fertile wadis in winter splendor,
> > lush germinating womb;
> ripening figs, grapes and pomegranates,
> > my fruitfulness aroused;
> proud cypress,
> > my nimble limbs;
> parched gold of thistled fields,
> > seasons of my wisdom,
> sand and shore,
> > my outer encasement;
> jasmine-infused Jerusalem evening,
> > carnal incense,
> azure blue sea and sky,
> > my crystal vision of creation.[11]

---

11. Bonna Devora Haberman.

Vibrantly alive, actively aware, acutely conscious, fully responsive in the moment – these are special attributes of the characters in the Songs. Sexuality is part of an encompassing arousal in the garden. Potency grows with the lengthening of the days as winter subsides, with the earth awakening in spring into flowering and summer fruit. The contours of the body trace the sea coast, follow the lines of mountains and streams, city towers rising from the plain. These outlines are textured and colored by the tones of seasons, and phases of day and light, ripening like fruit, thirsting like desert, leaping wild on hills, soaring in flight. Concentrating on the land of Israel, the Songs articulate a unique celebration of human life, breathing and beating with the rhythm of earth and creation. Through their distinct and precise attention to a specific relationship among people with a specific land, the Songs achieve vast human resonance.

Alongside personal relationship, the Songs refer to social institutions through intricate symbols. In the garden of the Songs, the urgency and priority of connection overcome traditional separations of people from one other. In the first chapter, for example, the woman resists her family's expectations that she protect the inviolate boundaries of her property and body. Rebelling against mistreatment by her family, she boldly declares that she has not guarded her "vineyard." She proudly discloses what would usually be considered female impropriety.

> Look not upon me, because I am black,
> because the sun has tanned me:
> my mother's children were angry with me;
> they made me the keeper of the vineyards;
> but my own vineyard have I not kept. (Song of Songs 1:5)

This woman lover is proud of her insubordination; she resists the discipline of class and sex. Outdoors in the sun, she is free from the demand for pale obedience. At another poetic moment, her lover likens her to a mare among Pharaoh's chariots – alluding to the havoc that she creates in the midst of an army arrayed for battle. She disrupts the male order of war and conquest, asserting the priority of love (1:9). In another Song, defying her rural agricultural class position, a woman lover seeks to penetrate into the elite enclosures of the palace to be with the man she desires (5:6–8).

These Songs depict the garden as a place of alternative norms.

Unbound by social hierarchies, both women and men enact their vivid, embodied will. The garden is a root of their passion and an erotic setting for their lives together.

Portable Love

Poetic elements of the Songs affiliate the sacred sanctuary, the royal court, the land and body. Though the garden would seem wild and unrestrained compared with the court, this joint frame of reference lends dignity and power to the lovers' Songs. The Songs describe a portable structure, a palanquin that resembles the Mishkan-Tabernacle- for the transport of the two lovers. The palanquin is a covered litter carried on poles on the shoulders of four or more bearers. King Solomon uses the same materials for the building of both the Temple and the palanquin. He builds both structures for a couple who represent the love shared between the Jewish People and the divine.[12] The following passage from the Song of Songs demonstrates the overlapping imagery of the Mishkan-Temple and the palanquin.

> King Solomon made for him a palanquin of wood from Lebanon.
> He made its posts of silver, its upholstery of gold.
> Its seat of purple wool, within it, it is decked with love. (3:9–10)

The similarity of the pair of human-like cherubs, *keruvim*, who flank the ark and the pair of lovers in the Songs is irresistible. In a Talmudic passage, Rav Ketina states that on each of the three pilgrimage festivals, the priests would pull back the curtain of the sanctuary of the Jerusalem Temple in order to let the assembled people see the *keruvim* embracing each other, displaying God's love for Her/His people.[13] Speaking about the *keruvim*, the Zohar teaches that one was male and the other female, like the lovers in the garden.[14]

In addition to the parallel between the Mishkan-Temple and the palanquin, the poem explicitly compares the body of the male lover with the Temple structure itself. He is symbolically crafted from the same materials as the sanctuary.

---

12. I Kings 7:58.

13. *Yoma* 54a–b.

14. "The word "equity" [*meisharim*, lit. equities] in the above quoted verse [Ps. 99:4] indicates that the *keruvim* were male and female." (Zohar, *Vayikra* 59a)

His thighs are pillars of alabaster, set in sockets of fine gold,
His appearance as Lebanon, choice as the cedars. (5:15)

These descriptions layer the metaphors of the body and sanctuary with the sacred garden, the land, and the divine and human lovers. The exquisite beauty of each envelops the others in vibrant and escalating desire. The divine presence abides between the wings of the *keruvim*, between the arms of the lovers' embrace. From between the two golden beings who inhabit the inner sanctuary of the Mishkan, the ongoing divine revelation emanates.[15]

(A)Scents

While all of the senses titillate in the Songs, fragrance has special prominence. In the Garden of Eden, Eve is attracted to the fruit by its appearance and flavor, by the wisdom that it yields, but conspicuously not by its smell. The garden of the Songs brims with seductive aromas. These disseminating smells arouse attentiveness and love.

My beloved is to me like a pouch of myrrh, between my breasts he lodges. (1:13)

Scent, according to literature and brain research, is the most primordial of human senses. Aromas arouse our earliest memories and feelings. The "Proustian phenomenon" is named after the French novelist Marcel Proust whose three-thousand page novel, *In Search of Lost Time* is triggered by the smell and taste of a small, rich cookie-like pastry, dipped in a cup of tea.[16] Psychologists demonstrate that memories triggered by smells can be more emotional, as well as more detailed. The direct link between odors and the amygdala – a part of the brain affiliated with emotion, may help explain the potency of smells.[17] Unfiltered by the cognitive brain, even ancient experience becomes present to our consciousness through scent. The garden of the Songs is replete with scents.

---

15. Ex. 25:18–22.
16. Marcel Proust, *In Search of Lost Time*, 1.
17. See for example, Simon Chu and John J. Downes, "Odour-evoked Autobiographical Memories: Psychological Investigations of Proustian Phenomena," *Chem. Senses* 25:111–116, Oxford University Press 2000.

Who is she who comes up from the desert,
Like columns of smoke
In clouds of myrrh and frankincense
All of the powders of the merchant? (4:6)
Nard and saffron, fragrant reed and cinnamon, with all aromatic
woods, myrrh and aloes – all the choice perfumes. (4:14)

These same spices are named among the ingredients in the incense of
the sanctuary.[18] Anointing is part of the preparation for the sanctuary
service. To sanctify the services of the Mishkan, the priests anoint the
utensils of the sanctuary as well as each others' bodies with oil infused
with exotic spices. Into the Holy of Holies, the High Priest takes a
special incense on Yom Kippur, the holiest day of the year. On Yom
Kippur, the holiest day of the year, the High Priest enters the Holy of
Holies with a panful of glowing coals scooped from the altar, and two
handfuls of finely ground aromatic incense.[19]

Dangerous Love

These olfactory parallels between the sacred service in the sanctuary
and the Song of Songs demonstrate how scent arouses loving partners.
In the Mishkan, the incense is an aphrodisiac to evoke divine attention. The parallels also point to the erotic dimensions of the sacred
service. Profound intimacy is the dangerous project of both the Songs
and the sanctuary, for unbounded union trespasses safety precautions.
Accordingly, the sacred incense affiliates with mortal risk. When two
of High Priest Aaron's children, zealous for the newly inaugurated
service, bring incense uninvited into the sanctuary, divine fire instantly
consumes them.[20] Beyond the risks of intimacy, in the garden of the
Songs, there is danger affiliated with amorous space.

The setting of the Songs alternates and contrasts between rural
fields and pastures and the urban enclosures of the walled city of
Jerusalem, the domain of the palace of the sovereign.[21] While the field

---

18. Ex. 30:23–30.
19. Lev. 16:12–13.
20. Lev. 10:1–3.
21. A biblical chapter in the book of Deuteronomy rules that if a man lies with a
betrothed woman in the field, then she is guiltless of the offense of adultery because

is usually thought to be a place of exposure and risk, the Songs invert this assumption of urban order: The garden is the place of security and freedom whereas the city is a place of danger. One female lover, seeking her beloved in town, is accosted by the night guards.

> I sought him, but I could not find him. I called out to him, but he did not answer.
> The guards who patrol the city found me; they struck me, they injured me. (5:6–7)

This violent incident wounds the lovers' scene. The poet declares that lovers must negotiate their passion in contested territories, within the confines of the (dis)order of society. Seeking the fulfillment of open and graceful, unbound and limitless desire entails risk. Similarly, the Jewish People needs to continually renegotiate the risks and dangers involved in pursuing the passion to be together and inhabit the land, for there is no "land without a people."[22] Mediating desire with the need to coexist in our surroundings is a constant responsibility of lovers.

Landed Reciprocity

According to rabbinic tradition, the land is itself animated by divine creation force. Therefore, it expresses and responds with great subtlety to the behavior of its inhabitants. When the relationship is good, rain falls in its proper season, and the land yields fruit. Rain in Israel is meant to express blessing – to fulfill God's yearning to meet the people in the land and to make their lives fertile and fruitful. Similarly, the growth of crops and trees expresses the longing of the land for heaven. As cited in the last chapter, drawing water from the spring of Shiloah outside the walls of ancient Jerusalem, and pouring it in the Temple intends to arouse the divine lubrication of the land, and bring rain to thirsty seeds. The intricate ordering of dietary, spiritual, sexual and

---

of the extra vulnerability of the open, uninhabited rural setting. If she had screamed, there would have been no-one to save her, argues the text. In the city, however, she is culpable because, assumes the text, someone would surely have come to her rescue if she would have screamed. Deut. 22:23–27.

22. An expression attributed to Israel Zangwill (1864–1926), an English-born Zionist, humourist and writer.

social conduct develops this symbolic relationship with the land. Through texts and practices, the land of Israel becomes a medium for God and the people of Israel to live and work in each other's imminent presence and to influence one another.

Extolling the arousing body and earth confounds the prudishness often affiliated with religion. The Songs are replete with desire for intimacy, yet there is never any explicit fulfillment of that desire.

> Draw me after you, let us run; the sovereign has brought me into his chambers, let us delight and rejoice in you. (1:4)

This verse, the most explicit in the text of the Songs, barely alludes to a sexual act. The extraordinary eros exudes precisely from the choreography of longing, drawing near and receding, from active searching, rebuff, momentary glimpses, recollection, confession, imagining the beloved, and anticipating. These modes contrast starkly with contemporary eroticism; pornography rushes to full exposure, to climax. In the Songs, the choreography is intricate, reciprocal, the motions refined, the separations filled with building desire and intention, with lingering attention to a rugged and unconventional beauty imbued with the potency of the land. Though the text prompts the presumption that these experienced lovers have been intimate with each other, the text broadcasts no ultimate consummation. Even dwelling in the proximity of the garden together, the lovers are constantly seeking more closeness. Their love is not an end, but the unfolding of passionate life in ardent connection with the cycles of creation. In the garden, the rain subsides, flowers follow, the fruit begin to sprout, grow and, gradually ripen. Implicitly, there is a quiet winter period of attentive nurturing of the relationship, absorbing the lush wet nutrients through the deepening roots of maturing love, preparing to again activate the exuberant joy of spring in the garden of Songs.

Throughout, the Songs express unbridled mutual eroticism. They assert an alternative to the inhibited, disembodied, individualist forms of our societies. The Songs appropriate symbols from nature into an ideology of love, locating us as witnesses to what is most often private, manifesting hidden emotional, aesthetic, and spiritual experience.

Discussing the early Zionists during the period of the "First Aliya," Yaffa Berlovitz writes that they were driven by a "fierce passion to *know* the land, to become familiar with her in an close and intimate way, like *knowing* a woman,"[23] like *knowing* a man (my emphasis). Zionist poets compose love songs to the land of Israel in the genre of the Song of Songs.[24] In the idealist period, Zionists set out to create social experiments based on an alternative ideology. While industrial capitalism was on the rise, the collaborative settlements – *kibbutzim* and *moshavim* – strived for agricultural sharing. The socialism did not weather shifting economic, social, and political conditions well. The younger generations turned from the ideal of community to more personal pursuits. The desire for union with an other, for oneness, divulges the inadequacy of individuality. While they are firmly rooted in the territory of the land of Israel, the Songs propose embodied sharing. Valuing connection and relationship defies the priorities of consumption and profit. Within the limits of human mortality, love aspires toward the eternal. The cultural resources of the garden fertilize different priorities in Israeli society.

Eco-Zionism

From love and desire spring responsibility for the well-being of the land, a full-fledged ecology based on reciprocity, sustenance, and flourishing. Such an ecology initiates a viable partnership with the land. Dedication to the fine quality of water, earth, air, vegetation, and fauna derives from caring rather than self-interest. Curbing waste, toxic emissions, pesticide use, chemical run-off, and pollutants of all kinds can become as obvious as concern for our beloved's health and well-being. Conserving and protecting natural resources and historic sites is akin to looking after our beloved's wellbeing and heirlooms. Daily loving also involves doing our beloved's laundry, washing the dishes, tidying the house. Israelis and visitors might actively clean up and cherish beach, forest, spring, desert, and wadi, as well as parks, streets, lots, and buildings. In this way, we attend to our beloved's needs and delight in our beloved's exquisite beauty.

---

23. Yaffa Berlovitz, *To Invent a Land, To Invent a Nation* [Hebrew] (Tel Aviv, 1983), 169.

24. See Yonatan Ratosh, *Shirim: Shirei Cherev, ha-holkhi ba-Choshekh, mizmor* (Tel Aviv: Hadar, 1977).

Love and Justice

The modern philosopher Emanuel Levinas (1906–1995) is a propo-
nent of love and empathy as the root for social institutions and ethics.
In one of his addresses to a Paris colloquium, Levinas discusses a
Talmudic passage that deals with the semi-circular arrangement of
the High Court, the Sanhedrin, which rules on cases of life and death.
The Mishna states:

> The Sanhedrin was like a semi-circle so that they would see each
> other.[25]

Seeking a biblical support for this seating arrangement, the text supplies the following verse,

> Your navel is like a round goblet full of fragrant wine, your belly like a
> heap of wheat hedged about with roses (Song of Songs 7:3).

The sages choose this verse to support the semi-circular seating pattern of the Sanhedrin from among numerous options. One verse in
the famous Psalm, "God is my Shepherd," combines references to the
round shape and to justice, the business of the High Court,

> S/He leads me in the *spheres*/ways of justice (Psalms 23:2)

About the choice of the verse from the Songs, Levinas comments,

> The nature of the text chosen for this purpose will still astonish us.
> The Sanhedrin with its magnificent semi-circle, making human faces
> show themselves to each other, with a perfect hierarchy, attesting to
> an objective and subjective absolute order, will find its basis in an
> erotic poem, in a verse of the Song of Songs.
>
> Of course the Song of Songs permits of a mystical interpretation,
> but for those who are forewarned – or, without prior assumptions,
> for the mysticism of the Song of Songs is not a mystification – it is
> an erotic text.
>
> Perhaps, justice is founded on the mastery of passion. The justice
> through which the world subsists is founded on the most equivocal
> order, but on the domination exerted at every moment over this
> order or disorder.

---

25. *Sanhedrin* 4:3.

> By speaking of justice in erotic terms, the eroticism of the terms
> has been overcome, all the while preserving in the meaning of the
> terms a fundamental link to the realm that has been overcome.[26]

Levinas acknowledges by name the eros in the text. He concludes that,
while it has been overcome, there remains a fundamental link to that
powerful emotional-physical realm of humanity. Yet, if he considers
eros and passion to be fundamental to justice, then why must they be
overcome?

The Mishnaic expression that connotes "semicircle" derives from
a semi-circular shaped threshing floor, the ground where wheat is
separated from chaff. Threshing wheat is a symbol of an erotic and
productive relationship with the land. The verse from the Songs fills
the flatness of the text with the roundness of the lover's belly. As we
have seen in the Songs, the subtle dynamic of revealing and concealing
creates erotic tension and arouses the lovers. Levinas preserves this
tension. He desires the love in justice and hesitates about its passion.
He claims that there is a fundamental link between eros and justice,
but asserts domination over eros. He sees eros at once as order and
disorder. To the verse from the Songs that reveals its power and beauty
in the midst of the Sanhedrin text, Levinas succumbs. His repeated
statement that it has been overcome invokes eros in the High Court,
in justice. Exploring what eros might mean for justice is not a challenge
that Levinas is prepared to meet in France. However, for Zionism, it is
a profound inspiration, for practice as well as theory.

In and Out of the Garden

The Songs are controversial because they disturb the composed surface of land and human being to reveal underlying passion. This passion is terrifying at the same time as it is irresistible. Rabbi Akiva is the
principle proponent of its value. On account of these challenges, the
sages debate the inclusion of the Song of Songs in the biblical canon.

> Rabi Yehuda says, "The Song of Songs transmits *impurity* to the
> hands; about Ecclesiastes, there is controversy." Rabbi Yossi says,

---

26. E. Levinas, *Nine Talmudic Readings*, Annette Aronowicz transl, University
of Indiana Press 1990, p. 75-76. I am grateful to Shmuel Wygoda for pointing to this
Levinas passage during his lecture on April 3, 2005, Hechal Shlomo, Jerusalem.

> "Ecclesiastes does not transmit impurity to the hands; about the
> Song of Songs, there is controversy."
>   . . . Rabbi Akiva said, "Heaven forbid! Not a single person among
> Israel disputes about the Song of Songs that it conveys impurity to
> the hands, because the entire world is not worthy of the day that
> the Song of Songs was given to Israel. All the writings are holy, but
> the Song of Songs is the Holy of Holies. If they argued, it was about
> Ecclesiastes." . . . And so they resolved. (Mishna *Yadayim* 3:6)

Counter-intuitively, the sages rule that a sacred text is not to be
handled directly because it conveys impurity – would one not expect
that a sacred document would convey, if anything, holiness? The sages
acknowledge the danger of sacred texts by warning that they convey
impurity: studying them urges toward change. With all of these con-
siderations, Rabbi Akiva emphatically asserts that the Song of Songs
belongs in the sacred canon of the Jewish People.

The Orchard

A famous Talmudic legend about Rabbi Akiva affiliates a sublime mystical experience with entering an orchard, a fruitful garden, perhaps
the garden of the Songs.[27] The only one of four sages to survive the
expedition into the orchard intact is Rabbi Akiva: The other three die,
go insane, and commit heresy. The text does not give details about
the special knowledge that protects Rabbi Akiva during dangerous
exposure to the divine. The only hint is the following comment,

> Rabbi Akiva said to them [prior to their ascent]: "When you come
> to the place of pure marble stones, do not say, 'Water! Water!' for it
> is said, 'Whoever speaks untruths shall not stand before My eyes.'"
> (Psalms 101:7)

One kabbalist explains that the separation between "water and water"
on the second day of creation (Genesis 1:6–8) is not applicable in the
divine orchard into which the sages enter. In the earthly domain, there
is separation. However, in the divine domain, the waters are indistin-

---

27. *Hagiga* 14b. The tale is also told in the *Zohar* (I, 26b) and *Tikunei Zohar*,
(Tikun 40).

guishable.[28] Rabbi Akiva perceives that separation is a temporary condition; union is the ultimate destination. He cites a verse from Psalms that clarifies the mortal peril of asserting the permanence or "truth" of separation. Kabbala conceives the separated waters as masculine and feminine forces that surge together. Rabbi Akiva's insight also applies to the matter of the universal and particular with which this chapter begins. While the entire creation articulates differences at all levels, among cells, elements, creatures, cultures, *et cetera*, at a sublime level, everything merges into a great oceanic Oneness.

Rabbi Akiva's garden view of the relationships of heaven and earth informs his determination to include the Song of Songs in the biblical canon. He seeks to reveal the divine-human connection and the potential unity of creation. Having entered the garden, he insists on enabling access for those who seek its fruit. Without elaborating further about this complex passage, suffice to say that from Rabbi Akiva's perspective, the Song of Songs offers passage into sacred domains.

Garden of Song: The Sephardic Bakashot

One Shabbat eve, a Jerusalem Sephardic synagogue invited well-known *paytanim*, liturgical singers, to lead songs in honor of a bar mitzvah, the Jewish celebration of a child attaining responsibility and full membership among her/his people. This event follows the tradition of singing *bakashot* every Shabbat morning in the wee winter hours. Traditional Sephardic synagogues would fill to the brim weekly at 3:00 a.m. Though this Baka community in south Jerusalem was paying homage to the ritual, many of its members, including young boys, are well-initiated – fluent with complex melodies, and comfortable leading and improvising solos.

The small women's area is on the side, blocked from the main section by a painting of fruit. Women peer between pomegranates. Some heavy-set women speak in Arabic about their various health ailments and trials. Some of the women are extremely literate in the tradition; their confident singing rallies others to join in.

Periodically, young boys enter the women's section bearing trays of peanuts and pastries, lemonade and diet cola. In the Ades Synagogue

---

28. Rabbi Moshe Cordevero (Ramak), *Pardes Rimonim,* Shaar Arachei HaKinuim.

and others in the Jerusalem neighborhood of Nachlaot where the *bakashot* are still sung every Shabbat morning throughout the winter, metal trays with glasses of strong sweet tea circulate.

The Sephardic synagogue is arranged with chairs around the perimeter facing inward, punctuated by tables. Some young men sit face-to-face, separated by a small table arrayed with snacks and drinks. The atmosphere in the main hall resembles a cafe or a casual bar, though decorum is strictly observed. Arak, an alcoholic beverage made with anise, is not brought into the women's section.

The melodies progress and spirits elevate. The sense of community converges in the fine rhythms and subtle elaborations. Egged on by the enthusiasm and artistic devotion of the soloists, the community soars into the mystical abode depicted by the sublime poetry of old Jewish communities of Turkey and Syria, "dwelling in the courtyards of the divine palace . . . this is your inheritance." Much of the poetry set to music issues from kabbalists, mystics who composed intricate love songs to the *Shekhina* filled with erotic passion for the divine. Rabbi Chaim Avraham HaKohen (1585–1655) was a student of Chaim Vital, the main disciple of the Ari, while he was teaching in Damascus. His poem, "My beloved has gone down into his Garden" is a centerpiece of the Moroccan supplications. The first stanza reads like verses from the Song of Songs, male and female lovers seeking one another in the garden, at the gates of Jerusalem.

My beloved has gone down to his garden to graze among the gardens	דּוֹדִי יָרַד לְגַנּוֹ לִרְעוֹת בַּגַּנִּים
For delightful play and to gather roses	לְהִשְׁתַּעְשֵׁעַ וְלִלְקֹט שׁוֹשַׁנִּים
My beloved's voice knocks – open for me, my beauty	קוֹל דּוֹדִי דוֹפֵק פְּתְחִי לִי תַמָּתִי
The gates of Zion that I love.	שַׁעֲרֵי צִיּוֹן אֲשֶׁר אָהַבְתִּי

The beloved is the adored Zion; his sensuous body is the threshold. The garden and Jerusalem blend into an ecstasy of anticipated union.

In the *piyyut* "*Agadelkha*," Ibn Ezra exalts the divine Glory with humble verses.

I will increase You, my God, Sovereign of every soul,	אגדלך אלהי, אלהי כל נשמה
	ואודך ברב פחד ואימה

and I will express gratitude to You with tremendous awe and trembling; As I stand among the fortress of Your community who elevate; to You I prostrate, bend my head and stature . . . Can a person possibly probe the secret of her/his creator?	בעמדי תוך קהלך צור לרומם לך אברע ואכוף ראש וקומה . . . היוכל איש חקור את סוד יוצרו

Each *piyyut* has its specific mood and timing in the Aleppo-Syrian four-hour cycle of early morning poems. The drama mounts as sunrise approaches, supplicating toward the arousal of dawn, the illumination. "We receive back our renewed divine soul that is temporarily deposited with us," warbles the *paytan*, "our hearts rejoice, the awesome presence among us."

A nation-wide Israeli project, "Kehillot Sharot" – Singing Communities, is sharing the liturgical music of far-flung Jewish communities. Young and old, men and women, observant and secular, Sephardic, Oriental and Ashkenazic Israelis meet in community centers to partake of this cornucopia of song and poetry. Kehillot Sharot restores dignity to members of communities whose culture has been dishonored by the privileging of Ashkenazi tradition. The majority of the Israeli population derives from the vast Spanish diaspora and the East. This revival is a blessing, and for some, a glimmer of hope that the songs and refined traditions will live on.

One of the founding musical leaders of Kehillot Sharot is Roni Ish-Ran. Roni grew up in the ritual embrace of the Halabi (Aleppo-Syrian)-Jerusalem community. He has also participated in academic research and rigorous training at the Jerusalem Music Academy. During his teen years, Roni had lapsed from his connection with the *bakashot*; he did not rise in the night with his parents. While serving in the Israel Defense Force, Roni was once stationed for a long period on a remote base in the Negev desert. Though in his army unit he found it onerous to observe the daily prayers and rituals, he had taken on the personal challenge to "stay religious" during his service. Having been denied leave for a number of weeks, he was finally anticipating a Shabbat at home in Jerusalem. At the last moment on Friday, his visit was cancelled. He was charged to remain on guard duty on the base.

Bound by his officer's order, he was stuck where he had no desire to be. There was no doubt that he would fulfill his duty. That evening, alone in a dark bunker, he lingered on the familiar Friday evening melodies of his childhood. Enclosed in the private space, time and the desert outside were an endless expanse. Finishing the traditional prayer service, he wanted more. The *bakashot* flooded him. He sang the full four-hour cycle of supplications from memory. The old minor key melodies and poignant lyrics voiced his longing for home. Though Roni was in Israel, the poetry voiced his personal sense of exile.

One of the greats of the last generations of Moroccan *paytanim*, liturgical poets, Rabbi David Buzaglo (1903–1975) lived most of his life in Morocco and immigrated to Israel in 1965 where he lived his last ten years. He weaves together the intense tone of humble personal entreaty with references to sacred texts and traditions. This particular *piyyut*, poem, is sung during the later part of the sequence, toward sunrise.

My God, Why Have You Abandoned Me?	אלי למה עזבתני
Rabbi David Buzaglo	ר׳ דוד בוזגלו

My God, why have You abandoned me
  dwelling in the wild – wandering in the
  desert?
See that my hands are weak for there is no
  judge for my cause
I have nodded my head with every crashing
  wave until it passed. . . .

אֵלִי לָמָה עֲזַבְתָּנִי
שׁוֹכֵן בָּר נָע בַּמִּדְבָּר.
רְאֵה כִּי אָזְלַת יָדִי וְאֵין דָּן דִּינִי
נִעְנַעְתִּי רֹאשִׁי לְכָל גַּל וּמִשְׁבָּר
עַד כִּי עָבַר. . . .

Composed eight centuries afterwards, the exile of the *Shekhina* and the destruction of the Temple frame this poem. Like many of the *bakashot*, this poem mourns. In Babylon, Syria, Persia, Yemen, Turkey, Greece, North Africa, Iberia, Jewish communities sang the anguish of their plight in terms of longing for the homeland. Though the Old City of Jerusalem and the Temple Mount had not yet fallen into Israeli hands, the Jewish People were certainly well installed within the borders of the land of Israel during Buzaglo's lifetime. Yet, like the Sephardic communities that gather in the Jerusalem night to sing, the *bakashot* reflect exile consciousness. They desire Jerusalem while they are actually in Jerusalem! When Yehuda HaLevi and Abraham Joshua Heschel expressed their desire for the homeland, they lived in exile from Israel.

They did not conceive the Jewish People at home. Though Israel has celebrated more than six decades of statehood, the night-time vigil continues; Kehillot Sharot – Singing Communities flourish. Why?

The material fulfillment of Zionism has clearly not resolved or sated the desire for homecoming. Indeed, while in the land, Jewish longing for the ideal state that Israel had once grown to symbolize persists. Israel is replete with creative potency and urging toward ever improving and more refined dreams, while at the same time, beleaguered by strife, unfairness, even suffering.

> I beseech – why is the redemption still blocked? Aman, aman, aman, aman.[29]

This supplication is as relevant to the Jewish People at home in Israel today as it was during the long exile. The desire for a more redeemed state in this material world and continuously laboring to fulfill it is an ongoing project of the Jewish People, of humanity. The onset of the Zionist movement and the unrelenting passion that Jews have invested toward its actualization marks a tremendous resurgence and empowerment to the enterprise of redemption in this world. Kehillot Sharot demonstrate how much the Zionist dream resonates among Israeli communities in the twenty-first century. But the dream is not a distant hope of return to Zion. It is also the work of communities in Israel joining together in a garden of love songs, knowing, appreciating, and caring for each other better.

Returning to Roni in his bunker on Friday night, he wants to go home. Like most Israeli young people, his years of young adulthood are dedicated to army service punctuated by visits home. Army is about obligation, responsibility, fear, discipline, camaraderie, obedience. Home is a place of nurture, love, warmth and acceptance, support, and freedom. A soldier often yearns for home with the fervor that Jews in exile have yearned for Israel. Compulsory army serve and annual reserve duty are necessary effects of the lack of fulfillment of Israel's fervent longing for peace. Insecurity in the land of Israel is an aspect of exile. The *bakashot*-supplications express Israeli striving for home. Living securely among one another and with our neighbors is one of the urgent unfulfilled desires of the *home*coming of the Jewish People.

---

29. Rabbi Rafael Antebi.

By contrast with Roni's experience, for many young Jews in the "Diaspora," home is a place to leave in order to gain independence, freedom, and seek adventure. At the same stage of life that Israelis yearn for home, many Diaspora young people are anxious to leave. Parents are often similarly impatient for their children to move on. Rabbi Shlomo Carlebach gives the blessing to parents that their young adult children should leave their home tracing slow steps backwards, with the same reverence and longing that one expresses when departing from the sacred Temple. This blessing, and Roni's experience proposing the sacredness of family life and home, have implications for the relationship of the Jewish People to our homeland.

Tending the Garden

On Yom Kippur, sacred time and sacred place converge in an awesome ritual. According to the ancient service prescribed in the Torah and elaborated in the Talmud, the High Priest, adorned in simple white linen garments, enters the innermost sanctum, the Holy of Holies, only once every year. There, with the community assembled outside, waiting in suspense for the High Priest to emerge intact from performing with precision and success the ritual of atonement, he offers supplication on behalf of the People of Israel. Lingering briefly after leaving the Holy of Holies, the High Priest intones one last prayer. A passage in Tractate *Yoma* – "The Day," Yom Kippur – discusses this last prayer.

Part 1

[Mishna: The High Priest] prays one short prayer in the intermediate courtyard (between the Holy of Holies and the Outer Court). [Gemara:] What does he pray? Rava, child of Rav Ada and Ravin, child of Rav Ada, both say in the name of Rav, "May it be Your will before You God, our Sovereign, that this year will be rainy and hot/dry." And what exactly is the blessing/value of heat/dryness? Perhaps you say it means that if it is hot/dry, let it be wet. Rav Acha, child of Rava, concludes it [the prayer] in the name of Rav Yehuda,

"May a ruler not depart from the house of Yehuda; May Your People Israel not need to support, one another [economically]; May the prayers of wayfarers/transgressors not come (enter) before You."

Part 2

Rabbi Hanina ben Dosa was walking along the road. S/He sent rain down upon him. He said,

"Sovereign of the Universe! The entire world is comfortable/at ease and Hanina is suffering!"

The rain stopped. When he arrived at his home, he said, "Sovereign of the Universe! The entire world is suffering and Hanina is comfortable/at ease!"

The rain came.

Rabbi Yosef said, "What use is the prayer of the High Priest in relation to Hanina Ben Dosa?!"

Part 3

Our sages taught, there is a story of a High Priest who prolonged his prayer. His fellow priests decided to enter after him. As they began to enter [toward the Holy of Holies, thinking that the High Priest must have failed fatally], he came out. They said to him, "On what account did you prolong your prayer?"

He said to them, "Is it difficult for you that I prayed for your sake, and for the Temple that it not be destroyed?!"

They said to him, "Do not accustom yourself to doing this, for we have learned, 'He would not prolong his prayer in order to avoid terrifying Israel.'" (*Yoma* 53b)

Rav's original version of the High Priest's prayer is a request for a wet *and* dry year. Rav is considered the first *amora* – he lived and taught in Babylon, where he established the great institute at Sura to redact the Babylonian Talmud. He tells the version of the prayer from the Temple period when Jews inhabited the land of Israel, farmed and conducted the service in Jerusalem. Praying for a year that is both rainy and dry reflects his familiarity with the ecology and agricultural cycle of the land. When the rain falls in its proper season, seeds germinate and tree roots soak up the nourishment they need. In the spring, the grains ripen for festive harvests, barley at Passover and wheat at Shavuot. Throughout the long dry season, the fruit matures on the trees; each variety ripens in its time. Grapes begin in the hot summer, then figs, pomegranates at the New Year, olives in the late fall after the first rains, in time to press oil for Chanukah – the winter festival of light, then dates in the winter. With the exception of the grains, this ripening sequence corresponds to the biblical verse listing the seven special species of the land of Israel.

> A land of wheat, barley, grape, fig, pomegranate, olive oil and [date] honey. (Deuteronomy 8:8)

Generations of Babylonian sages living outside of Israel during the early centuries of the last millennium query the prayer, "What exactly is the blessing of heat/dryness?" For the exiles in Babylon who do not garden, the harvest cycle is an abstraction, not a livelihood. They assume that rain is a blessing and that dryness is not. According to the later books of Isaiah, the exiles in Babylon live with despair and a sense of abandonment by God.[30] Dryness becomes a symbol for the barrenness of exile – by contrast with rain, a sign of blessing, fertility, and divine connection. This text reflects the shift in consciousness from being at home in the land during the Temple period to exile after the destruction. The text transforms the Israeli agricultural process into a symbolic system, separate from the land. The Babylonian sages reinterpret the prayer from their exile perspective that focuses on rain and loses sight of the fruitfulness of the dry season. The earlier Palestinian layer of the text, rooted in the garden, values both wet and dry.

This text also suggests aesthetic values. Along with the Babylonian sages who over-value wetness, the image of verdant fields and vistas has also seduced our own eyes. Desiring signs of fertility and potency, we soak our lawns and gardens during the dry season and drought periods, thirsting for the illusion of continuous fertility. By contrast, the ancient Jewish Palestinian sages acknowledge the value and blessing of the dry season. During these months, fruit ripen. Fields after the harvest, in the menopausal stage of the fertility cycle, are blanketed with golden hues and crowned with thistles. As I type, Jerusalem municipality gardeners are unfurling rolls of fresh sod, carpeting a former train route with thirsty grass. Drought-resistant planting is a sound alternative to heavy irrigation. Today, we need to curb our desire for lush green, to grow to appreciate the summer beauty of arid landscapes, and to value the whole yearly cycle of life and land. In this way, we will put our scarce water resources to better and more equitable use.

The second part of the Talmudic passage expands upon the third of

---

30. Isa. 40:27; 49:14; 50:1.

the concluding blessings, "May the prayers of wayfarers/transgressors not come (enter) before You." The text reflects on the tension between private and public interests, between farmer and traveler. The farming community understands how sustenance depends upon the blessing of rain in its season. For a traveler, rain is an inconvenience, causing muddy roads and difficult passage. Here the physical discomfort of the winter rain is palpable. Hanina Ben Dosa is a first-century Palestinian sage – renowned for his piety and miracles – who lived in the lower Galilee. Hanina's privileged access to divine favor undermines the Temple ritual that aims for the seasonal nurturing of the land for its inhabitants. Rabbi Yosef, teaching in exile more than two hundred years after the destruction of the Temple, cautions about the power of charismatic figures. Personal interests must be subordinated to sustenance for the inhabitants of the land. For the talmudic redactor, the garden is the highest priority.

Beginning in the Bible, Judaism emphasizes the fruitful production of the land of Israel. The agricultural seasons set the festivals, Temple services, and prayer cycles, and reflect the ethics of living on the land. The intricate garden system engages the spirit and the body of Israel. Agricultural self-sufficiency was one of the goals attained by the Zionist pioneers during the first decades of statehood. As government priorities have shifted, the cooperative settlements and their indigenous agricultural production declines. The extent to which Israel eats from the land is not only an economic choice; it is bound up with the cultural identity of the Jewish People and the meaning of Zionism. Outsourcing the Israeli food supply lessens exposure to the special labors and inspiration of the garden. In view of limitations of space and water, and the fragility of the ecology, our sustenance is one of the important challenges facing Israel today.

Below the Line

Sustenance is on the Israeli agenda. Conceived initially as a socially responsible democracy, under current political and economic conditions, aggravated by government policy, a significant and growing proportion of Israelis lives in poverty. Among the thirty-five member countries of the Organization for Economic Cooperation and Development, Israel has one of the highest rates of child poverty – one in five children lives below the poverty line. The ignominious American child poverty standard is 37 percent.[31] The growing gap between the rich and poor diminishes the morale of Israeli society. This deepening divide alienates communities from one another and distributes society's resources and responsibilities in increasingly inequitable ways. According to Reb Yair, founder and director of *Chelev HaAretz*, "the fat of the land" [an initiative to feed hungry children and elders and improve the lives of troubled youth], in the Israeli poverty "business," political and entrepreneurial interest groups compete for the profits from service to the needy. A biblical passage depicts abuse of power on the basis of hunger.

> Esau came in from the open field, exhausted. Esau said to Jacob, "Please, give me some of that red stuff to gulp down, for I am exhausted . . ."
> Jacob said, "First, sell me your birthright."
> Esau said, "Here I am about to die, what's my birthright worth to me?!" (Genesis 25:29–32)

The patriarch Jacob manipulates his brother to improve his position and increase his wealth. Hunger is political. The blessing for which Jacob and Esau contend is a blessing of nourishment from the earth. In the end, through Rebecca's intervention, Isaac bestows the blessing upon Jacob instead of his firstborn brother.

> May God give you from the dew of heaven, from the fat of the earth, plenty of grain and juice of grape. (Genesis 27:28)

Entering Isaac's chamber, bearing his carefully prepared feast in anticipation of receiving his father's blessing, Esau learns that Isaac

31. Ruth Eglash, "OECD report rates child poverty in Israel among highest," *The Jerusalem Post*, Retrieved Jan. 12, 2012, http://www.jpost.com/Headlines/Article.aspx?id=219031. 16% of American children – more than 11 million – lived in poor families in 2002, meaning their parents' income was at or below the federal poverty level. These parents are typically unable to provide their families with basic necessities like stable housing and reliable child care. 37% of American children – more than 26 million – lived in low-income families in 2002. These families often face material hardships and financial pressures similar to those families who are officially counted as poor. National Center for Children in Poverty (NCCP), Columbia University, School for Public Health, http://www.nccp.org/pub_cpf04.html.

has already given the blessing to Jacob. Isaac is fear-struck; Esau is inconsolable.

> Isaac was seized with very violent trembling. . . . [Esau] burst into wild and bitter sobbing, and said to his father, "Bless me too, Father!" But he answered, "Your brother came with guile and took away your blessing." (27:33, 35)

To Esau's desperate plea, Isaac responds with compassion. He bestows a blessing of nourishment not dissimilar to the one he had given to Jacob. The only difference is the subordination of Esau's firstborn status to Jacob.

> See, your abode shall enjoy the fat of the earth
> And the dew of heaven above.
> Yet by your sword you shall live,
> And you shall serve your brother (27: 39–40)

In spite of his preferential treatment of Jacob, Isaac does not deprive Esau of a dignified livelihood. Every person is entitled to sustenance from the same divine source, the "fat of the earth, and the dew." Like many so-called *developed* nations, in Israel, some children go to bed hungry. The sages famously remark, "If there is no flour, then there is no Torah; if there is no Torah, then there is no flour" – we need to eat in order to study Torah.[32] There is another meaning – neglecting dignified sustenance for every person in our midst diminishes the authenticity of Torah study and ritual observance. In Israel, we must apply refined Jewish codes about social obligation to the structures of poverty.[33]

Fanatical Sabbatical

The Torah addresses the relationship between ritual and nurture. Parallel to sanctifying the seventh day, Shabbat, the Torah prescribes a sabbatical year for the land – *shmita*. As humans are enjoined to desist from creative and productive labor on the seventh day, Shabbat,

---

32. *Avot* 3:17.

33. See, for example Maimonides *Eight Degrees of Charity*, Jonathan J. Baker, trans., retrieved July 19, 2011, http://www.panix.com/~jjbaker/rmbmzdkh.html.

in honor of Creation, the land of Israel is to rest from production on the seventh year. In this way, the Torah transposes time onto space. Comparable to the rest of Shabbat, the land and its inhabitants are meant to renew and revive their strength. On Shabbat, people enjoy their harvest after a week of work; during the *shmita*, people take a break after six years of cultivating. These themes are conjoined in the legend of the manna. After leaving Egypt, the Israelites, in the desert, receive one portion of manna daily. They are not permitted to keep it overnight, for when they did "it became infested with maggots and stank." But on Friday, they receive two portions.

> God said to Moses, "I will rain down bread for you from the sky, and the people shall go out and gather each day that day's portion – that I may thus test them, to see whether they will follow My instructions or not. But on the sixth day, when they apportion what they have brought in, it shall prove to be double the amount they gather each day." (Exodus 16:4–5)

The sabbatical year is similarly meant to be sufficiently sustaining without laboring.

> And should you ask, "What are we to eat in the seventh year, if we may neither sow nor gather in our crops?" I will ordain My blessing for you in the sixth year, so that it shall yield a crop sufficient for three years. (Leviticus 25:20–21)

In *shmita*, time unites with space – a Shabbat for the land. Both Shabbat and the *shmita*-sabbatical year call to desist from production. The *shmita* frees inhabitants who labor productively for six years to appreciate the contentment of basic sustenance on the seventh. The Torah assures everyone of a basic standard of living and security while resting. The Jubilee year, a cycle of seven sabbaticals, legislates against the perpetuation of an inherited landed aristocracy and landless/ homeless class.[34] The Torah curbs incentive to earn excessively and honors simplicity. According to the Jubilee manifesto, the blessing of subsisting on the land pertains to every inhabitant. Redistributing material resources among all strata of society releases people from the suffering brought on by economic inequity and restores human

---

34. Lev. 25:8–13.

dignity. "You shall proclaim freedom throughout the land for all its inhabitants."

The Jewish year 5767 (2007–2008) was one of the most observed of any *shmita* year in the history of the State of Israel: by municipalities, private businesses, and individuals. There was, however, much controversy about how to observe the *shmita*.

Before Rav Kook arrived in Israel, prior to 1904, he romanticized *shmita* as one of the commandments connecting Jewish resettlement of the land with redemption. He fantasized the nation liberated from daily labor, studying and pursuing all manner of meaningful activities. Once he was in the land, he became acquainted with farmers struggling in the young settlements. Identifying with their plight, he permitted a legal loophole to allow Jews to symbolically sell their land in order to continue to work it during *shmita*. Rav Kook's ruling bound the Israeli chief rabbinate to uphold the sale procedure so that Israeli farmers can earn their living, and the Israeli public can afford to buy food. Ultra-Orthodox halakhic authorities do not feel bound by this decision. The controversy affects today's economy and society:

> As in the past, and after investigating the situation of agriculture in this country, Israel's Chief Rabbinate is instructing Jewish farmers in Israel to sign deeds of sale for the lands they possess so that Jewish farming can continue in Israel. However, at the same time, the Rabbinate has informed the chief rabbis of Israeli cities that they are not bound by this instruction, thus enabling the ultra-Orthodox community to follow a line of conduct that zealously protects – and focuses exclusively on – the interests of ultra-Orthodox consumers. As a result, we find chief rabbis of cities issuing instructions forbidding restaurants and other establishments from using Israeli agricultural produce and requiring them to work only with suppliers importing foreign produce.[35]

In response to the hardship caused by the strictures, a group of Zionist rabbis mobilized dissent against the chief rabbinate. Their Tzohar organization issues its own *shmita* certificates to institutions and businesses where the local rabbis would not honor the land sale agree-

---

35. Benjamin Lau, "Observing shmita sensibly," *Haaretz*, 10/09/2007, http://www.haaretz.com/hasen/spages/902515.html.

ment. Rabbi Rafi Feuerstein, chairman of Tzohar, says, "We believe it is important to strengthen Jewish farmers and provide reasonably priced produce to the Jewish nation."[36] After protracted deliberation and appeal, the Supreme Court ordered the chief rabbinate to replace any municipal rabbi refusing to accept the symbolic sale, the *heter mechira*.[37] In the wake of the ruling, the Israeli justice minister commented that he would oppose the adoption of an Israeli constitution that prohibited the Supreme Court from ruling on conflicts between the state and religion.

One proponent of religious Zionism, Rabbi Benjamin Lau concludes about *shmita*,

> We must apply the original idea of the shmita, a year when commercial competition is suspended and we refine our qualities, to other channels relevant to most Israelis. It is neither correct nor moral to subjugate our small community of Jewish farmers to a commandment whose observance is no longer possible.[38]

Lau advocates for a humane religious solution – to circumvent the laws through the necessary manipulations. This has become a mainstream approach to *shmita* observance – finding halakhic solutions to enable people to carry on with their personal and business lives as usual. At the same time, he advocates to apply the values of *shmita* to non-agricultural realms of economic activity, in order to make *shmita* more meaningful to Israeli society.

Some view the *shmita* debate as a contest between the ultra-Orthodox and mainstream religious authorities. Others view it as an exercise in modernizing halakha to respond to twenty-first century conditions. While both of these are true, the debate also reveals the difficult process of Zionism – applying Jewish ideals to contemporary Israeli reality. Organized today as a modern urbanized nation, there is

---

36. Steven Erlanger, "As Farmers and Fields Rest, a Land Grows Restless," *New York Times*, October 8, 2007, http://www.nytimes.com/2007/10/08/world/middleeast/08shmita.html.

37. "Israel's Top Court Backs Loophole in Farming Law," *New York Times*, November 27, 2007, *http://query.nytimes.com/gst/fullpage.html?res=990CE2DB1 23FF936A15753C1A9619C8B63&n=Top/Reference/Times%20Topics/People/E/ Erlanger,%20Steven.*

38. *Op. cit.*

no doubt that adhering to the utopian *shmita* principles jeopardizes the well-being of many. However, there is not enough acknowledgment within the Zionist camp of how circumventing the laws betrays profound goals in the texts. The *shmita* laws themselves acknowledge their own difficulty. For example, the Torah foresees the need to encourage people to continue to lend money even as the *shmita* cancellation of debts approaches. The Torah commands people to overcome inclinations to protect their self-interest at the expense of the needy.[39] When the Torah warning proved insufficient, Hillel, a sage who lived at the beginning of the first millennium, instituted the *prosbul*, a mechanism to circumvent the *shmita* debt cancellation. The Mishna records this innovation.

> Seeing that the law which prescribed the release of all debts every seventh year brought about the harmful consequence that people refused to loan to one another and thus violated what was written in the Torah, namely, that a money loan should not be withheld because of the approach of the *shmita* year, Hillel instituted the *prosbul*.[40]

This *prosbul* benefited the rich by protecting them against loss of property, and the poor by enabling them to obtain a loan when they needed it. The Talmud reasons that the innovation was made for *tikkun ha'olam* – for the sake of fixing the world, i.e., for the better working of society.[41]

Like the *prosbul*, the symbolic sale agreement-*heter mechira* aims to ensure people's well-being. Both allow the *status quo* to proceed in spite of biblical obligations to redress class divisions in society. Whereas the *prosbul* was a legal innovation for Jews in exile who had little control over their economy, the need for the *heter mechira* arises when Jews own land in Israel. Precisely for this situation, the *shmita* laws apply. Their purpose is not to perpetuate the status quo, but to subvert its unfairness.

This section begins by citing the connection between *shmita* and

---

39. Deut. 15.
40. *Shevi'it* 10:3. The formula of the *prosbul* is: "I deliver to you ... judges of ... [place], that I may at any time I choose collect my debts." This declaration was attested by witnesses or by the judges of the court before whom the declaration was made (*Shevi'it* 10:4).
41. *Gittin* 37a.

Shabbat. The biblical intentions of Shabbat are twofold: to memorialize creation and to liberate every being from labor. This second aim is explicit in the version of the Ten Commandments in Deuteronomy:

> Observe the sabbath day and keep it holy, as the Lord your God has commanded you. Six days you shall labor and do all your work, but the seventh day is a sabbath of the Lord your God; you shall not do any work – you, your son or your daughter, your male or female slave, your ox or your ass, or any of your cattle, or the stranger in your settlements, so that your male and female slave may rest as you do. Remember that you were a slave in the land of Egypt and the Lord your God freed you from there with a mighty hand and an outstretched arm; therefore the Lord your God has commanded you to observe the sabbath day. (Deuteronomy 5:12–15)

Like the epic Exodus from Egypt, each Shabbat intends the release of families, their servants, animals, and guests from servitude. All are equal in the liberation. Similarly to the collection of the manna, all are equal in the harvest – each according to her/his need. The *shmita* rules intend to fulfill the Shabbat goal of release from labor – for an entire year on the land. The release from debt and, on the Jubilee-*yovel*, from landlessness, intends an even more radical leveling.

While exile confines Shabbat observance to time, in Israel, *shmita* transpires in space. While exile limits the Jewish People to symbolic liberation, Israel affords the possibility of actualizing liberation. A religious Zionist reflects about the challenges of *shmita*.

> [W]e regretfully admit that no other commandment in the Torah (ranging from the Sabbath to the commandments concerning personal status) is so utopian in its vision yet so pathetically far from ideal in its practical realization, both at present and in the foreseeable future, as the commandment of *shmita*. Therefore, one must work to promote social equality and minimize societal gaps in Israel by means of progressive legislation that will lend expression to this aspect of the law of *shmita*.[42]

---

42. Amnon Shapira, "Ideological Issues in the *Shemitta* Controversy," Bar-Ilan University's Parashat Hashavua Study Center, May 19, 2001, http://www.biu.ac.il/ JH/Parasha/eng/bahar/sha.html.

At the Periphery

Mini Israel, a model at Latrun, exhibits historic sites, buildings and landscapes from around the country. Well-dressed tiny people relax on the beach, stroll down a Tel Aviv street, pray at the Kotel. The goal of the park is "to create a kind of living 'picture album' that will reflect the reality of life in this small strip of land."[43] "The reality of life in this small strip of land" is deeper than the glossy outer surface that Mini Israel exhibits. Israel teems with invention, is shattered by brokenness, foments with innovation, cringes with poverty, hums with prayer, engrosses with debate, abounds with vision. Mini Israel does not make visible the many faces of creativity, need, and desire that elicit caring and responsibility, the possibility of commitment and connection to the current joys and challenges of Zionism.[44]

While the era of draining malarial swamps, rendering the earth arable, and building the physical infrastructure has passed, the present generation of young Israelis is defining new concepts of "pioneering" and "settlement" of the land of Israel. Young adults – yeshiva and university students – are social pioneers. The Ayalim project concentrates its efforts in the Negev and Galilee. Working with weakened communities, endangered youth, new immigrants, handicapped and bereaved families, thousands of students tutor and mentor, putting their Zionist values to work. In Dimona, they build their own homes together and open their doors to Jewish and Beduin adolescents to help them to feel "a part of this place and start to instill a sense of social responsibility."[45]

In 1988, a group of graduates from a yeshiva in Yerucham (a development town in the Negev desert), established Midreshet BeYachad (the "Together Institute"). This yeshiva emphasizes social action and responsibility, encouraging its students to get involved in poverty in Yerucham. Students join local employees to support their struggles for decent living wages, for example. The project develops leadership, promotes settlement and local involvement in Yerucham and the

43. Mini Israel website, http://www.minisrael.co.il/about/a_en.htm.

44. See Michael Feige, "Mini Israel: The Israeli Place between the Global and the Miniature" in *Jewish Topographies: Visions of Space, Traditions of Place*, Julia Brauch, Anna Lipphardt, Alexandra Nocke, ed. (Aldershot, England; Burlington, VT: Ashgate, 2008), 328–342.

45. Shelly Paz, "O, pioneers," *The Jerusalem Post*, Jan. 25, 2007.

Negev region. Midreshet BeYachad and the yeshiva have increased the population of Yerucham by more than six percent, including teachers and university graduates. They run programs that reach as many as 12,500 students annually.

These initiatives educate toward Jewish values, constructive national identity, tolerance and community responsibility, bridging gaps between populations. Rather than staking out territories in the West Bank and Gaza for their strategic, symbolic religious and historical value, today's young pioneers opt for the frontiers of social justice.[46]

In the summer of 2011, Israeli young people launched a national Social Justice Movement. Student-led rallies amassed an unprecedented number of Israelis in the streets. Tent encampments sprang up in a main Tel Aviv boulevard and throughout the country. The growing movement calls on all citizens and the government to enable affordable living and housing, quality education, health care, and fairer economic distribution. Young orators quote from ancient biblical prophets Isaiah, Amos, and Jeremiah.

> Hear this, O you who would swallow the needy, and destroy the poor of the land, saying: "When will the new moon be gone, that we may sell grain? and the sabbath, that we may set forth corn? making the *ephah* [measure of flour] small, and the *shekel* [measure of money] great, and falsifying the balances with deceit; That we may buy the poor for silver, and the needy for a pair of shoes, and sell the refuse of the corn?" (Amos 8:4–6)

Itzik Shmuli, head of the National Student Council, calls for a new social order where corruption abates and equality obtains regardless of religion, race, or gender.[47] An antidote to cynicism, a new optimism wafts in Israel as people gather in parks and living-rooms, giving voice to hopes and organizing to fulfill them together.

Until Zionism, the garden has been a figment of our fertile imagination. Israel affords the extraordinary opportunity to dig into the inspiration of the garden, to plant, tend, and reap the fruit with the fullness of our humanity.

---

46. Nadav Shragai, "Moving from settlement of the hilltops to settlement in the hearts," *Haaretz Online*, 02/12/01.

47. At Afula rally, *The Marker* (Hebrew), Aug. 13, 2011, retrieved Oct. 10, 2011, http://www.themarker.com/news/tent-protest/1.682536.

5   Sacred Action

KODESH, THE SACRED, has fascinated humanity from the beginning. Where people apply sacredness to space, the outcome is often fatal. Competing claims to conquer, possess, and control sacred places have stained many history pages with blood. Today, claims to sacred space mobilize the resources of reckonable powers that threaten regional and global stability, and the security of the world's populations. In 1998, Osama bin Laden called world Muslims to religious duty, justifying war and killing to capture the Temple Mount in Jerusalem.[1] Prominent Palestinian activist and president of Al-Quds University, Sari

---

1. "[I]n compliance with Allah's order, we issue the following fatwa [Islamic religious obligation], to all Muslims: The ruling to kill the Americans and their allies – civilians and military – is an individual duty for every Muslim who can do it in any country in which it is possible to do it, in order to liberate the al-Aqsa Mosque and the holy mosque [Mecca] from their grip, and in order for their armies to move out of all the lands of Islam, defeated and unable to threaten any Muslim. This is in accordance with the words of Almighty Allah, 'and fight the pagans all together as they fight you all together,' and 'fight them until there is no more tumult or oppression, and there prevail justice and faith in Allah,'" (citations from Qur'an, 2:190–193), "Jihad Against Jews and Crusaders," World Islamic Front Statement issued by Shaykh Usamah Bin-Muhammad Bin-Ladin, Ayman al-Zawahiri, amir of the Jihad Group in Egypt, Abu-Yasir Rifa'i Ahmad Taha, Egyptian Islamic Group, Shaykh Mir Hamzah, secretary of the Jamiat-ul-Ulema-e-Pakistan, Fazlur Rahman, amir of the Jihad Movement in Bangladesh, "Al Qaeda's Fatwa," PBS Newshour, Feb. 23, 1998. Retrieved Feb. 24, 2012, http://www.pbs.org/newshour/terrorism/international/fatwa_1998.html.

Nusseibeh, denies that the sacredness of the Temple Mount or any place justifies killing.[2] While Osama bin Laden's rhetoric is extreme, a common assumption about territorial sovereignty underlies his statement – conquest is a legitimate way to possess and control land. The same assumption also underlies American and European sovereignty. Once Western nations had mainly secured their territories through long and terrible wars, they crafted a consensus that opposes forceful conquest and supports a *status quo* favorable to their power.

Holiness has been accumulating in Jerusalem for thousands of years. On Mount Moriah, Avraham is said to have prepared to sacrifice Sarah's and his child Isaac in accord with a divine command. This episode, known as "the binding of Isaac," is one of the formative chapters of Jewish faith. On that site where human sacrifice was annulled, the first and second Jewish Temples – the center point of Jewish ritual life – were built. For Christians, the Temple Mount is a site that Jesus visited and taught. A few meters away, he ate his last supper and walked his last steps along the Via Dolorosa. Known to Muslims as *Haram al-Sharif*, the Temple Mount is the place from which the prophet Muhammad is believed to have ascended heavenward – where the Dome of the Rock was later built, and beside it the al-Aqsa Mosque. At the nexus of these events, the Old City of Jerusalem is the territory most charged with sacredness for the biblical religions.

Israel made Jerusalem her capital in 1948 with the declaration of the State on the grounds of the sanctity and centrality of the place in Jewish tradition.[3] From the biblical period onward, Jerusalem has been a principle feature of the material, spiritual, aesthetic, ritual, and emotional life of the Jewish People. The Palestinian national movement that emerged over the recent decades desires its capital in East Jerusalem. The Arabic name for Jerusalem is *al-Quds* – the sacred city. Some argue that the motives for the Muslim religious claim to Jerusalem are political – the Qu'ran does not mention Jerusalem or Zion once.[4] Sari Nuseibeh considers the sacredness of Jerusalem to

---

2. "The Haram Al-Sharif," in *Muhammad's Ascension from Jerusalem's Rock to Heaven*, Khusraw Dihawi, ed. (*Kahmseh*, Topkapi Museum, Hazine 798, 2007), 368, retrieved July 19, 2011, http://sari.alquds.edu/doc/where_sky_earth_meet.pdf.

3. Some variant of "Jerusalem" appears in the *Tanakh* 669 times and "Zion," referring either to Jerusalem or to the land of Israel appears 154.

4. Daniel Pipes, a controversial pro-Israel academic and activist published,

come from two roots: Islam's respect for Judaism and Christianity, and the one miracle recorded about Muhammad's life – his ascent to Allah. "Jerusalem is thus the gateway to the heavens and to divine knowledge, the medium through which to reach the divine – in short, the spiritual threshold of the divine paradise."[5] Nuseibeh's words have an ecumenical tone consonant with a prophetic verse referring to the Jerusalem Temple, "for My house will be a house of prayer for all peoples."[6] In spite of the spiritual openness of these attitudes, people contest hegemony over the sacred place. War over sacred ground is based on a belief that it *is* sacred, that sacredness inheres in a specific geographic place – in the earth, air, and water.

Investing in the Sacred

Since the initial biblical divine promise to Avraham and Sarah through the exile that lasted until the modern period, Jewry has been investing the land of Israel with sacredness. Judaism directs intention and expectation toward the land – to celebrate presence in it, and to anticipate and yearn to return when absent from it. Unlike any period in Jewish history since the exile in 70 CE, today a large portion of the Jewish People lives in the homeland and almost every Jew has physical access. Zionism's fulfillment of the long-standing desire for the land often gets lost amidst the high volume of anti-Zionist rhetoric. Too many people lose sight of what Zionism achieves. Except among religious camps, many vestiges of the *sacred* idea of the land have succumbed to the siege of *post*-Zionism. For many, Israel has become tainted by impure intentions, rather than sacred ones. Attitudes about the land shape Israel's internal life and policy, her relations with the Palestinians, with

---

"The Muslim Claim to Jerusalem," *Middle East Quarterly*, VII(4), fall 2001, http://www.meforum.org/article/490. Christopher Hitchens rebukes Pipes, "Pipes the Propagandist: Bush's Nominee Doesn't Belong at the U.S. Institute for Peace," *Slate*, Monday, Aug. 11, 2003, http://www.slate.com/id/2086844/. In 2001, Nadia Abu El-Haj published her argument that Israelis fabricate the evidence of the sacred history of the land – *Facts on the Ground: Archaeological Practice and Territorial Self-Fashioning in Israeli Society* (Chicago: University of Chicago Press, 2001).

5. "Jerusalem, Holy City of Islam," *New York Times*, April 25, 1982, retrieved Aug. 3, 2010, http://www.nytimes.com/1982/04/25/travel/jerusalem-holy-city-of-islam.html.

6. Isa. 56:7.

her neighbors, and her prospects for peace and war. We need to open the topic of sacredness to more diverse views and ethical sensibilities than currently dominate the conversation.

According to the Torah, the sacredness of a place has both literal and symbolic meanings. Moses's first encounter with the divine comes about when he notices an extraordinary sight in the desert: a bush aflame but not burning up. Drawn close, he must remove his shoes because the ground upon which he stands is sacred (Exodus 3:5). Moses relates to sacredness by focusing and changing his behavior. In this case, sacredness imbues a specific place at a particular moment: when and where a person notices God revealing Godself. There is no indication that the place where the bush burns had been sacred before the divine apparition there, nor that it remains sacred after the divine presence departs. Of what does the sacredness of the land of Israel consist? Is it relevant? And what if anything does sacredness require of the inhabitants of Israel – today and onward? Continuing with the Mishkan-Temple model, we explore meanings of the sacredness of land.

Ten Holinesses

In one tractate of the Mishna, *Kelim*-Vessels, sages set out a concept of the sacredness of the land of Israel. Tractate *Kelim* is part of the Jewish purity code that aims for the sanctity of divine service. *Kelim* draws on an assortment of biblical passages dealing with *purity*. In the Torah and rabbinic literature, purity is a gateway to holiness. The Mishna maps a sacred spatial system of ten concentric circles onto the land of Israel. These circles define zones into which access is increasingly restricted with passage into the deeper inner spaces, as the intensity of *kedusha*-sacredness rises. The innermost, enclosed, private sanctuary within the Temple is the Holy of Holies.[7]

The text limits entry to the sacred space on the Temple Mount according to a person's ritual *purity* status-*taharah*. In different states of readiness, ritual fitness, people participate at different proximities to sacred zones. The text deals in such topics as skin disease, contact

---

7. As we saw in the discussion of the garden in the previous chapter, Rabbi Akiva holds the Song of Songs to be a spiritual abstraction of the spatial Holy of Holies.

with dead reptiles, and corpses. Here is the relevant section from the Mishna – redacted in the second century CE.

Mishna 6

There are ten [degrees of] holinesses: The land of Israel is holier than all lands. What constitutes her holiness? From her they bring the *Omer* [an offering of grain](Leviticus 23:10f], the *bikkurim*-first-fruits (Deuteronomy 26:2ff), and the two loaves [of bread offerings] (Leviticus 23:17), which they do not bring from all lands.

Mishna 7

Cities [of Israel] which are surrounded by a wall are still more holy, for people with skin diseases are sent out from them; and, a corpse may be carried within the city as much as they want, but once it has gone out, they may not bring it back in.

Mishna 8

Within the wall [of Jerusalem] is still more holy, for only there the Lesser Holy Things and the Second Tithe may be eaten [offerings brought to feed the priests who serve in the Temple] (Deuteronomy 12:17).

The Temple Mount is still more holy, for no men or women who had a flux [unhealthy genital discharge], menstruants, or postpartum women may enter there.

The rampart is still more holy, for no gentiles and none who has become impure from [contact with] a corpse may enter.

The "Women's Court" is still more holy, for none who has immersed that day [and is waiting for sunset to complete the purification cycle] may enter . . .[8]

The Israelite Court is still more holy, for no-one whose atonement is incomplete may enter . . .

The Priests' Court is still more holy, for Israelites may not enter except when they perform the laying of the hands [on a sacrificial animal] (Leviticus 3:2), slaughtering and waving (7:30).

---

8. The designation "Women's Court" does not delimit women's access to the inner courts. Men and women intermingled in the Women's Court in the Temple, and performed ritual functions in the inner courts as well.

Mishna 9

Between the Porch and the Altar is still more holy, for no-one who has a blemish or whose hair is loosed [signs of mourning] may enter.

The Sanctuary is still more holy, for no-one may enter there with hands and feet unwashed.

The Holy of Holies is still more holy, for no-one may enter except the High Priest on the Day of Atonement at the hour of the [Temple] service. (*Kelim*, Chapter 1)[9]

The purity codes are among the most confounding of Jewish ritual.[10] The terse language of the Mishna needs interpretation. One of the unique features of the text is the connection it unsqueamishly assumes between sacredness and the living body. Whereas Western culture deems matters such as menstruation and ejaculation discreet and private, here they bear on public ritual functions. This system propels *kedusha*-holiness and its requirement for purity into intimate daily bodily function. Rather than seeking purification *from* the body, escape from the corporeal into the spiritual, Leviticus instructs about entering the spiritual *in* bodily process. The texts combine the study of sacred Temple functions with care and maintenance of the sanctity of the body and the utensils in every individual Israelite home. Not transcending the body, but in the fleshy materials and acts of life and death, in seepages, the Mishna negotiates the meaning of sacredness.

Many of the conditions of *impurity* are transient physical states. While death is final – the corpse can never be returned into the sacred enclosure – skin heals, menstrual bleeding ends, semen washes away. Certain periods of healthy, normal physiological cycles require ritual action to prepare to participate in the sanctuary. These rituals define access to sacredness in terms of prescribed purifications that draw attention to the body and our life processes.

The Temple incorporates (re)productive life into holiness. The Mishkan-Temple rituals of sanctification are cyclical – they relate to the monthly cycle of fertility, gestation, and childbirth, healing from illness, the agricultural seasons of harvest, and ultimately, life and

---

9. Translation by Philip Blackman, with my modifications.

10. Mary Douglas, *Purity and Danger: An Analysis of Concepts of Pollution and Taboo* (New York: Praeger, 1966) is a landmark study of Leviticus.

death. Many of the instructions in the text direct motion, progressing inward toward more intense sacredness, circling, and going out from the enclosure. These directions define a dynamic of interaction: approaching, drawing nearer, then receding – a sacred choreography. Desire for connection with the Creator and creation implicitly propels the choreography. The rhythm of the ritual moves deeper into the inner enclosures. It often culminates in a mortal act of offering, sacrifice, substituting a gift in place of one's own life. Then it retreats from the intensity of the encounter, soon to return again after proper preparation. In this system, sacredness is a dance of intimacy between creature and Creator. The Temple service performs rituals aligned with personal and national life-cycles, expressing gratitude and supplicating for the gifts of life and sustenance, and sanctifying human functions and nurture with offerings.

Aside from restricting peoples' access to the sanctuary while they are experiencing transient conditions of impurity, the text also mentions some permanent exclusions. Gentiles are not permitted to enter past the outer perimeter of the Temple Mount. According to the sages, the biblical sacred purity system does not apply to non-Jews. The Temple system defines sacred activity in terms specific to the Jewish People. It does *not* claim superiority over other cultures. Excluding non-Jews from the inner sacred spaces stems from the need for commitment to and initiation into the system as pre-requisites for participation. The Temple functioned as a headquarters for Jewish sacred operations. A person who is unfamiliar with proper and safe procedures is not admissible to an operating room. Most sacred practices require commitment, study, mentoring, and extensive preparation, and therefore, exclude the uninitiated. One reason for the exclusion is that the acts and rituals cannot be understood by observation – study, preparation, identification with the process, and initiation are required.

In the Mishnaic system, some of the permanent exclusions are more troubling to our sensibilities. Whereas becoming a member of the Jewish People is open through the conversion process, the priestly class is hereditary. Disqualifying people with "blemishes" from leadership is highly problematic. With the exception of the Orthodox streams, all of the denominations of Judaism have redressed the biases in the ancient text by including women and people with disabilities in sacred services. Contemporary Jewish voices advocate for the full participation of those of us who are excluded by biological criteria – sex and physical disability. These revisions demonstrate the capacity of sacred systems to evolve with evolving ethics.[11]

First-Fruit

The first Mishna in the sequence defining the sacred territories of the land cites three agricultural items: the *Omer* [grain offering], the *bikkurim*-first-fruits, and the two loaves – food brought *from* the land to an unstated destination. The verb "to bring" implies a Temple-centric ritual – these items are to be brought *to the Temple*. One aspect of the holiness of the land is that only fruit grown in Israel is suitable for the Temple service. A possible explanation for this exclusivity is that the earth of Israel is uniquely and inherently sacred. Only produce grown in that earth is permitted into the sacred Temple ritual because it absorbs the sacredness. The texts that describe the first-fruit ritual open other possible explanations for the sanctity of the fruit. Upon entry into the land of Israel, the first commandment to the Jewish People is to bring the *bikkurim*-first-fruit offering. Here is the biblical source.

> When you enter the land that God is giving you as a heritage, and you possess it and settle in it, you shall take some of every first fruit of the soil, which you harvest from the land that your God is giving you, put it in a basket and go to the place where God will choose to establish His/Her name. You shall go to the priest in charge at that time and say to him/her, "I acknowledge this day before your God that I have entered the land that God swore to our forebearers to give us."
>
> The priest shall take the basket from your hand and set it down in front of the altar of your God.
>
> You shall then recite before your God the following: "My father was a fugitive Aramean. He went down to Egypt with meager numbers and sojourned there; but there he became a great and very populous nation. The Egyptians dealt harshly with us and oppressed us; they imposed heavy labor upon us. We cried to the God of our ancestors, and God heard our plea and saw our plight, our misery, and our oppression. God freed us from Egypt by a mighty hand, by

---

11. See Tzvi Marx's landmark study, *Disability in Jewish Law* (London; New York: Routledge, 2002).

an outstretched arm and awesome power, and by signs and wonders. S/He brought us to this place and gave us this land, a land flowing with milk and honey. Wherefore I now bring the first fruits of the soil which You, God, have given me."

You shall leave it before the Lord your God and bow low before your God. You shall enjoy, together with the Levite and the stranger in your midst, all the bounty that your God has bestowed upon you and your household. (Deuteronomy 26:1–11)

This passage describes the ritual in detail, including the text that the farmer recites inside the Temple compound. The recitation affirms a personal biographical link between the first-fruit and the liberation from slavery in Egypt, the grand narrative of Jewish Peoplehood. The *bikkurim* represent the fulfillment of the divine promise to settle the Jewish People in the land. Rather than serving a human oppressor in Egypt, the farmer willingly offers the produce of the earth toward the national sacred practice of her/his People. In comparison to enslavement, bringing forth fruit from the earth symbolizes the freedom and autonomy of the Jewish People to labor freely for sustenance – material and spiritual.

The Mishna specifies which fruit are admissible for *bikkurim* and when they are to be brought.

> One does not bring first-fruit offerings except from the seven species [of the land of Israel]; not from dates which grow on the hills, not from the fruit in the valleys, and not from olives for oil which are not the choicest. One does not bring the *bikkurim* before Shavuot. (*Bikkurim* 1:3)

The finest specimens from the seven species of the land of Israel, grown under optimal conditions are to be brought. These fruit grow wild throughout the land; they can all be found and enjoyed today. The Mishna describes the process of selecting the first-fruit.

> How does one choose first-fruit? A person goes down to her/his field and sees a fig that has sprouted forth [emerged from within the flower], a cluster of grapes that has sprouted forth or a pomegranate that has sprouted forth – s/he ties a reed around them and says, "Behold, these are first-fruits!" after s/he breaks them from the [connection to the] ground. (3:1)

This passage instructs the farmer to pay attention to the gradual process of growth in the orchard. In the spring, as the flower petals are finishing, one checks from behind which flower the earliest fruit has begun to appear. At the instant of recognizing the first sign of fruit, the farmer marks it and declares it *bikkurim*-first-fruit. This declaration signifies the human intention to sanctify. Marking the fruit signifies the intention to take it to the sanctuary in order to fulfill a divine command. In these descriptions, the worthiness of the produce from the land of Israel to enter the sacred domain does not stem from the *inherent* sacredness of the land. Instead, the texts describe a subtle and intentional process: tending fruit trees, carefully observing their development, flowering and sprouting, designating and declaring first-fruit, nurturing the trees to fruition, picking the ripe fruit, taking the fruit in a basket to the sanctuary, reciting the special first-fruit declaration, and delivering the fruit into the hands of the priest who lays them at the altar. According to this example, the sacredness of the land comes from fulfilling a series of actions that cumulatively sanctify reaping the harvest. These actions make the person worthy for sacred service.

The Mishnaic text in *Kelim* describes sacredness in terms of *human relationships* to the land and its produce. The Mishna refers to activities that relate to materials and space. Mindfulness, acts of purifying and sanctifying the work of the earth generate holiness. The rabbinic text maps motion inward toward smaller, more contained, and exclusive space. The process emphasizes meticulous attention. People prepare to approach the sacred realm incrementally, and to participate at each stage in the healthy function of the sacred system. Entering implies an intention to contribute toward fulfilling divine service precisely and thoroughly. One enters with fear, awe, and trepidation, to offer gifts, arouse divine attention, secure blessing, or attain atonement.

At the surface, this mapping of the holiness of Israel seems to assign sacredness to physical space, earthly territory. However, the text deals with sacredness not in terms of territory, but in terms of distinctly human acts: growing food, giving birth, menstruating, enduring illness, honoring the dead, seeking spiritual connection. There is no territorial or ownership claim made about the sacred enclosure. The sole justification for entering into the sacred realm is desire to sanctify the activities and materials of life. The physical borders of the Mishnaic scheme rely upon the discipline of the participants to sanctify the space through their efforts.

This interpretation of the passage in *Kelim* suggests an alternative to sacredness as transcendence, exclusion, or possessiveness. Seeking the sacred is not a matter of going beyond this world, but of entering more deeply into this world. While penetrating into the enclosed sacred realm alludes to a symbolically male act, the texts reveal the complexity of sacred symbolism. There is no evidence of conquest, possession, or ownership – *ba'alut*. Interacting with sacred space entails a set of reciprocal actions: offering implies receiving. The sacredness of the physical place relates to human intentions and activities of preparing, approaching, engaging, and receding from the space. The divine is conceived as an active participant, receiving, and responding to a human partner, conducting an intense and erotic relationship.

Limits to the Infinite

One Hasidic commentary on the Torah, the *Mei Shiloah* by Mordecai Yosef Leiner of Ishbitz (1804–1854), offers insight about the nature of spatial sacredness. He discusses the sacredness of space before and after the Mishkan is completed. Based on his close reading of the relevant Torah passage, he claims that until the erection of the outer defining boundary, the entire territory of the desert had the potential for sacredness. Here is his interpretation:

> HE SET UP THE ENCLOSURE SURROUNDING THE MISHKAN (Exodus 40:33): When the Torah says throughout the preparation of the elements of the Mishkan, "According to God's commandment to Moses," it means that the thing was obvious and explicit to Moses, each element according to its character as it was at the moment that God spoke about it to him. As the sages said, every aspect that was told to him, he was sprite to fulfill immediately and for all generations.
>
> Behold, up until the erection of the Mishkan, the entire desert is fit for [divine] speech, but after the Mishkan is erected, the desert becomes unfit for [divine] speech. Therefore, when the enclosure is erected, that is at the total completion of the Mishkan, there is no need to say "According to God's commandment to Moses" because

the matter of God's command applies when [divine] speech is clear and explicit as it was at the moment that the Creator commanded. This is impossible with the erection of the enclosure because from that moment, the desert becomes unfit for [divine] speech. Therefore, the text does not say "According to God's command to Moses" in relation to the enclosure.[12]

The *Mei Shiloah* observes that the Torah comments, "according to God's commandment to Moses," for every detail of the construction of the Mishkan – with one exception: the final curtains enclosing the courtyard. Here, the expression is missing.[13] Therefore, he interprets, the erection of the courtyard signals an important change. The *Mei Shiloah* suggests that creating a sacred enclosure concentrates sacredness inside the Mishkan, and thereby diminishes the capacity for divine encounter outside it. The *Mei Shiloah* points out that God reveals a model to guide the creation of the Mishkan. This model is only available during the construction. Once the Mishkan is complete, the divine template is no longer relevant or helpful. The Hasidic master does not indicate why.

The divine template reveals the Mishkan in its static form, as an architectural model. Based on the template, the Israelites build the physical structure for the sacred service. Just as an architect cannot model the functioning of the building s/he designs, the divine template can not model the Mishkan functioning. Human activity is subject to human will, individual intentions, approximations, misunderstanding, errors and innovations. Therefore, immediately upon completion of the Mishkan, with the cordoning off of the enclosure, the divine template for the sacred space becomes obsolete, and a new more contingent situation begins. The sacred work becomes the responsibility and opportunity for the Israelite community. While the prototype for the structure of the Mishkan emanates from a divine command, the use of the structure – the service itself – is human.

These interpretations can also apply to contemporary Israel. Rather than thinking of the land as inherently sacred, independent of people and our actions, sacredness depends upon human behavior. Sacred-

---

12. *Mei Shiloah*, Pekudei, 32, my translation.
13. Ex. 40:33.

ness is a potential to be actualized through sustainable living with respect for human dignity and the integrity of creatures and creation. The text of the ten holinesses defines sacredness in terms of scrupulous attention to the mortal process of the Jewish People living in the land. Since the founding of the modern State of Israel, the sacredness of the land is more fully in the hands of its Jewish inhabitants than ever before. Whatever sanctity pertains to the land depends on human will and action, on our worthiness.

"Acquiring" the Land

As we have seen, giving form to sacredness in material and social space requires discipline and will. Sanctifying brings human life into contact with core concepts of creation. According to Jewish mystical sources, creation begins with the divine infusing the infinite into a finite world – a fantastic undertaking. Fraught with breakage and shattering, ultimately the creation process sets the stage for an extraordinary relationship between people and land. Possessing the land is one of the contested keys to its sacredness and to its desecration.

Jewish concepts of acquisition begin in and develop from biblical sources. According to the Torah, Avraham transacts the initial land purchase in Israel. He buys a plot to bury his spouse, Sarah. The Torah recounts the story in Genesis.

> "Hear us, my lord: you are the elect of God among us. Bury your dead in the choicest of our burial places; none of us will withhold his burial place from you for burying your dead." Thereupon Avraham bowed low to the people of the land, the Hittites, and he said to them, "If it is your wish that I remove my dead for burial, you must agree to intercede for me with Ephron son of Zohar. Let him sell me the cave of Machpelah that he owns, which is at the edge of his land. Let him sell it to me, at the full price, for a burial site in your midst." Ephron was present among the Hittites; so Ephron the Hittite answered Avraham in the hearing of the Hittites, all who entered the gate of his town, saying, "No, my lord, hear me: I give you the field and I give you the cave that is in it; I give it to you in the presence of my people. Bury your dead." Then Avraham bowed low before the people of the land, and spoke to Ephron in the hearing of the people of the land,

saying, "If only you would hear me out! Let me pay the price of the land; accept it from me, that I may bury my dead there." And Ephron replied to Avraham, saying to him, "My lord, do hear me! A piece of land worth four hundred shekels of silver – what is that between you and me? Go and bury your dead." Avraham accepted Ephron's terms. Avraham paid out to Ephron the money that he had named in the hearing of the Hittites – four hundred shekels of silver at the going merchants' rate. So Ephron's land in Machpelah, near Mamre – the field with its cave and all the trees anywhere within the confines of that field – passed to Avraham as his acquisition, in the presence of the Hittites, of all who entered the gate of his town. And then Avraham buried his wife Sarah in the cave of the field of Machpelah, facing Mamre – now Hebron – in the land of Canaan. Thus the field with its cave passed from the Hittites to Avraham, as a burial site. (Genesis 23:6–20)

In spite of Ephron's generous offer to give the land for free, Avraham insists on paying. The formal purchase of the cave becomes part of the burial ritual.

While Avraham is the first in the Torah to purchase land, this is not the first time that the concept of "acquisition" is used in the Torah. The first occurrence is in a statement by Eve, when she gives birth to Cain: "Adam had sexual relations with Eve his woman; she conceived and bore Cain. She said, 'I have *acquired* a man with God.'"[14] Both of these stories relate to the connection between spouses at life transitions – death and birth. Avraham seeks to honor his deceased spouse Sarah with a fitting burial; he is a mourner shaken by the impermanence of human life. Avraham strives for a sense of permanence to soothe his loss by establishing an eternal resting place for a mortal body. The land, more precisely, the cave, stands for Sarah – long dry, once fertile, and finally, lifeless.

Eve's obscure statement comes at the opposite end of the life cycle to Avraham's – at the initial human moment of life-giving, at the first birth of a child. She experiences the miracle of creation and gives credit to God for the new life. She uses the word "acquiring" to describe

---

14. Gen. 4:1.

her parenting relationship with her child, suggesting a creating role, responsibility, connection, sustenance.

The second biblical occurrence of the Hebrew root "acquire" is used by a non-Jewish priest who refers to acquisition of the world by the Creator of it.

> King Melchizedek of Salem brought out bread and wine; he was a priest of God Most High. He blessed him saying, "Blessed be Abram of God Most High, *Acquirer of heaven and earth.*And blessed be God Most High, Who has delivered your foes into your hand." And [Abram] gave him a tenth of everything. Then the king of Sodom said to Abram, "Give me the persons, and take the possessions for yourself." But Abram said to the king of Sodom, "I swear to the Lord, God Most High, *Acquirer of heaven and earth*: I will not take so much as a thread or a sandal strap of what is yours; you shall not say, 'It is I who made Abram rich.'" (Genesis 14:18–23)

Melchizedek refers to the Creator as the One who *acquires* the universe. Neither of these cases of *acquisition*, Eve or Melchizedek, relates to the contemporary sense of *purchase* or *ownership*, certainly not to exclusive possession, use, or control. These texts indicate that *acquisition* refers to co-creation and entails responsibility, connection, and sustenance. As Eve is not the owner or acquirer of her child, so God is not the *owner* nor acquirer of heaven and earth, but the Creator.

These biblical sources for *acquisition* raise questions about our sense of possessing the land. According to many sources in the Torah, it is not actually possible to possess the land with any sense of permanence; the land is not subject to human ownership.

> The land shall not be sold in perpetuity; for the land is Mine; for you are strangers and residents with Me. (Leviticus 25:23)

Yet God promises Avraham, "God appeared to Abram and said, 'To your seed I will give this Land.'"[15] Yakov recalls the promise to his grandparents, "I will give this Land to your seed after you for an everlasting possession."[16] These verses complicate the relationship to the land. On the one hand, the land is within divine jurisdiction; on the

---

15. Genesis 12:7.
16. Ibid., 48:4.

other hand, it is a gift to the Jewish People. A passage in the *Shema* – a credo of Jewish faith, contributes insight to this paradox; possession of the land is conditional upon observing the divine commands.

> *If* you will obey . . . *then* your days will be lengthened on the land . . . but, *If* your heart be seduced and you turn away . . . *[then]* you will swiftly be banished from the good land that God gives you. [italics – my emphasis] (Deuteronomy 11:13–17)

This text expresses a divine intention for the Jewish People to inhabit the land of Israel. However, the intention is not to be abused or taken for granted – it is a privilege to be earned. At any moment, the privilege can be rescinded. Yeshayahu Leibowitz, a modern Israeli theologian, emphasizes that Jewish sovereignty in the land depends on the commandments – fulfilling the commandments renders the land sacred. "The country has no intrinsic holiness . . . It is the *mitzvot* [commandments], when observed, that confer sanctity upon the land."[17] Read narrowly, Leibowitz undercuts the possibility of secular Zionists, for they do not have the intention to perform the commandments. However, he does interpret the holiness of the land deriving from human action. An Israeli inhabitant of Efrat, a large settlement in the Gush Etzion area outside of Jerusalem, beyond the Green Line[18] comments,

> Whoever *sanctifies* the land in such a way that it endangers human life, blatantly transgresses the prescription, "It is preferable to die rather than to commit a vile forbidden act." The blood of those killed and murdered is on his/her head.[19]

This opinion subordinates the value of control and possession of land to the value of protecting life, a clear statement of ethical priorities. In decisions about how to sanctify the land – life is more precious. Period. Such a hierarchy of values appears orderly and sane to a person who is cozy within safe borders. Yet, Israel arose with the unbearable need to take mortal risks for the sake of the safety and future of the Jewish People. From the outset, the sanctity of life and

---

17. *Judaism, Human Values and the Jewish State* (Cambridge: Harvard University Press, 1992), 120–121.

18. The Green Line is the pre-1967 border of the State of Israel. It excludes the West Bank and Gaza Strip.

19. יעל משאלי, http://news.walla.co.il/?w=/77/544636/@opinion.

land are inextricable from one another. The tidy principle of life over land could not have applied during the period of the founding of the State of Israel, nor has it ever been tenable in the presence of enemies who seek Israel's destruction. Israel is a home that must be defended by a capable army of soldiers who risk their lives for the sake of the security of nearly eight million Jews, Muslims, and Christians. The choice is not whether to risk life and limb – for that is a regrettable given, but how to minimize risk and suffering for all parties. As much as possible, the goal must be to take steps to de-escalate conflict and to progress toward peace. This is the general thrust of most parties to the Israeli political scene. The differences are a matter of how to negotiate risk and territory occupied in the 1967 Six-Day War, and held in the 1973 Yom Kippur War fought in defense against threats to the existence of the state. Much of the Israeli policy debate involves balancing intersecting claims about security, the sanctity of the land, and contemporary Palestinian nationalism.

Recent generations have grown up with the State of Israel as an assumption. Though from the current vantage point, the permanence of Israel seems certain, history teaches impermanence. So far, Jews have lost sovereignty over the land every time we have lived in it. When the first destruction of Jerusalem and exile from the land are imminent, the biblical prophet Jeremiah undertakes a symbolic act of land acquisition.[20] At the moments preceding destruction, the prophet faces the terrifying end of the Temple, a symbol of the eternal in this world. Like Avraham in his personal life who seeks connection with the Infinite at a moment of loss, Jeremiah addresses the same finitude of mortality at a national level. Obtaining a deed to property in the land of Israel, Jeremiah attempts to defy the limits of military power and defeat. The ritual purchase symbolizes the spirit and will to return to worthiness to inhabit the land.

Historians explain the destruction of the Temple and the exile in terms of the ambitions and conflicts of imperial powers – the foment of rebellion in the kingdom of Judah while Babylon and Egypt contest imperial sovereignty. These explanations attend to a political layer of life. Meanwhile, at another layer, the prophets of Israel hold the people accountable for their failure to demonstrate their merit to remain. In

---

20. Jer. 32.

an earlier chapter, before the purchase agreement, Jeremiah explains his frustration and sets out his prophecy.[21] The prophecy asserts full human responsibility. Worthy behavior is the only admissible ground for living in the Promised Land. This is one of the meanings of the promise. According to the prophet, destruction and exile are outcomes of unethical action. Regardless of its historicity, the prophetic version of events urges toward personal accountability and social improvement rather than disaffection, apathy, anger, vengeance, remorse, or violence. The prophet's disposition is reflexive, turned inward to prescribe changes in society, rather than aiming outward to blame others and call for political or military retribution. Though territorial control is impermanent, Jeremiah's land deed concretizes eternal hope and symbolizes the prospect of returning to the land. Even as the adversary advances, the prophet is contracting a hope for redemption. On the basis of such a hope – a metaphysical deed to the land – the Jewish People conceives the desire for Israel in the modern period.

For centuries, Jewish culture has stressed the goals of intellectual achievement combined with social justice. These priorities have informed Jewish communities and their actions. Excellence in social responsibility has been a defining trait of Jewish identity. "There are three characteristics that distinguish the Jewish People – they are merciful, they are bashful and they are performers of acts of kindness."[22] Egged on by texts that obligate social betterment, Jews contribute to the infrastructure of social justice in America and throughout the world. In his treatise, *To Mend the World*, philosopher Emil Fackenheim states that, "*tikkun olam* [healing the world] depends on Jewish collective, particular response to history." When Fackenheim envisions strengthening and cherishing the state of Israel as part of the work of *tikkun olam*, he invokes a disposition for Diaspora Jews.[23] The "Jewish collective, particular response to history" that he advocates is binding both *inside* Israel – for Jews currently inhabiting an autonomous and sovereign Jewish state, and outside of Israel.

The wanderings of Jewry on the "Zion Cycle" – the choreography of

---

21. Ibid., 25.

22. *Yevamot* 79a.

23. Emil Fackenheim, *To Mend the World*, (New York: Schocken, 1982), 250–313. For a textual analysis of *tikkun olam*, see Gilbert S. Rosenthal, "Tikkun ha-Olam: The Metamorphosis of a Concept," *Journal of Religion*, Apr. 2005, Vol. 85:2, 214240.

homecoming and exile – demonstrate the precariousness of dwelling in the land. Rather than a fixed and stable sacred destination, these texts view the land as both opportunity and obligation to sanctify the practices of daily life. This chapter interprets sacredness less as a quality of the land than a function of human intentional action. Sacredness involves continuous refinement in all realms of society. These texts teach heightened responsibility in relation to Israel, to invest in sacredness. The legitimacy of Jewish presence in the sacred domain depends on collective and ongoing sanctifying action. The sacredness of the land, therefore, is neither a fact nor a right, but a privilege to be continuously earned by the Jewish People and by Israeli society. Every group and nation on earth has the possibility to continually introspect, critique, and refine itself, its priorities and strategies, and upgrade its contributions to humanity.

6 Inner Fires: Parallel Cases

BEFORE THE DECLARATION of the State of Israel in 1948, the most recent time that the Jewish People held political sovereignty was during the era of the Maccabees, more than 2,000 years ago. From the time of the death of Alexander the Great in 325 BCE, Seleucid kingdoms dominated Judaea. In the second century BCE, the official policy of the ruling Hellenist Syrians was to suppress Jewish practice. Under the yoke of the Hellenizers, Judaism and the Jewish People were on trial in the land of Israel. Then as now, incentives to assimilate into a dominant culture accelerated the abandonment of Jewish life and identity. The Maccabean rebellion against imperial power won the Jewish population in ancient Judaea a stint of independence. Like the modern Zionists, the Maccabees waged a struggle for political autonomy, and for the meaning of Jewish life. Applying insights from previous chapters, here we explore this historic episode and its implications for contemporary Israel and Jewry.

Jewish Autonomy in the Land

Having suffered defeat at the hands of Rome in 188 BCE, the Seleucids of Syria owed a heavy indemnity.[1] Syrian King Antiochus IV Epiphanes connived to replenish his coffers with the treasure from the splendid

---

1. Primary sources for this period are Josephus, *Antiquities* and *Against Apion*; Livy, *History of Rome* and Appian, *History of Rome* and *Syrian Wars*.

religious temples in his kingdom. The Jews were positioned between him and Ptolemaic Egypt, his foe. Seeking religious and cultural uniformity, Epiphanes viewed the Jews of Judaea as a stubborn thorn in his realm. He resolved to force Hellenism on them. Antiochus deposed the High Priest Onias in Jerusalem and installed his Hellenist-friendly brother Jason to promote his agenda. As head of the Jewish religious establishment, Jason officially embraced assimilation and apostasy and imposed Hellenism. Many Jews joined the popular trend and abandoned their traditions for the lifestyle of their oppressors. Dubbing the Hellenistic practices "evil," the pro-Jewish redactor of the First Book of Maccabees offers his perspective,

> In those days lawless men came forth from Israel, and misled many, saying "Let us go make a covenant with the Gentiles round about us, for since we separated from them many evils have come upon us."
>
> This proposal pleased them, and some of the people eagerly went to the king. He authorized them to observe the ordinances of the Gentiles. So they built a gymnasium in Jerusalem, according to the Gentile custom, and removed the marks of circumcision, and abandoned the holy covenant. They joined with the Gentiles and sold themselves to do evil.[2]

With the Jewish observance of circumcision prohibited, this text mentions a painful operation to *reverse* it. Later, when the Maccabees take power, they forcefully circumcise boys of assimilated Jewish parents.[3] These acts – defiling sacred covenantal insignia – embody the struggle between Hellenism and Judaism.[4] The Maccabean insurrection engages main themes of Zionism raised in this book – mind-body dualism, sacred home and land.

---

2. I Maccabees 1:10–15. The redactor choses a phrase that echoes a biblical statement about the corruptions of the Israelites in the period of II Kings (17:17).

3. "Mattathias and his friends went around and tore down the altars; they forcibly circumcised all the uncircumcised boys that they found within the borders of Israel." First Book of Maccabees, 2:45–6.

4. Circumcision is also corrupted by the slaughter of the Shechemites (Gen. 34) and the 100 Philistine foreskins that King Saul demanded from David for the hand of his daughter, Michal (I Samuel 18:25–27).

Spoiling the Sanctuary

The First Book of Maccabees describes Antiochus's incursion into the Temple enclosure, the sacred home, ravishing the fine implements.

> After subduing Egypt, Antiochus returned in the one hundred and forty-third year. He went up against Israel and came to Jerusalem with a strong force. He arrogantly entered the sanctuary and took the golden altar, the lamp-stand for the light, and all its utensils. He took also the table for the bread of the Presence, the cups for drink offerings, the bowls, the golden censers, the curtain, the crowns, and the gold decoration on the front of the Temple; he stripped it all off. He took the silver and the gold, and the costly vessels; he took also the hidden treasures which he found.

In this narrative, force prevails. The raiders steal vessels for their precious material value without regard for what is invisible and worthless to them – their sacred purpose. The conquerors draw after them the minds and spirit of many.

Though referred to as "Greek," Hellenism is far removed from the classical Greece of Odysseus, Socrates, and Oedipus. Hellenism is a distant heir to the refined Greek culture of the 5th century BCE, the golden age of Athens. After the demise of the Greek city-states, the conquests of Alexander the Great left behind a sprawling empire. The Hellenists simplified and popularized a version of the Greek culture that had seeped into the Eastern states during Alexander's expansions. Not that the Jews completely resisted cross-fertilization with other cultures. Synthesis of Greek and Jewish traditions was already advancing in Alexandria, Egypt.[5] However, in Judaea, the Seleucids replaced the Greek ideals of beauty, truth, and goodness with adoration of the body, idols, and their own aggrandizement.

> Then the king wrote to his whole kingdom that all should be one people, and that each should give up his customs. All the Gentiles accepted the command of the king. Many even from Israel gladly adopted his religion; they sacrificed to idols and profaned the sabbath. And the king sent letters to Jerusalem and the cities of Judah; he directed them to follow customs strange to the land, to forbid

---

5. Philo of Alexandria (20 BCE–50 CE) is a stellar example of this trend.

burnt offerings and sacrifices and drink offerings in the sanctuary, to profane sabbaths and feasts, to defile the sanctuary and the priests, to build altars and sacred precincts and shrines for idols, to sacrifice swine and unclean animals, and to leave their sons uncircumcised. They were to make themselves abominable by everything unclean and profane, so that they should forget the law and change all the ordinances. "And whoever does not obey the command of the king shall die."[6]

Hellenism offered Jews a rare and irresistible opportunity to meld into the majority. Escape from the rigorous demands of Jewish life – ritual commandments and strictures – held a certain attraction. The Hellenizers succeeded to entice many Jews to abandon their beliefs and transgress their sacred tradition. Jews who did not comply willingly, Antiochus Epiphanes coerced with violence.

Among some Jews, the Hellenist oppression triggered resistance. Particularly the priests – who had the most invested and feared for the demise of Jewish sacred service – mobilized opposition and fomented armed rebellion. In the First Book of Maccabees, the onset of the revolt is a spontaneous showdown between Syrian officials and a bold priestly family whose head, Mattathias "saw the blasphemies being committed in Judah and Jerusalem."

> Then the king's officers who were enforcing the apostasy came to the city of Modiin to make them offer sacrifice. Many from Israel came to them; and Mattathias and his sons were assembled. Then the king's officers spoke to Mattathias as follows: "You are a leader, honored and great in this city, and supported by sons and brothers. Now be the first to come and do what the king commands, as all the Gentiles and the men of Judah and those that are left in Jerusalem have done. Then you and your sons will be numbered among the friends of the king, and you and your sons will be honored with silver and gold and many gifts."
>
> But Mattathias answered and said in a loud voice: "Even if all the nations that live under the rule of the king obey him, and have chosen to do his commandments, departing each one from the religion of his/her ancestors, yet I and my children and my siblings will live by

---

6. I Maccabees 1:41–50.

the covenant of our forebearers. Far be it from us to desert the law and the ordinances. We will not obey the king's words by turning aside from our religion to the right hand or to the left."

When he had finished speaking these words, a Jew came forward in the sight of all to offer sacrifice upon the altar of Modiin, according to the king's command. When Mattathias saw it, he burned with zeal and his heart was stirred. He gave vent to righteous anger; he ran and killed him upon the altar. At the same time he killed the king's officer who was forcing them to sacrifice, and he tore down the altar. Thus he burned with zeal for the law, as Pinehas did against Zimri the son of Salu.[7]

Then Mattathias cried out in the city with a loud voice, saying: "Let every one who is zealous for the law and supports the covenant come out with me!" And he and his sons fled to the hills and left all that they had in the city.[8]

Flouting the order to transgress the most grave Jewish prohibition, idolatry, Mattathias seizes the momentum of his defiance to rally support. A relatively small band of Jewish zealots mounted a revolt against Antiochus's well-outfitted forces. The rebels sought to take action against their oppressors as well as against their fellow Jews who had succumbed to Hellenism.

Like many Jews throughout history, the Maccabees forge their community and Jewish life in a hostile environment, in mortal combat. Then as now, there is no neutral ground for a minority – the choice is to succumb and assimilate or to struggle to hold on. By education, behavior, language, and dress, Jews pass on and evolve sacred traditions from generation to generation. Unity against oppressors creates a shared purpose. For Jews in the ancient Hasmonean and modern Israeli eras, and many years in between, peace has been but a remote hope.

Passionate for their homeland, the Maccabees prevail and achieve Jewish autonomy in Judaea. Purifying the Jerusalem Temple from the idolatry that the Hellenizers had instituted and rededicating it to Jewish rituals, the Maccabees restore public Jewish society. These military, political, and spiritual accomplishments, akin to the Zionist

---

7. Num. 25:6–13.
8. I Maccabees 2:15–28.

accomplishment of statehood, came to be celebrated by the festival of Chanukah.

Among the festivals of the Jewish calendar cycle, the sages institute Chanukah to commemorate post-biblical events. Outside of Israel, many relate to Chanukah as a children's holiday, a time of gift-giving that corresponds with Christmas winter cheer. Beyond the brightly-colored candles and foil-wrapped chocolate coins, Chanukah holds together challenging tensions. Between the values of military heroism and subtle spirituality, between the passion of the few and the force of the many, between sameness and difference, between particularity and universalism, the Maccabean period pulses with the challenges that contemporary Jewry faces – in Israel and abroad.

At one level, Chanukah celebrates the excitement of freedom to practice Judaism in sacred space. Chanukah festivities during the early Zionist period and in the modern state of Israel resonate with this inspiration for Jewish sovereignty in the land. The Maccabean revolt endorses the goal and actuality of full self-determination for the Jewish People. Israelis continue to celebrate Chanukah as a nationalist festival. During recent decades, "post-Zionists" criticize this version of the story as a selective and retroactive fitting of history with Israeli interests. The ancient sages also took issue with the Chanukah emphasis on military bravado.

After the destruction of the Jerusalem Temple, and the loss of political and religious autonomy in 70 CE, the sages popularize a different version of Chanukah from the one in the Books of the Maccabees. Having suffered at the hands of the Romans, the sages in exile do not identify with the military story. They harbor no hope for material power, let alone political autonomy. In place of the Maccabean military victory, the sages tell a more subtle story of Chanukah. In the wake of utter defeat in terms of land and politics, they choose to assert the survival of the inner fire of the Jewish soul through subtle symbolic rituals – they invent a new narrative of *spiritual* autonomy. While the Jewish body is conquered by the Roman destruction that followed the Hasmonean period, the sages harbor no vengeance. They take responsibility for the corruption and transgressions that had weakened Jewish autonomy.[9] Their soul is alive with commitment

---

9. See, for example, the long literary passage in the Talmud, 55b–58a of BT *Gittin*.

to Jewish survival and flourishing. With this perspective, Chanukah presents an opportunity to explore the relations between the material and spiritual body of the Jewish People, Israel and sacredness, and the contemporary political narrative.

The concept of Chanukah relates to the rededication of the Jerusalem Temple after it had been defiled by the Hellenizers. Historical documents recount different traditions concerning the initial impetus for the festival. The principal textual sources are narratives in the *Books of Maccabees*, the *Antiquities of the Jews* by Josephus Flavius, and a passage in Tractate *Shabbat* of the Babylonian Talmud. Relating to the same events, the texts voice different interpretations.

Maccabean Dedication

The canonized Hebrew Bible, the *Tanakh* excludes some texts contemporary to the later biblical books, the "apocrypha."[10] The first two Books of Maccabees are preserved in the Septuagint, the Greek version of the Bible. The First Book of Maccabees, composed in Hebrew during the same century as the revolt, is the best extant historical source for the period. The author records a full and detailed description of the rededication of the sanctuary – the restoration of the Jerusalem Temple, its material structure and appointments.[11] Completing the missing elements, crowning the outer walls of the sanctuary with gold, and celebratory music express the joy of the new-found freedom to worship. The text exudes celebration at the recovery of the space, the preparations and recommencement of the service. With all of these details, including the specific mention of kindling the lamp, the *menorah*, no special attention is drawn to any incident involving the scarcity of oil. The text conceives the events as large gestures – removing the altar that had been profaned, restoring, building, and fortifying.

> The Second Book of Maccabees describes the events from a slightly different ideological perspective – in support of Judas Maccabeus and his rebels. After the success of the revolt, The Second Book of Maccabees records the purification of the Temple sanctuary.

---

10. "Apocrypha" means "hidden" in Greek.

11. *The First Book of Maccabees* 4:36–61, translation from New American Bible © 1991, 1986, 1970 Confraternity of Christian Doctrine, Inc., Washington, DC.

Now Maccabeus and his followers, the Lord leading them on, recovered the Temple and the city and they tore down the altars which had been built in the public square by the foreigners, and also destroyed the sacred precincts. They purified the sanctuary and made another altar of sacrifice. Then striking fire out of flint, they offered sacrifices, after a lapse of two years, and they burned incense and lit lamps and set out the Show Bread. When they had done this, they fell prostrate and besought the Lord that they might never again fall into such misfortunes, but that if they should ever sin, they might be disciplined by Her/Him with forbearance and not be handed over to blasphemous and barbarous nations. It happened that on the same day on which the sanctuary had been profaned by the foreigners, the purification of the sanctuary took place, that is, on the 25th day of Kislev. They celebrated it for eight days with rejoicing, in the manner of the Feast of Booths, remembering how not long before, during the Feast of Booths, they had been wandering in the mountains and caves like wild animals. Therefore bearing ivy-wreathed wands and beautiful branches and also fronds of palm, they offered hymns of thanksgiving to Her/Him who had given success to the purifying of Her/His own holy place. They decreed by public ordinance and vote that the whole nation of the Jews should observe these days every year.[12]

These two different accounts of the origin of the festival of Chanukah emphasize the delight in returning to the sanctuary, and rededicating it for sacred service. There is another version of the Chanukah events preserved in the writings of Josephus Flavius.

Josephus Flavius

Josephus Flavius wrote his histories under the supervision of the Roman emperor Vespasian while he was a prisoner after the destruction of Jerusalem. Having participated in the Jewish revolt against Rome as a general of Jewish forces in the Galilee who surrendered during the defeat, his account of the struggle is a unique and invaluable first-hand record of a tumultuous period. Though his scholarship of

---

12. *The Second Book of Maccabees*, 1:1–9 and 10:1–8.

both Jewish and Greek texts contributes erudition and insight to his work, the conditions under which he wrote and his tendency to trust rumors probably detract from his reliability. He records an account of Chanukah in his *Antiquities of the Jews*.

> Now Judas celebrated the festival of the restoration of the sacrifices of the Temple for eight days; and omitted no sort of pleasures thereon; but he feasted them upon very rich and splendid sacrifices; and he honored God and delighted them by hymns and psalms. Nay, they were so very glad at the revival of their customs when after a long time of intermission they unexpectedly had regained the freedom of their worship, that they made it a law for their posterity, that they should keep a festival on account of the restoration of their Temple worship for eight days. And from that time to this we celebrate this festival, and call it Lights. I suppose the reason was, because this liberty beyond our hopes appeared to us; and that thence was the name given to that festival. Judas also rebuilt the walls around the city, and reared towers of great height against the incursions of enemies, and set guards therein. He also fortified the city Bethsura, that it might serve as a citadel against any distresses that might come from our enemies.[13]

These three similar accounts of the Chanukah festival bear little resemblance to the version of the story that became popular among the Jewish People from the Talmudic period until the modern State of Israel. Neither the Books of Maccabees nor Josephus mentions the central event of the legend: the miracle of a tiny cruse of oil. Though Josephus has an obvious opportunity to launch into the oil narrative when he explains the name of the festival, "Lights," he does not refer to any miracle at all. Instead, he associates the lights with *freedom*.

These texts stress the battle, cleaning, purifying, feasting, rebuilding, and public rituals. Without exception, all of these activities involve massive materials and control of physical and political realms. The celebration is on account of a military victory. Josephus himself expresses reservations about the festival having to do with lights – perhaps discomfort with the strident materialism. Seeking some spiritual significance, he *supposes* that the lights indicate liberty.

13. Flavius Josephus, *Antiquities*, Book 12, Chapter 7, Part 7.

Blood to Oil

The spiritual story of the miracle of the oil overpowers the warrior texts, and comes to represent Chanukah. Only at the end of the passage do the sages explain the origin of the ritual.

> Our sages taught: The commandment of Chanukah requires one light per household; the zealous kindle a light for each member of the household; and the extremely zealous – Beit Shammai maintain: On the first day eight lights are lit and thereafter they are gradually reduced [by one each day]; but Beit Hillel say: On the first day one is lit and thereafter they are progressively increased. Ulla said: In the West [Eretz Yisrael] two *amoraim*, R. Jose child of Abin and R. Jose child of Zebida, differ concerning this: One maintains, the reasoning of Beit Shammai is that it should correspond to the days still to come, and that of Beit Hillel is that it shall correspond to the days that are gone. But another maintains: Beit Shammai's reason is that it shall correspond to the bullocks of the Festival [of Tabernacles; i.e., Sukkot], while Beit Hillel's reason is that we increase in matters of sanctity but do not reduce.
>
> Rabbah child of Bar Hana said: There are two old men in Sidon: One did as Beit Shammai and the other as Beit Hillel: The former gave the reason of his action that it should correspond to the bullocks [sacrifices] of the Festival, while the latter stated his reason because we increase in [matters of] sanctity but do not reduce.
>
> Our sages taught: It is incumbent to place the Chanukah lamp by the door of one's house on the outside; if one dwells in an upper chamber, place it at the window nearest the street. But in times of danger it is sufficient to place it on the table. Raba said: Another lamp is required for its light to be used, yet if there is a blazing fire it is unnecessary. But in the case of an important person, even if there is a blazing fire another lamp is required.
>
> What is [the reason for] Chanukah?
>
> Our sages taught,
>
> On the 25th of Kislev begin the eight days of Chanukah on which eulogies and fasting are prohibited. When the Hellenizers entered the Temple, they defiled all of the oils in the Court. When the sovereign power of the Hasmonean dynasty overpowered and defeated

the Hellenizers, they searched and found only one cruse of oil that had on it the seal of the High Priest. Though there was only enough oil in it to burn one day; a miracle occurred, and they lit the *menorah* from it for eight days. The following year, they appointed these days a festival with Hallel and thanksgiving. (*Shabbat* 21b)

The apocryphal books and Josephus purport to tell history, focusing on large-scale, public actions and the battle for sacred territory. Performing cultural interpretation, the sages create a meaningful ritual from within their narrative. Using discreet domestic materials, they reconceive the Chanukah miracle.

At the outset, the text interprets the Chanukah commandment to light candles for eight days. The object of kindling is to publicize a miracle – not the military victory, the recovery of the Temple, or political autonomy, but, surprisingly, a humble miracle about a tiny amount of oil burning for eight days. After the destruction, when there is no public Jewish center, the sages make each home stand for the Temple. Each Jew acts as a priest entering the sacred sanctuary, preparing the pure shining vessels, and lighting the *menorah*. The text purposely discloses a controversy about the ritual. Important sages, Hillel and Shammai, teach opposite approaches – one increases the number of lights with each passing day of the festival; the other decreases them. Each is based on a different vision of the lights. For Shammai, the lights correspond with the now defunct sacrifices of the Temple. Kindling lights in one's home reminds of the public offerings once performed by the priests in the Temple on behalf of the nation.

Hillel's view is that lights must increase like holiness. Once we kindle a certain number, we cannot decrease. The reluctance to lessen the amount of light as the days progress illumines the next segment of the text – how to observe Chanukah under conditions of fear. If lighting candles in the window might attract the attention of persecutors, then it is permissible to light on the table where the *menorah* will not be seen by passers-by. During oppression, Jews cannot risk publicly demonstrating their faith. The purpose of lighting the candles is to publicize the miracle of Chanukah – to Jews and non-Jews,[14] and to

---

14. Rav Yosef Dov Soloveitchik, *Beit Ha'Levi al ha'Torah* (Jerusalem: *Oz ve-Hadar*, 1990).

express gratitude for Jewish sovereignty and freedom to worship. While wanting to draw attention to the candles, the sages are sensitive to life predicaments. For both sages, the candles enact the Temple ritual on a personal level. For the sake of safety, the sages make it paradoxically possible to *publicize* the miracle in *private*, inside the home. On the table, the lights represent the fears and constraints of exile.

In the atmosphere of danger that permeates the text, the sages downplay the power and might in the story, and portray the Hasmoneans as witnesses to a divine miracle. For the sages, the miracle abides in the spiritual quality of faithful service that defies the oppressor with symbols, and resists conquering militias inwardly. For the Shabbat of Chanukah, the sages choose a reading from the prophet Zecharia. The divine message to the exiles who return and rebuild the Jerusalem Temple after the Babylonian exile admonishes against the use of might and power, "This is the word of God to Zerubbavel: Not by might, nor by power, but by My spirit – said the God of hosts."[15] This verse counteracts Maccabean militarism – it is enshrined on the bronze menorah at the Knesset-parliament as motto of the State of Israel. The prophets prevail upon their leader, Zerubbavel to rebuild the Temple. For a period of a century and a half, the Jewish community succeeds to maintain peaceful relations with the powerful Persian Empire without compromising Jewish religious and spiritual self-determination. Even as this vision is compelling, there is an unstated limit to its validity. So long as Jews do not have political autonomy and capability to protect ourselves, religious freedom and life are subject to the whims of the governing power. Unfortunately, tolerance does not always materialize, and Jews are oppressed. A children's Holocaust book tells the story of inmates in a concentration camp who risk their lives to steal one potato and a spoonful of margarine to kindle a light in their bunk during Chanukah. They tear threads from their garments to make a wick that burns for a bold instant of hope in their dark lives.[16]

The sages invent a way to replicate a massive miracle using tiny symbolic materials – oil and thread.[17] They transform the victory

---

15. Zech. 4:6.

16. Eve Bunting, K. Wendy Popp (illustrator), *One Candle* (New York: Harper Collins, 2004).

17. The worn linen garments of the Temple priests were used for wicks, (*Shabbat* 21).

won by grand motions of war into a subtle act of lighting candles; they transform the blood of war into oil and light. The Chanukah flames burn at the fragile boundary between matter and spirit – each tiny flame represents the resilient soul of the Jewish People, persevering, increasing hope every day, not diminishing.

Biblical and rabbinic sources support the sages' emphasis on spiritual refinement and humility as credentials for participating in sacred acts. The sages see war compromising sanctity. Violence interferes with closeness to the divine. Insofar as humanity behaves in the image of God-who-is-Creator, humanity fulfills more of the divine aspect. Insofar as people act as destroyer, they distance themselves from the Creator. For this reason, David is prohibited from building the Temple – his hands are stained. The biblical text prefers hands that are pure from the acts of war, "God said to him [David], you shall not build a house to My name for you are a man of war and have spilt blood."[18]

According to Maimonides, Jewish law requires a military general to exhaust the possible options for peace before pursuing war. Maimonides interprets this concept from the example of the Israelites preparing to cross the Jordan valley into the land under the command of Joshua.

> Joshua sent three letters before he entered the land. The first one that he sent to them inviting anyone who wants to flee should flee; again he sent offering anyone who wants to make a peace agreement should make peace; again he sent saying that anyone who wants to make war should do so.[19]

However fervent the desire to avoid war, Jews have sometimes fought to survive. Zionism, the project of Jewish self-determination, has been fraught with struggle. Military conflicts have brought with them profound conflicts of value, and, sometimes the need to subordinate religious practice to face imminent danger. The Israeli rabbinic authorities base their justification for the IDF to fight, and thereby defile the sacred Shabbat, on Judah's argument in the Book of Maccabees.

> It was reported to the officers and soldiers of the king who were in the City of David, in Jerusalem, that certain men who had flouted the

---

18. I Chr. 28:3.
19. Maimonides, *Mishneh Torah, Melachim* 6:5.

king's order had gone out to the hiding places in the desert. Many hurried out after them, and having caught up with them, camped opposite and prepared to attack them on the sabbath. "Enough of this!" the pursuers said to them. "Come out and obey the king's command, and your lives will be spared." But they replied, "We will not come out, nor will we obey the king's command to profane the Shabbat."

Then the enemy attacked them at once; but they did not retaliate; they neither threw stones, nor blocked up their own hiding places. They said, "Let us all die without reproach; heaven and earth are our witnesses that you destroy us unjustly."

So the officers and soldiers attacked them on the sabbath, and they died with their wives, their children and their cattle, to the number of a thousand persons. When Mattathias and his friends heard of it, they mourned deeply for them. "If we all do as our kinsmen have done," they said to one another, "and do not fight against the Gentiles for our lives and our traditions, they will soon destroy us from the earth."

On that day they came to this decision: "Let us fight against anyone who attacks us on the sabbath, so that we may not all die as our kinsmen died in the hiding places."[20]

In order to avert slaughter, Mattathias asserts the priority of defense over observance of Shabbat. After all, the Torah teaches that we should *live* by its precepts, not die on account of them.[21] In the modern period, Rabbi Shlomo Goren (1917–1994), the rabbinic authority for the Israel Defense Forces, takes a further leap to justify armed combat on Shabbat. In addition to survival, Goren speaks about the commandment to "sanctify and conquer the land."

> Permission to fight on Shabbat is not based on the requirement to save life. It is based upon the permission that is granted uniquely for war, for the conquest of the land of Israel. Deuteronomy 20:20 supports my claim:
>
> "Only trees that you know are certainly not food-bearing may you cut down; build bulwarks against the city that has made war against you *until it is subdued*."
>
> "Until it is subdued" – even on Shabbat. After all, why would we

---

20. The First Book of Maccabees, 2, 31–41.
21. Lev. 18:5.

need special permission to defend ourselves on Shabbat, since saving life always overrides Shabbat? The requirement to fight on Shabbat derives from the commandment to sanctify and conquer the land. The commandment to sanctify and conquer the land overrides the commandment to save life.[22]

The requirement to fight in order to save life is self-evident, Rabbi Goren argues, though the Maccabees did not think so at the outset of their rebellion. They justified that view only after many lives were lost due to faithfulness to Shabbat. Concerning the Israeli army, Goren posits that the commandment to "sanctify and conquer the land" is even a higher order obligation than the obligation to save life. Sacrificing life for the sake of autonomy in the land, even on Shabbat, is acceptable, according to his argument.

Goren's view might appear territorial or militaristic to those who have been blessed with peace in their land. Americans have known no act of war on home turf between the Civil War (1861–1865) and September 11, 2001.[23] On the grounds of the September 11 attack, America and her allies wage an ongoing global war on terror – battling international networks such as al-Qaida, conquering the regime in Iraq, and fighting in Afghanistan, the Philippines, Somalia and many parts of Africa, and Pakistan. By contrast with prevailing peace in America, Zionism was forged in the crucible of long-term persecutions throughout the world, and ongoing aggression against the citizens of Israel. These have conditioned Israel to the necessity to use force at any hour when life and land are at risk. The need for Israel to protect the Jewish People has been amply demonstrated. Like the Maccabees, Israelis learn from cruel experience to defend life even during sacred hours. On the holiest day of the Jewish Year, Yom Kippur 1973, a coalition of Arab states backing Egypt and Syria mounted a surprise attack against Israel on two fronts, threatening Israel's existence. Israelis grow up aware of the battle for survival. Compared with some periods in

---

22. Rabbi Shlomo Goren, former Chief Rabbi of the IDF and Chief Rabbi of Israel, *Meshiv Milchama*, a halakhic guide for the Israeli army, Vol. 1 (Jerusalem: Ha-Idra Rabba, 1982), 85.

23. The Japanese attack on Pearl Harbor, Hawaii in December 1941, though it caused substantial losses and constituted a declaration of war, was far from the US mainland.

Jewish history when Jews were slaughtered like sheep, Jewish self-defense is a bold innovation. Anti-Semitism and anti-Zionism have not only inflicted suffering but forced Israel to harm others. Former Israeli Prime Minister Golda Meir poignantly stated this pain after the Yom Kippur War and before the peace talks with Anwar Sadat, President of Egypt, "I can forgive you for killing my sons, but I cannot forgive you for forcing me to kill *your* sons."

Passionate Criticism

The Maccabean rebellion unites Jewish body and soul. While the sages inspire and cultivate tremendous spiritual resources, they also retreat into private space when there is danger, and discorporate. Talmudic advice to kindle Chanukah lights on the table does not suffice when the table is also breached. Both the Maccabees and in contemporary times, Zionists dare to face that contingency and opt to protect life. Military defense raises difficult ethical challenges – how to engage in civilian areas, the acceptable extent of risk to soldiers compared with non-combatants, the admissibility of assassinating terrorists, intelligence and detention procedures, *et cetera*. In war, soldiers face dilemmas that test humanity to its limit. Many armies commit abuses and atrocities, and some governments support terrorism outright, yet they are rarely held accountable for the harm they cause to humanity and the environment.[24] Usually soldiers are recruited from the lower, more "dispensable" classes of society; they take orders and mainly wage battle off-camera and far away from public scrutiny.[25] By

---

24. The American, British, Indian, Russian, Chinese, Pakistani, Azerbaijani, Jordanian armies, to name a few examples, have been accused of extreme ethical abuses – few are investigated, let alone spotlighted globally or daily. The current American list of countries that sponsor terrorism includes Cuba, Iran, Sudan, and Syria. Libya, Iraq, North Korea, and South Yemen have been on the list. American warfare causes extreme harm to civilians. "Agent Orange" in Vietnam is one blatant example. See André Bouny, "The effects of Agent orange and its consequences," *Global Research*, Jan. 16, 2007, retrieved Aug. 26, 2010, www.globalresearch.ca/index.php?context=va&aid=4490.

25. Amy Lutz, "Who joins the military?: A look at race, class, and immigration status," *Journal of Political and Military Sociology*, Winter 2008, retrieved Sept. 2, 2010, findarticles.com/p/articles/mi_qa3719/is_200812/ai_n31513217/?tag=content;col1.

comparison, civilians from every sector of society comprise the Israeli Defense Forces (IDF); all Israelis are obliged to serve.

Thirty-five years after Israel took control of the West Bank and Gaza Strip during the 1967 war, more than 550 Israeli soldiers and officers signed a public "Combatant Letter." The signatories, many of whom formed the "Courage to Refuse" organization (CTR), affirm their Zionism and proven commitment to defend and strengthen the State of Israel. They claim that they were issued commands and directives during their service in the IDF that have as their "sole purpose" to "perpetuate our control over the Palestinian people." They declare their refusal to serve missions of "occupation and oppression" on the grounds that such directives "destroy all the values we had absorbed while growing up in this country." The soldiers propose to distinguish between what they consider necessary defense and conquest. They further state that they "know that the Territories are not Israel, and that all settlements are bound to be evacuated in the end."[26] This claim states their political opinion and implies their assessment of future Israeli security arrangements. Their refusal to participate further in what they consider moral compromises vocalizes a cutting public critique of government policy.

A group of Israeli settlers brought a case to the Supreme Court to challenge the legality of the CTR. The lawyer representing CTR summarized the January 2006 Supreme Court ruling, "All three judges accepted CTR's distinction between an organization that supports refusniks and an organization that calls for an act of refusal. The ruling also distinguishes legitimate conscientious acts of individuals from illegal acts of incitement. Thus, this verdict is actually a warning to the Settlers' Rabbis, who explicitly ordered their congregations to refuse orders throughout The Disengagement [from Gaza], and might try to evoke rebellion during the next withdrawals."[27]

Both soldiers and settlers exercise the protections of democracy and the openness of the public discourse to assert contradictory opinions that bear on their actions and lives. They seek to refine the Jewish body, land and soul, to separate murky blood from purer oil. Their

---

26. Combatant Letter, 2002, www.seruv.org.il/defaulteng.asp.

27. Courage to Refuse, retrieved Feb. 21, 2012, http://www.seruv.org.il/english/article.asp?msgid=255&type=news.

passionate critiques well up from deep conscience and responsibility, from visions of the character and quality of Israeli society – a sign of the extent of accountability that Israeli citizens and soldiers expect. This discourse is available to people who hold a stake in and contribute responsibly to Israeli society – such as soldiers who serve in the IDF and citizens whose homes and communities are subject to national policy. The IDF operates under the watchful eyes of a vocal political opposition, a multitude of Israeli and international human rights organizations, a pro-active Supreme Court, wildly free media, and a public that takes its protests to the press, the internet, the courts, and to the street. Democratic, accountable instruments of justice mediate and monitor claims. This extreme openness renders Israeli controversies transparent and vulnerable, particularly in contrast with the authoritarian and coercive regimes in the region and throughout the Arab world. Individuals, organizations (NGOs, the UN, et cetera), and states abuse the openness of Israeli society to express self-righteous rage against the State of Israel. This kind of attention would be better addressed to self-critique and to issues for which the critics are responsible, involved, more informed, and personally invested.

The Rambam demands that force must only be permitted when all options have been exhausted, and military defense is required. Facing ideologies of hatred and terror in an atmosphere of aggression and rejection requires vigilance to ensure that defense does not turn to excess. Israel has pioneered systems to minimize civilian casualties. During the 2008–9 Gaza War, the IDF notified thousands of civilians to evacuate buildings where weapons were warehoused and combatants were headquartered. Israel electronically relayed tens of thousands of phone messages and dropped harmless "knock on the roof" sound bombs. The US army studies and learns from Israeli methods in their war against terror.[28] In spite of its unique accountability to a critical democratic society and the stringency of the ethical code of the IDF, the international community singles Israel out for condemnation.[29]

---

28. Jonathan F. Keiler, "Who Won the Battle of Fallujah?," *Proceedings of Naval Institute, the Independent Forum on National Defense*, January 2005, retrieved July 20, 2011, www.military.com/NewContent/1,13190,NI_0105_Fallujah-P1,00.html.

29. See Maj. Gen. Amos Yadlin, "Ethical Dilemmas in Fighting Terrorism," *Jerusalem Issue Brief*, vol. 4, no. 8, 25 November 2004, retrieved Aug. 16, 2010, www.jcpa.org/brief/brief004-8.htm.

Secretaries General Kofi Annan and Ban Ki Moon, the United Nations Human Rights Council's president Doru Costea, the European Union, Canada and the United States accuse the council of focusing disproportionately on the Israeli-Palestinian conflict.[30]

Such a campaign by states, international bodies including the UN and NGO's to delegitimize Israel's right to exist has never been undertaken against any other sovereign state among the nations of the world. The campaigners selectively target Israel while they neglect abuses and oppressions, brutal policies and war tactics, fierce race and religion-based oppression practiced by many nations. Committed and creative engagement and respectful criticism are better contributions. Recrimination and hate-filled messages feed feelings of persecution, and arouse defensiveness and intransigence. Among the nations that freed themselves from European colonialism during the twentieth century, the Jewish People is entitled to self-determination.

From the beginning of Israel, many forward-looking analysts understood the significance of the relationship between Zionism and the Arab inhabitants of Palestine.[31] Until recently, mainstream Zionism attended mainly to Jewish destiny in the land. Having achieved consistent military victories against her assailants, Israel has succeeded to negotiate peace with two of her former foes, Egypt and Jordan – only from a position of strength. Fuller regional stability and peace have yet to materialize. The Arab Spring of 2011 might lead to the reformation of monarchies, dictatorships, oligarchies, and totalitarian regimes in the region, and create more promising partners for peace. These fruit are yet far from ripe, and Israel must continue to attend assiduously to her defense.

Palestinians suffer the dispute over the territories daily, unfulfilled political autonomy, corruption and violence, and the machinations of Arab states. All of these drain energy and good will away from resolving

30. Since March 1948, more than 225 United Nations Security Council resolutions deal with Israel. See Secretary-General address, UN Department of Public Information 08-12-2008, www.un.org/News/Press/docs/2006/sgsm10788.doc.htm; Human Rights Council president wants reform, SwissInfo 29-09-2007, www.un.org/News/Press/docs/2006/sgsm10788.doc.htm.

31. See for example, Martin Buber, Judah Leon Magnes, Akibah Ernst Simon. Ihud [Organization], *Towards union in Palestine: Essays on Zionism and Jewish-Arab Cooperation* (Ihud [Union] Association: Jerusalem, 1947).

the Middle East conflict and detract from the pursuit of wholesome national goals, Israeli and Palestinian. Palestinian leaders – in Gaza and the West Bank – need to denounce violence, recognize the Jewish State, and make peace. Sami Awad is one of the leaders of non-violent practice and theory in the Palestinian community; he and his Holy Land Trust are educating about the spiritual, political, economic, and social benefits of living non-violence.[32] With humility and longing, I offer these tenets of Israeli society as an agenda to share with the people of Gaza and the West Bank: sustainable economic development, universal education for civic responsibility and respect for all peoples, women's liberation from systemic oppression and full participation in public life and leadership, a comprehensive, high quality universal health care system, academic institutions that promote open, critical thinking and innovation, the critical study of history, pursuit of science, technology and medical research and development, vibrant and uncensored media, culture, and arts. On such a basis, Israel will surely support the flourishing of Palestinian civil society, a state living side-by-side with us in peace, with dignity and security.

In our day, much of the world's population lives with fear and instability. Relatively few people feel safe, that their needs are met, and that they enjoy freedom and the resources to pursue their life choices. Even for those with the blessings of material plenty, the barrier separating them from a harsher fate is gossamer thin. After the 9/11 terrorist attacks on the New York City twin towers and the Pentagon, American psychologist and social critic Phyllis Chesler commented, "now we are all Israelis" – referring to an American awakening to vulnerability.[33] Ultimately, we cannot fully protect against those who choose to hurt and destroy.

Both Maccabean and modern Zionism seek to ensure the security of the Jewish People to exist, practice freely, and continue to develop our gifts to humankind. While defending Jewish life, both Maccabees and Zionists resort to territorial battle. Eventually, the Maccabees devolve into a violent and factionalized regime that succumbs to Roman control under Herod and, finally to destruction and exile. In our era, sovereignty in our land challenges our capability to pursue our

---

32. Retrieved Jan. 12, 2012, http://www.holylandtrust.org/.
33. Retrieved July 20, 2011, www.phyllis-chesler.com/180/now-we-are-all-israelis.

finest purposes. For both the Maccabees and contemporary Zionists, military action both secures Jewish life and practice and tests Jewish values. In the process, pure oil is tainted with the blood of war.

Both in the Maccabean period and today, the military enterprise occupies too much of Israel's energy; war wastes life and resources. Similarly to the Maccabees, Israel has internalized the demand to use force to ensure Jewish existence. The effects of military culture on Israeli civil society are pervasive and problematic, but neither inevitable nor eternal.[34] The conundrum of persistent violence is much bigger than Israel and the Middle East. Humanity as a whole must learn to resolve conflict by skillful use of peaceful means – desisting from the myopic profits and manipulations of war, and empowering bold, capable, and visionary leadership. Israel shares with the West the mission to protect open society – without compromising the values and practices that are in jeopardy. We must dedicate more resources to creative, collaborative, and sacred service rather than destruction. Israel is among the nations for whom moving humanity beyond violence is a vital interest. Collaborative and creative work to disarm threats is on the Zionist agenda. The time is ripe for Israelis and Palestinians to innovate in peacemaking, and to fertilize seeds of peace throughout the world.

War and Miracle

The sages are not naïve about power. Aside from lighting candles, they also acknowledge the necessity of war and compose songs of gratitude for the victories. Chanukah celebrates the hard-earned opportunity to sanctify spiritual will and freedom. In prayers, the sages explicitly acknowledge the military victory among the miracles of Chanukah.

> **These Lights – *HaNerot Halalu***
> We light these lights
> For the miracles and the wonders, for the redemption and the battles
> That You performed for our forebearers in those days, at this season,

---

34. Shlomo Swirski, "The Price of Occupation: The Cost of the Occupation to Israeli Society," *Palestine - Israel Journal of Politics, Economics & Culture*, 2005, 12(1), 110–120. Also Orna Sasson-Levy, Sarit Amram-Katz, "Gender Integration in Israeli Officer Training: Degendering and Regendering the Military," *Signs: Journal of Women in Culture & Society*, 2007, 33 (1), 105–133.

Through Your holy priests.
During all eight days of Chanukah, these lights are sacred
And we are not permitted to make ordinary use of them,
But only to look at them;
In order to express thanks and praise to Your great Name
For your miracles, Your wonders and Your salvations.

This poem mentions both *holy priests* and battles as media for miracles – an oblique reference to the Maccabees. Another prayer, "*Al HaNissim*" – "About the Miracles" – the rabbinic insertion into the daily liturgy during Chanukah, explicitly mentions the Hasmoneans, the Maccabees. These texts interpose the military narrative with the miracle of oil. While they accept the importance of the mortal power, the Chanukah prayers praise miracles of redemption and refocus on humility. No human choice, ideology, or victory is ultimate truth. The prayer registers opposites: defiled and pure, wicked and righteous, insolent sinners and students of Torah. Usually, we find ourselves in transition between one and the other. For the sages in exile, military matters become a metaphor. Divine light triumphs over darkness with every new dawn. With no possibility of independence, the rabbinic texts propose a subtle spiritual form of rededication. The sages turn the blood of military victory into pure oil. These Chanukah texts shed light on the darkness of fear and conflict, and on military and religious excesses. The textual interplay between soldier and scholar inspires us to lubricate the flesh and blood of daily sovereignty with the refined sacred spirit of Chanukah oil.

Both Maccabees and Zionists alike call upon us to find and test the meaning of our lives beyond our own personal interest, and to accept responsibility for the flourishing of Jews and Judaism now and in the generations to come. Both undertake to contribute toward the ongoing project of Jewish Peoplehood to the fullest extent possible. "The Zion Cycle" connects us with those who proceeded us, those who are our contemporaries, and those who will yet inherit Jewish destiny from us – if we opt to pass it on.

> Not with you alone do I make this covenant, this undertaking, but both with those who are standing here with us this day before the Lord our God, and with those who are not with us here this day.
> (Deuteronomy 29:13–14)

These verses describe a covenant extending to the entire collectivity of Jewish People throughout time and space. Zionism conceives our personal lives in a flow of Jewish experience, imbued with national aspiration. Both the Maccabees and contemporary Zionists rebel against the dominant *status quo* in order to develop a uniquely Jewish society. Israel reactivates the ancient experiment of building the Jewish homeland. Zionism today has a tremendous agenda that invites participation and contribution. Rooted in Jewish sources, this worldview might puzzle some who are reared in a Western climate of individualism. Zionism focuses on shared destiny and interdependence – current values for a sustainable world.

7   Journeying Onward

SOME SOUND AN alert about the weakening connection between the Jewish People and Israel.[1] Professionals, philanthropists, media people, and educators are working to strengthen Jewish identity – in Israel and throughout the world, buttressing against turbulent anti-Israel sentiment. People drift away from Judaism and Zionism because they do not find them inspiring, valuable, or even relevant enough to perceive the significance of their lives to these great projects of humanity. Concern is not only about numbers – the meaning and destiny of the Jewish People and Israel are in our hands. For these generations, the relationship to Israel is far from a simple vector pointing upward to Zion – the bull's-eye in life's target. Instead, Zionism stands accused. The Zion Cycle invokes committed engagement to the full-bodied process of interpreting texts, people, and land at this historic moment, mobilizing world Jewry toward creative, responsible state-building. This chapter begins by taking stock of some of the critiques of Zionism, consolidates some of the proposals of this book, and suggests further directions.

---

1. As cited in chap. 3, Peter Beinart, "The Failure of the American Jewish Establishment," *NYT Book Review,* retrieved June 10, 2010, www.nybooks.com/articles/archives/2010/jun/10/failure-american-jewish-establishment/.

Inverted Exodus

Nations asserting their autonomy is one of the main features of Western modernity. Revolutions and emancipation brought masses of people forth from the dark poverty of feudal serfdom, from the absolute despotism of divinely ordained monarchy, and from the racism and paternalism of colonizers. During the modern period, a considerable portion of the world's population at least nominally shook off the old regimes – kings and queens, church, colonialism, and slavery. In this climate, nationalism and the drive for political autonomy intensified. By the end of the Second World War, the trend toward self-determination for national, ethnic, and religious groups swelled. Newly independent states proliferated.

Recognition of the right to practice and educate in one's heritage emerges from the ravages of World War II. The so-called *enlightened* cultures of Europe had unleashed violent racism and ethnic supremacy that proved the dire need for a global corrective. On December 10, 1948, the United Nations adopted its International Declaration of Human Rights. The preamble proclaims that "disregard and contempt for human rights have resulted in barbarous acts which have outraged the conscience of [hu]mankind."[2] As a result, Article 18 clarifies,

> Everyone has the right to freedom of thought, conscience and religion; this right includes freedom to change his [sic] religion or belief, and freedom, either alone or in community with others and in public or private, to manifest his [sic] religion or belief in teaching, practice, worship and observance.[3]

During the first two decades after the Second World War, 1945–1962, almost every Muslim country in the world gained independence from European powers. Similarly the European empires that had controlled South Asia, Africa, and Latin America were dismantled as national groups wrested freedom from foreign rulers. While the momentum of anti-colonialism peaked, the Zionist movement also achieved statehood for Jews. The Yishuv – the Jews who lived in Palestine under

2. United Nations Department of Public Information, www.unhchr.ch/udhr/lang/eng.htm.

3. United Nations Department of Public Information, www.unhchr.ch/udhr/lang/eng.htm.

the British Mandate – declared independence, offering refuge to the remnants of the Jewish People who survived the afflictions of the first half of the twentieth century.

For thousands of years, the Jewish People drew succor and hope from the biblical Exodus tradition of liberation toward freedom. With the establishment of Israel and the opening of the former Soviet bloc, the Passover message, "Let my people go," applies less to Jews as a people than ever.[4] By providing a homeland for refugees, and rescuing those afflicted, Israel has mainly succeeded to relieve world Jewry of the oppressions of thousand of years.

Israel was not a gift, nor compensation for suffering. There were few supports and no safety net. The same America that barricaded its borders against Jews seeking refuge from Europe before and during the Holocaust enforced an arms embargo on Israel during the War of Independence that threatened to destroy the foundling state.[5,6] Zionism did not ride a wave of national autonomy but earned it by indomitable will and effective action. The Zionists' military, economic and political strategy, determination, and success against overwhelming odds achieved the State of Israel. Many offered themselves limitlessly to achieve our freedom to live as Jews.

Up until and including the Six-Day War in 1967, Israel was a favored character in a modern Exodus drama. Leon Uris's novel *Exodus*, named after the ship that rescued Holocaust survivors from Europe

---

4. Many Jews direct their sentiments of responsibility and civic values gleaned from the Exodus to work toward justice for disadvantaged and oppressed groups. *Tikkun olam* – repair of the world – has become a motto for Jewish communities, an identity marker.

5. The 1924 National Origins Quota legislation restricted the number of immigrants allowed into America to no more than two percent of the number of each nationality residing in the U.S. in 1890. This policy prevented Jews from entering the USA during the period of extreme persecution. Shiploads of desperate Jewish refugees were turned away from American ports back to Europe for decimation in the concentration camps. The tragic journey of the S.S. *St. Louis* is one case. Many shiploads of Jewish refugees fleeing from Europe were denied visas into Palestine by the British under the provisions of the 1939 White Paper quotas. The ships *Struma* and the *Exodus* are famous examples.

6. On December 5, 1947, the U.S. imposed an arms embargo on the region, including Israel, while Britain was supplying weapons to Iraq and Jordan. Shlomo Slonim, "The 1948 American Embargo on Arms to Palestine," *Political Science Quarterly*, 94(3), Fall 1979, 500.

and took them to Palestine, sold more than five million copies in the first five years. The three and a half hour-long film version starring Paul Newman as Ari Ben Canaan was a box-office home-run. According to one reviewer on Amazon, "The joyously pro-Israel strains of *Exodus* will probably now draw more cynicism than solidarity."[7] From the mid-1970s and into the last decades of the twentieth century, Israel's detractors inverted the Exodus script. With the protracted territorial dispute over the West Bank and Golan Heights (and, until 2005, the Gaza Strip), many view Israel as a colonial power, preventing the Palestinians from achieving the same self-determination and freedom that Israel enjoys. Israel has been cast into the Pharaoh role in the biblical Israelite liberation drama.

From the perspective of most contemporary young people, Zionism is more an oppressor than a liberation movement. On campuses, in the media, among liberal circles, organizations and nations, agitation against Israel and her policies rampages. So-called *progressive* voices accuse and condemn Israel: apartheid, fascism, brutality, even insinuations of Nazi-like behavior are among the litany. Lobbies advocate sanctions and divestment of funds from Israel. Academics have organized boycotts of Israeli institutions and scholars.[8]

While public rallies, boycotts, and divestment schemes target Israel and her institutions, Israeli contributions to sciences, agriculture, medicine, arts, literature, and social innovation are in constant use and enjoyment throughout the world. Among the popular Israeli inventions are drip irrigation, Intel Pentium chips, core components of MS Windows, XP and Vista, Firewall software (by the IDF), Google's search algorithm, the first instant messaging platform, tsunami detection systems, Clear Light Acne treatment, Copaxone treatments, Mirabel breast cancer detection, GiVen PillCam for GI imaging, computerized prescription systems, pilotless drones, cell phone, camera and phone chip technology, voicemail, and the cherry tomato.[9]

---

7. Jason A. Miller, retrieved Oct. 20, 2010, www.amazon.com/Exodus-Leon-Uris/dp/B000IZTZ9O.

8. On April 22, 2005, The High Education Union of the UK, AUK, enforces an academic boycott of Israeli institutions. www.aut.org.uk/index.cfm?articleid=1201.

9. The cherry tomato, *tomaccio* is the result of a 12-year breeding program by Hishtil nurseries on Moshav Nehalim, retrieved July 25, 2011, www.raker.com/doc/raker.tomaccio.handout.pdf.

In spite of the popular image of Israeli economic strength and military prowess, Israeli Jews continue to see ourselves as vulnerable. Worst-case scenarios depicted by enemies unnerve generations in the shadow of the Holocaust and accumulated Jewish suffering. Destruction, loss of life, the obliteration of precious culture – all of these have instilled deep fear among Jews, a fear that feeds concerns about survival. Persistent wars, terror, and threats of annihilation condition Israelis to feel isolated in a hostile region.

(Dis)Placing Nationalism

Anti-Zionism I: Ancient Oaths

Since the Hasmoneans in the second century BCE, no other generations of the Jewish People have merited to grow up in a world where Jewish political autonomy is a fact of life. Zionism inaugurated an unfathomable shift in the trajectory of Judaism. Indeed, the shift was so dramatic that until the Holocaust, the vast majority of world Jewry opposed the establishment of Israel. Israeli historian Yosef Salmon writes about Jewish attitudes toward Zionism at the beginning of the nineteenth century.

> But it was the Zionist threat that offered the gravest danger, for it sought to rob the traditional community of its very birthright, both in the Diaspora and in Eretz Israel, the object of its messianic hopes. Zionism challenged all the aspects of traditional Judaism: in its proposal of a modern, national Jewish identity; in the subordination of traditional society to new life-styles; and in its attitude to the religious concepts of Diaspora and redemption. The Zionist threat reached every Jewish community. It was unrelenting and comprehensive, and therefore it met with uncompromising opposition.[10]

Leader of the Satmar Hasidic movement, Rabbi Yoel Teitelbaum, crystallizes religious opposition to Zionism in his treatise, *Va-Yoel Moshe*.[11] He bases his main argument on a Talmudic passage interpreting three

---

10. Quoted by Yakov M. Rabkin, author of *A Threat from Within: A Century of Jewish Opposition to Zionism*, (Black Point, N.S.: Fernwood, 2006), on Haaretz.com, www.haaretz.com/hasen/pages/rosnerGuest.jhtml?itemNo=796902.

11. *Va-Yoel Moshe* (ויואל משה) (New York: "Jerusalem," 1961).

verses from the Song of Songs, the "three oaths." King Solomon thrice appeals to the daughters of Jerusalem not to arouse love until it is ready.

> I adjure you, O daughters of Jerusalem, by the gazelles, and by the hinds of the field, that you awaken not, nor stir up love, until it please.[12]

The Talmud explains how these oaths bind the Jewish People to wait patiently for God before initiating any movements to return to sovereignty in the land.

> These three oaths, what are they about? One, that the Jewish People are not allowed to ascend [to Eretz Yisrael] against a wall [by force]; one, that the Holy One swore the Jewish People not to rebel against the nations of the world; and one, that the Holy One swore the nations of the world not to oppress the Jewish People too much. (*Ketubot* 111a)

Setting the conversation in the garden of the Song of Songs, the sages express both the frustration of their desire and their acceptance of divine rejection. Evidence of rejection is ample in the historical suffering that Jewish communities endured in exile. Though the sages refer explicitly to the return of the exiles from Babylon to Israel in the sixth century BCE, implicitly they refer also to their own exile. The Jewish People waits while the divine lover is inattentive, unaroused – "until it please." This Talmudic passage blatantly states the passive demeanor of Jewry, a passivity that endured for millennia. Communities dealt with their vulnerability, suffered oppression when it befell them, and did not disrupt the divine beloved. From the time of the second destruction of Jerusalem in 70 CE, in spite of wars and anti-Semitism, until modern Zionism, world Jewry had no viable means of self-defense. The third oath states the only remedy – to rely on those who rule over them to exercise restraint. Neville Chamberlain was not alone espousing appeasement.[13] Teitelbaum even blames Zionism for causing the Holocaust by breaking the oaths.[14] By all accounts, the nations violated the third of the Talmudic criteria and oppressed the Jewish People far too much.

---

12. Song of Songs 2:7 and 3:5, with a slight variation in 8:4.

13. Chamberlain signed the Munich Agreement in 1938 to appease Adolf Hitler by ceding a region of Czechoslovakia to Germany.

14. *Va-Yoel Moshe*, section 110.

During the twentieth century, Zionism completely transformed Judaism and the Jewish People. Zionism proclaims the full dignity of Jews and all peoples. To a great extent Zionism is an antidote to terrible scourges of humanity – anti-Semitism in particular and racism in general. While Zionism invests Jewry with an active posture with respect to Jewish fate, anti-Zionism seeks persistently to undermine it.

Anti-Zionism II: Recognition

Saeb Erekat, the senior Palestinian Authority negotiator at the Annapolis international summit, captures the demeanor of disrespect for Israel as a Jewish state. In November 2007, he declared his refusal to recognize Israel's Jewish identity on the grounds that "it is not acceptable for a country to link its national character to a specific religion."[15] While Article 4 of the Basic Law of the Palestinian Authority declares that, "Islam is the official religion in Palestine," Palestinian negotiators resist recognizing the Jewishness of Israel.[16] More than fifty countries of the Organization of the Islamic Conference are recognized and respected as Muslim states. Indeed, most modern nations inscribe religion in their constitutions.[17] German Chancellor Angela Merkel declares, "Europe's 'Christian values' should be enshrined in a new version of the EU constitution."[18] Her declaration is particularly bold in view of the multiple non-Christian religious communities within the European Union, the most populous being Muslim.[19]

---

15. Jeff Jacoby, "Is Israel a Jewish state?," *The Boston Globe*, November 14, 2007, www.boston.com/bostonglobe/editorial_opinion/oped/articles/2007/11/14/is_israel_a_jewish_state/.

16. See memo to Palestinian drafting team, "Strategy and talking points for responding to the precondition of recognizing Israel as a 'Jewish state,'" retrieved Aug. 7, 2011, http://transparency.aljazeera.net/files/2021.pdf.

17. Argentinean law mandates government support for the Roman Catholic faith. Queen Elizabeth II is the supreme governor of the Church of England. The constitution of the Himalayan kingdom of Bhutan proclaims Buddhism the nation's "spiritual heritage." The Greek Constitution declares the Eastern Orthodox Church of Christ to be the prevailing religion in Greece. Part I, Article 3.1, retrieved Aug. 4, 2011, www.cecl.gr/RigasNetwork/databank/Constitutions/Greece.html.

18. Nicholas Watt, "Merkel backs more Christian EU constitution," *The Guardian*, Aug. 29, 2006, www.guardian.co.uk/eu/story/0,,1860140,00.html.

19. According to Nabil Shebai of *Islam Online*, the ratio of Muslim youth (between

Withholding recognition of the core identity of one party to the conflict discredits the sincerity of the peace process. Anti-Zionist and anti-Jewish rhetoric undermines prospects for resolution between Israel and the Palestinians, and among her Arab neighbors.

Anti-Zionism III: Internal Offensive

The offensive against Zionism is rife both outside and within Israel's borders. During the late decades of the twentieth century, Israeli academics and intellectuals promoted a new historical revisionism, seeking to debunk what they came to regard as Zionist *mythology*. Some revisionists deny the ethical validity of the Zionist idea, its Jewish roots and associate Zionism with colonialism and imperialism. Another position is *post*-Zionism – a claim that the establishment of the State of Israel extinguished the need for Zionism.

Some aspire to a secular democratic Israel focused neither on Jews nor Judaism. Though the rhetoric sounds progressive, universalist, and innocuous, it amounts to eradicating the Zionist purpose. Statehood has never and does not now require cultural or religious neutrality or uniformity. Jews have lived as a minority under the religious, political, and cultural order of non-Jewish societies for millennia. Among the nations of the world, Israel implements an open, accountable, pluralist, and egalitarian society, and is committed to betterment. There is no need to jettison Zionism in order for Arab, Muslim and Christian minorities to flourish within Israeli society. Israel is an historic and precious undertaking: one Jewish homeland on earth.

While embracing Zionism, there are legitimate grounds for critique. Critique ought to engage the many players in the Israeli-Palestinian and Middle-East struggles, local and international, state and non-governmental. Humanizing Israelis as well as Palestinians – learning to distinguish camps, views, and policies – will also help to nuance the discourse. Some critics appropriately draw attention to issues that were previously neglected by Israelis and our leaders. Unfortunately, many critics often over-compensate, and lose perspective on the purposes

---

45 and 50% of the Muslims) to EU youth is between 16 and 20%, retrieved Aug. 4, 2011, www.islamonline.net/servlet/Satellite?c=Article_C&cid=1156077742293& pagename=Zone-English-Muslim_Affairs%2FMAELayout.

and accomplishments of Israel. It is possible to support Israel while empathizing with the pain of all parties to this conflict *and* enable progress toward productive peace in the region. Western critics are too often poorly informed or selectively oblivious to their own and other countries' laws and practices in such areas as immigration and trade; justice and prison policy; intelligence, security, and war procedures; foreign aid; police and border control practices. Many base their views of Israel on naïve assumptions and insufficient knowledge. An organization of queers marched against Israel in a Toronto Gay Pride parade.[20] Israel is the only country in the Middle East that protects free lifestyle choices and prohibits discrimination on the basis of sexual preference. Under Palestinian authority, homosexuality is a crime punishable by law.[21] Israeli policy and practice must be seen more thoroughly in context through comparative analysis, and more realistically in relation to her neighbors and other states facing similar challenges, not according to platitudes, empty rhetoric, and trendy incriminations.

Consider one example of how anti-Israeli ideology functions within an academic setting. In 2006, Hebrew University awarded a master's degree in anthropology to Tal Nitzan based on a thesis entitled, "The Limits of the Occupation: The Rarity of Military Rape in the Israeli-Palestinian Conflict."[22] Not finding incidents of rape of Palestinian women by Israeli soldiers, Tal proposes that "the lack of organized military rape is an alternate way of realizing [particular] political goals." She continues, "In the Israeli-Palestinian conflict, it can be seen that the lack of military rape merely strengthens the ethnic boundaries and clarifies the inter-ethnic differences – just as organized military rape would have done." Tal argues that, "[t]he rejection of, just like the use of, intentional military rape can serve to reinforce group boundaries."[23] Published and awarded a prize by the Hebrew

20. See the Jewish Telegraphic Agency report, retrieved Aug. 4, 2011, www.jta.org/news/article/2011/05/26/3087895/toronto-rules-for-anti-israel-group-in-gay-pride-parade-flap.

21. See the Freedom House Report on Palestine (Palestinian Authority and Israeli-Occupied Territories), retrieved Aug. 4, 2011, www.freedomhouse.org/template.cfm?page=180.

22. Supervised by Prof. Eyal Ben Ari and Dr. Edna Lomsky-Feder, (in Hebrew), www.upfree.net/3100688.

23. The thesis attributes the absence of rape to a governmental program instilling

University's Shine Center, the thesis also received honorable mention by the Israeli Sociology Association for the Advancement of Scientific and Professional Sociology.[24] Tal Nitzan has proposed that, in terms of its racism and systematic dehumanization, the *absence* of rape by the Israeli military is equivalent to actually perpetrating rape. Where Israel is concerned, not rape *is* rape. Many theories might better explain the absence of rape. In spite of the research findings, this thesis justifies predetermined, circular conclusions.

There is increasing isolation of camps within and outside Israel. A self-effacing, even self-degrading demeanor permeates many sectors of Jewish and Israeli society and informs education.[25] At the same time, extreme nationalists assert expansive territorial claims. Settlers in the West Bank sometimes flaunt the institutions of democracy, including the Supreme Court. While reflection and self-criticism indicate a healthy and dynamic society intent on betterment, anti-Zionism disables confidence and commitment to the vital meaning and relevance of Israel. The void sometimes fills with trendy, purposely shocking rhetoric. The respected Israeli daily *Haaretz* published the following poem by Aharon Shabtai, indicating the currency that despondency has gained in Israeli society.

> Already from the window of the parked airplane one can see that we have returned to the same excrement from which we came.

racism in IDF soldiers who come to believe that Arab women are sub-human and not worthy rape victims. The basis of the research and analysis is 25 personal interviews with reserve soldiers, ages 23–32, who served as combat troops in the West Bank and Gaza during the second *intifada*-Palestinian Uprising. None of the soldiers supports or even indirectly confirms Nitzan's conclusions. Tal Nitzan, abstract, www.upfree.net/3693668.

24. Prof. Zali Gurevitch, head of the Shaine Center, made the decision to honor the thesis and defended it to the media iss.moonsite.co.il/index.aspx?id=1944.

"This was a very serious paper that asked two important questions: Is the relative lack of IDF rapes a noteworthy phenomenon, and if so, why is it that there are so few IDF rapes when in similar situations around the world, where rape is so much more common?" Hillel Fendel, "Hebrew U. Paper Finds: IDF Has Political Motives for Not Raping," *IsraelNationalNews.com Arutz Sheva*, 12/23/07, www.israelnationalnews.com/News/News.aspx/124674.

25. See an academic historian's reflection about one of the new textbooks, Eyal Naveh, "Memory and History and the Problem of Reconciliation: The Public Uproar over an Israeli History Textbook," www.fl.ulaval.ca/celat/histoire.memoire/histoire/cape1/naveh.htm.

But to complain, to lament, to cry,
Is only a part of the tax-package required of the educated citizen.
The country's corrupt, dishonorable and stuttering rulers want the
freezer to be filled with delicate literary meat. Therefore, I propose to
shorten the soul to a line that connects between two points:

A. To know that there is no difference between Yitzhak Rabin and
Benjamin Netanyahu . . .

B. The poet, the intellectual, is not one who reads Kafka or Marcel
Proust when liberty and justice are being trampled on in the markets.
No, in a forever-young body he stands, lowering his pants, and uri-
nates on the dying bonfire of Zionism . . .[26]

Shabtai refers to Israel with disdain, mocking the Ashkenazi leaders'
conceit about their Western literature while their society abuses its
own principles – justice and liberty. His tone reminds of the biblical
prophets rebuking the corruptions of the ancient Israelites. Yet his
message is neither hope nor encouragement to repair ailments, but a
smug denigration of Zionism. Rather than a glowing bonfire around
which the Zionists sing and dance the *hora* of old, the youth of this
generation pee on the last smoldering coals. This poem draws the
reader to the outside of the circle – to witness aloft while defiant youth
shun Jewish state-building.

In place of *post-* and *anti-*Zionist alienation, this book proposes involvement in the ongoing formulation of Jewish Peoplehood at home.

Alternate Odyssey

One of the foundation myths of Western culture is the Odyssey.
Homer's ancient epic conceives life as a journey. Odysseus departs
reluctantly from his native Ithaca, Greece, to join the Trojan campaign.
Paris, son of King Priam, had abducted and taken Helen to his father's
land. Helen was the much-sought daughter of Zeus and Leda. One of
Helen's original wooers, Odysseus had lost the contest for her hand.
Menelaus, the victorious suitor and king of Sparta, rallies the former
suitors to bring Helen back. The goal of the journey is the conquest
of a woman and, by extension, a land and her people. Relinquishing

---

26. Aharon Shabtai, "*Shtei Nekudot*," *Haaretz*, Oct. 11, 1998.

Helen would have been an insufferable humiliation, her capture a blow to Greek honor and potency. Homer's epic opens with a statement of Odysseus's purpose.

> Tell me, O muse, of that ingenious hero who traveled far and wide after he had sacked the famous town of Troy.
> Many cities did he visit, and many were the nations with whose manners and customs he was acquainted;
> moreover he suffered much by sea while trying to save his own life and bring his men safely home.[27]

The war and the journey stem from Helen's wrongful displacement; she must be returned *home*. Therefore, the Odyssey follows a circular route. After the war, the hero sets off from Troy on his adventures to return home to Ithaca. His spouse, Penelope, faithfully waits for him. Putting off the suitors who vie for her hand, by day, she spins a funeral robe, and at night she unravels her work. Her perpetually unproductive labor is a futile struggle against time and mortality, striving to hold life still. Odysseus expects to reintegrate into his former life with Penelope who yearns for the man who set out. She does not know the transformed warrior and adventurer. Penelope symbolizes a static *home*. Though Odysseus voyages, he concludes at his starting point.

The concept of a circular odyssey contrasts dramatically with epic journey narratives of the Jewish People. Throughout the *Tanakh*, in rabbinic, mystical and Hasidic texts, people are called upon to set forth from their specific and familiar territory toward an unseen destination, an unknown land, to an un-anticipatable state. The journey does not return to the point of departure. *Lekh lekha* is the paradigm case. In Genesis, God instructs Avram to leave his native land, his kin, his family home, and go to a land that God will show him.

> God said to Avram, "Go out from your native land and from the house of your kin to the land that I will show you. I will make of you a great nation, and I will bless you; I will make your name great, and you shall be a blessing." (Genesis 12:1–2)

Enigmatically, this command supplies no justification for the choice of Avram. Advocating for his worthiness, tales abound of Avram early

---

27. Homer, *The Odyssey*, opening lines.

monotheistic tendencies. They tell of how he deduces the divine Creator by observing creation. He smashes idols in his father's shop to demonstrate their impotence and the iconoclasm of his new faith. The text indicates Avram's readiness to journey toward the unknown. Movement through space symbolizes Avram's movement in consciousness. Hasidic masters suggest that the divine constantly beckons us toward more meaningful, spiritual, and adventurous living. The question is whether we free ourselves from the mundane to embark on our life adventure. Avraham and Sarah are both willing recruits. Their identities, symbolized by their changed names, transform with the journey; returning to their starting point is inconceivable.

The biblical Rivka is similarly an adventurer, sprite and eager. Invited to leave her kin and all that is familiar, to immigrate to an unknown land and spouse, Rivka opts to take the risk.

> They said, "Let us call the young woman and ask for her reply." They called Rivka and said to her, "Will you go with this man?" And she said, "I will." (24:57–58)

Ruth, a Moabite bereft of her spouse, chooses to accompany her Jewish mother-in-law, Naomi, to her homeland. She leaves her family to travel to Canaan. There Ruth redeems lost lives in bleak exile. In Israel, she gives birth to the messianic lineage. With brazen commitment and trust, she forges ahead into the unknown.

> Ruth said, "Do not entreat me to leave you, and to return from following after you. For wherever you go, I will go; and where you lodge, I will lodge. Your people shall be my people, and your God my God. Where you die, will I die, and there will I be buried. God does so to me, and more also, nothing but death will separate me from you." (Ruth 1:16–17)

In these narratives, the journey away from one's point of origin toward Israel is an act of faith, a vision. Unsettled, the voyager relinquishes illusions of control and becomes more vulnerable to the world and its inhabitants. The road away from the familiar brings fresh perspective, induces introspection and self-improvement.

Though he leads them out of slavery, Moses, the greatest prophet of Israel, does not succeed to enter the Promised Land. This aching failure frames the narrative of the Israelite Exodus from Egypt – the

Torah concludes on the far side of the river. Yet, the journey does not end at the border. The land of Israel becomes the destination, not only in terms of geography, but as an aim toward ever-increasing fulfillment.

This book demonstrates how the journey continues *into* the land. Native-born Israelis are as much part of the *lekh lekha* journey as immigrants. All partake of the historic opportunity to contribute toward a better, more fulfilled Zion(ism).

Freedom

Many young nations that declared political autonomy from the imperial powers of the northwestern hemisphere have yet to achieve proper sustenance for their citizens and/or open and free society. These nations are now part of the *two-thirds* world where development and the distribution of resources are major challenges in the post-modern era.[28] At the intersection of continents, of East and West, *developed* and *developing*, Israelis build and strive toward an ever more sustaining, thriving civil society, economy, and politics.

In her early stages, Israel instituted social democratic institutions to provide for and develop her population, and advance scholarship, arts, agriculture, and technology. Israeli governments made highly subsidized public education available to all citizens – from kindergarten through university. Before and even with the rise of anti-Zionism, Israel assists other young nations, particularly in Africa. Zionists pioneered a society and economy – the *kibbutz* and *moshav* – to address the exigencies of the land, malarial swamps, and Arab attacks on Jewish settlements. To some extent, Western economic values – profit motives and individualism – erode the spirit of collaborative settlement. The gap between the affluent and those who suffer unemployment, hunger, and poverty grows increasingly to resemble the American condition with pockets of poverty and under-development. Yet, this oft-cited indicator must be taken in perspective. Social services, including medical coverage, have always been universal in Israel. Israel continues to offer a unique opportunity to express and refine Jewish approaches to social responsibility.

---

28. "Two-thirds world" describes the so-called *developing* world that comprises two-thirds of the world population and geographic territory.

Israel's radical democracy functions with a heterogeneous population descended from survivors of traumas, and refugees. From the outset, Israel has been absorbing massive immigrations from all quarters of the earth, and initiating people into civil society – political participation and accountability, due legal and democratic process, openness, tolerance, critical media, and entrepreneurism. The global trend toward splintering of discreet ethnicities makes it more difficult to integrate disparate people into a shared civil and political frame. Combining multiple and contradictory human commitments into a coherent society continues to be one of the challenges and blessings of Israel. In Israel, cultures and languages of the East and West converge. Judaism, Christianity, and Islam coexist; closed communities of ultra-religiosity and theocracy share space and administration with spiritual and secular communities from dozens of ethnicities. Jews, Druse, Christians, and some Muslims – women and men, serve together in the Israel Defense Forces, and in the Border Police.[29] Israel has become a cutting-edge experiment in multiculturalism.

Iconoclasm

Beginning with Avraham breaking the idols in his father's shop, iconoclasm has long been a feature of Jewish identity. Ending the long struggle for freedom *from* authority, from the state, the current challenge is to express Jewish yearning and freedom with and through the instruments of the state. Israel is the destination to which the Israelite people arrived in order to actualize ourselves and not a place to escape from or rebel against. With the birth of Israel, Jews are suddenly meant to become emotionally, politically, spiritually, and economically committed to their state and its institutions. Moral action is relatively easy to contemplate in opposition to state policy, but much harder to effect when seated in government. The transformation of Jews from object of state policy to empowered subject demands a complete change in consciousness. Whereas in biblical Egypt, God mediates Jewish

---

29. See, for example, "First female Arab soldier joins elite unit 669," Ynet, 4.4.08, retrieved Aug. 7, 2011, www.ynet.co.il/english/articles/0,7340,L-3527584,00. html, and "Minorities in the IDF," *Jewish Daily*, 27.08.2011, retrieved July 27, 2011, http://www.jewishideasdaily.com/content/module/2011/7/27/main-feature/1/minorities-in-the-idf.

responsibility, in Israel, the Jewish People are directly responsible. One aspect of enslavement is lack of responsibility; the taskmaster directs a slave in all details of life. Liberation moves people toward responsible self-determination.

Israel aspires to express the collective freedom of the Jewish People, "the initial flowering of the redemption," in such a way that does not infringe any person. This tremendously difficult project – never accomplished by any nation in the history of humanity – requires nurture, support, and perseverance. Israel is at once a conscionable member of the global ruling establishment, while at the same time profoundly experimental. The attainment of Exodus mandates change not only from oppressed to empowered, but from rebel to responsible citizen. This change beckons beyond fear and survival.

Jewish Continuity?

Many Jewish organizations have adopted two principle strategies to ensure the *continuity* of the Jewish People:

1 Jewish text study, including all forms of Jewish literacy; and
2 Israel experience.

The widespread campaign for Jewish "literacy" has made the study of Jewish texts a priority in Jewish schools, synagogue adult education programs, *midrashot* and *yeshivot*, as well as in post-secondary institutions, universities, and colleges. In Israel, the government is instituting enhanced text study throughout the national school system. Post-secondary, pre-army study programs multiply. The first "secular yeshivot" are established in Tel Aviv and Jerusalem.[30] In general, the programs of study tend to emphasize the beauty, intellectual rigor and complexity, history, and in some places, spiritual wisdom to which Jewish texts give access. Another goal of the contemporary renaissance of Jewish text study, particularly outside of Israel, has been to place Jewish books on the shelves of Western culture. In addition to the *Tanakh*, the Talmud, rabbinic and mystical treatises, and legal codes, Jewish philosophic, literary, ethical, legal, and political works rank among the great books in the Western canon. Jewish leaders use

---

30. The BINA Center for Jewish Identity and Hebrew Culture, www.bina.org.il/english.htm.; HaYeshiva HaChilonit BiYerushalayim, http://www.hayeshiva.org.il/.

text study to reflect and affirm the worthiness and dignity of Judaism and the Jewish People. This goal is best achieved by studying affirming texts that make people feel proud to be Jews.

Often, the approach to Israel echoes this approach to texts. Corresponding to the choice of texts, Israel curriculum focuses on affirmation, endorsement of Israel and her policies. Widening the lens would capture difficulties of present society and a more complex picture of both the state and texts of the Jewish People. While so many young people feel more critical and disenchanted with both Judaism and Israel, guided Israel experiences mainly glorify the past, and feature a lustrous, romanticized present. To a large extent, these images are presented in congenial texts and contemporary cultural artifacts. Often, education about Israel deals with the period from the early Zionists through the establishment of the State and the first couple of pioneering decades. The years of social and agricultural entrepreneurialism, military heroism, and youthful democracy are indeed inspiring. Overcompensating for anti-Zionism, many take recourse to idealized versions of Judaism and Israel. The Jewish establishment broadcasts mottos of unflinching support – "We Are One," "We Stand Together." Though these sentiments are edifying, we also need focused, caring engagement. Pressing the priority of survival often justifies overlooking crises of faith and purpose. Reacting to and defending against the vicious ideological onslaught, simplistic messages arrest the struggle for the meaning and relevance of contemporary Zionism. This emotional-political climate of defensiveness invites reactionary responses. The religious and political right and fundamentalist Christians who harbor hopes that the Jewish state will hasten the apocalypse have become major Israel supporters. These factions alienate the majority of Jews, young and old. We need refined, responsible, and constructive Zionist alternatives.

"Difficult" Texts and Life

Israel is a multi-dimensional text – extending in space and through time. The comparison between texts and Israel clarifies advantages to dealing with difficulties in both.

While some passages in the Torah and Talmud are gratifying, others chafe against our contemporary sensibilities. Jewish texts that mandate us to give charity, deal fairly in business, and prescribe Shabbat rest from the hectic week affirm us and our faith in the goodness of Judaism and the Jewish People. Similarly we feel pride and validation when we learn about Israelis making the Negev desert bloom, about the bold Israeli rescue of hostages taken by terrorists to Entebbe, and the inventive and prolific Israeli silicon wadi – the high-tech industry. We can also feel moved when we visit places where events in our ancient texts transpired: in Elijah's cave in the Carmel mountain ridge, the "still small voice" of the divine echoes.[31]

By contrast, some texts and events provoke, exasperate, make us cringe and revile, feel frustrated and furious, excluded, embarrassed, defensive, offended, even wounded and alienated. Every tradition and nation has its "difficult passages." Sometimes we euphemize difficulties, sometimes we ignore them, sometimes we become obsessed with them and denigrate ourselves on their account. The question is how to genuinely engage with them. Choosing to study difficult texts and face difficulties in life proposes a different role for text study and for our relationship with Israel. Beyond the goal of affirming Jewish identity, the commitment to wrestle is an unsettling but worthwhile proposition, a step on a journey into mature commitment and responsibility.

Conquest and Power

Living in the land of Israel embroils Jews in the dilemmas of power. Passages in the Bible prescribe violent treatment of the inhabitants and their possessions. Consider a passage about Joshua's initial conquest of the land.

> They [the Israelites] took the field against Midian, as the Lord had commanded Moses, and slew every male. Along with their other victims, they slew the kings of Midian: Evi, Rekem, Zur, Hur, and Reba, the five kings of Midian. They also put Balaam son of Beor to the sword.
>
> The Israelites took the women and children of the Midianites captive, and seized as booty all their beasts, all their herds, and all their wealth. And they destroyed by fire all the towns in which they were settled, and their encampments. They gathered all the spoil and all

---

31. II Kings 19:12.

the booty, man and beast, and they brought the captives, the booty, and the spoil to Moses, Eleazar the priest, and the whole Israelite community, at the camp in the steppes of Moab, at the Jordan near Jericho.

Moses, Eleazar the priest, and all the chieftains of the community came out to meet them outside the camp. Moses became angry with the commanders of the army, the officers of thousands and the officers of hundreds, who had come back from the military campaign. Moses said to them, "You have spared every female! Yet they are the very ones who, at the bidding of Balaam, induced the Israelites to trespass against the Lord in the matter of Peor, so that the Lord's community was struck by the plague. Now, therefore, slay every male among the children, and slay also every woman who has known a man carnally; but spare every young woman who has not had carnal relations with a man. (Numbers 31:7–18)

Seeking to protect the Israelites from the temptations of idolatry, the *Tanakh* states vicious policies against the dwellers of Canaan. Two chapters later, the text relates further to the religious practices of the inhabitants of the land.

In the steppes of Moab, at the Jordan near Jericho, the Lord spoke to Moses, saying: Speak to the Israelite people and say to them: When you cross the Jordan into the land of Canaan, you shall dispossess all the inhabitants of the land; you shall destroy all their figured objects; you shall destroy all their molten images, and you shall demolish all their cult places. And you shall take possession of the land and settle in it, for I have assigned the land to you to possess. You shall apportion the land among yourselves by lot, clan by clan: with larger groups increase the share, with smaller groups reduce the share. Wherever the lot falls for anyone, that shall be his. You shall have your portions according to your ancestral tribes. But if you do not dispossess the inhabitants of the land, those whom you allow to remain shall be stings in your eyes and thorns in your sides, and they shall harass you in the land in which you live; so that I will do to you what I planned to do to them. (33:50–56)

These biblical passages narrate scenes attributed to the Bronze Age – three thousand years ago – that might or might not be historical.

Fearing for the vulnerability of early Israelite faith and practice, these texts show no tolerance for *otherness*.[32] They bring us face-to-face with excess zeal and ethnocentrism and demand our attention to choices about how to relate to difference. The same Torah records the requirement to treat strangers in our midst with justice and caring because "once we were strangers in Egypt" on four different occasions.[33] The Exodus teaches awareness of *others*, strangers, on account of our own suffering in exile. On these grounds, argues the Torah, we need to be particularly fastidious about kindness to "others" when we are at home in our own land. Safeguarding and fostering uniqueness while respecting and embracing difference is one of the tasks of multicultural society in general, and Israel in particular.

Chosenness

While in this twenty-first century, the diversity of human faith and practice has been well-established, many religious groups maintain their teachings of superiority. Jewish liturgy is replete with the doctrine of *chosenness*. The blessing recited on the public Torah reading includes the divine attribution, "Who has chosen us from among all the nations – אשר בחר בנו מכל העמים." The private sanctification of the morning prayers, "Uva leZion," includes the statement, "who has distinguished us from those who are [mistaken] lost and given us the true Torah." Every Jewish prayer session concludes with the "Aleinu," an ancient formula originally recited on the High Holy Days. According to Hai Gaon, the head of the Pumbedita Talmudic academy during the eleventh century CE (modern-day Fallujah in Iraq), Joshua composed it when his army captured Jericho.[34] The prayer praises the Master of All,

> ... who did not make us as the nations of the lands, and did not place us like the families of the earth who prostrate to vanity and emptiness, and pray to a god who does not save.

---

32. In 2001, the Muslim extremist Taliban regime dynamited the monumental sixth-century stone Buddhas of Afghanistan. The 55- and 37-meter-high statues had been carved into the side of the Bamyan cliffs.

33. Ex. 22:20, 23:9; Lev. 19:34; Deut. 10:19.

34. תשובת הגאונים, שערי תשובה סי' מד.

In these texts, the Torah and the land bear witness to chosenness. During the exile, these claims evoked the ire of nations. In 1703, the Prussian king decreed the erasure of the phrase on the grounds that it insults Christianity (and all other religions). He demanded that the leader chant the prayer aloud in order to ensure that the Jews did not secretly utter the offensive phrase. The king appointed supervisors to be present in synagogues during the recitation. No longer subjected to the supervision of a foreign censor, many communities today recite the most offensive part of the *"Aleinu"* prayer intact. Some Ashkenazi communities accept the erasure. Some recite the line unabashed; others cringe while they recite it. Liberal Jewish movements expunge the ethnocentrism.

The first Prime Minister of Israel, David Ben Gurion, cited a phrase from biblical Isaiah's prophesy of peace, "light unto the nations," to describe his vision for the State.[35] Ben Gurion regarded the statement as a privilege and responsibility, yet its tone of superiority rankles. Partly in defiance of taboos and ethnocentrism, many post-modern Jews, particularly Israelis, abandon Judaism and/or seek their spiritual home in *other* religions and spiritual traditions, in Hinduism, Buddhism, yoga, meditation, and many alternative paths.

Zionism inherits the need to address Jewish ethnocentrism responsibly. No longer a disempowered minority dispersed throughout the world, Israel installs Judaism among the faiths of the global community of nations. Jewish and Israeli dignity can coexist with religious tolerance and respect for other traditions and nations. Zionist claims to inhabit Israel need not debase the culture, religion, or ethnicity of any people. Jewish and Israeli schools, and all formal and informal institutions, must work harder to achieve more humility and respect for peoples, their beliefs, and practices.

Diagnosis and Loving Critique

The "difficulty" in our texts and behaviors is bound up with the relationship between the Jewish People, our homeland, and the rest of the nations of the world. Facing these kinds of texts relates to some of the difficult challenges facing Israel today. Questions about territo-

---

35. Isa. 42:6, 49:6, 60:3.

rial entitlement, Jewish destiny, relations among different ethnic and religious populations, relationships between Jewish monotheism and other religions, justifications for and the extent of the use of force – are among the issues at stake.

Palestinian nationalism and rebellion against the Israeli occupation increasingly call into question some of the old Zionist assumptions and practices. Social stratification of classes, economic unfairness and poverty, discrimination against minorities – all of these coexist with and contradict the ethical visions of the prophets, of the sages, and of the Zionist movements. With the waves of Ethiopian immigration, racism is more pervasive in Israel. These ailments are particularly troubling in the wake of the Zionist dream of an equal, fair, and open society. The ideal of Jews building our homeland, and being built by that labor has capitulated to the market temptation to use cheaper Palestinian, and more recently, international migrant workers in the building and manufacturing industries. Whereas agriculture and self-sustenance were a primary occupation of both the biblical settlers and the Zionist pioneers, non-Jews principally perform the manual labor of food production in contemporary Israel. Israel has become a hub for trafficking in women for the purposes of prostitution. Political corruption is rampant: an Israeli Jew assassinated our own Prime Minister; the office of the President of the State of Israel has been disgraced. A former Prime Minister stood accused of corruption and bribery. Though facing serious ecological perils, particularly in relation to water resources, Israel often implements environmentally irresponsible policies.[36]

We need to work with the difficulties in the texts and in life face-to-face, and refine ourselves according to the most rigorous ethical standards for this age. By tackling our difficult texts and interpreting our tradition critically, we refine and enrich our Zionist ideas and practices. This is part of the revolution of Zionism and the significance of reviving the Jewish nation after millennia of exile.

At certain moments of stock-taking, often prompted by public outcry, the Israeli establishment expresses awareness and will to

---

36. See for example, Miriam Haran, Rana Samuels, Shoshana Gabbai, Uri Mingelgrin, "Quality indicators of the state of chemical pollution in Israel," *Israel Journal of Chemistry*, 2002, vol.42 (1), 119–132.

scrutinize and seek to improve public ethical standards and policies. Investigating the decision-making and conduct of the 2006 Lebanon War, the Interim Report of the public Winograd Commission, states:

> The Commission was appointed due to a strong sense of a crisis and deep disappointment with the consequences of the campaign and the way it was conducted. We regarded and accepted this difficult task both as a duty and a privilege. It is our belief that the larger the event and the deeper the feeling of crisis – the greater the opportunity to change and improve matters which are essential for the security and the flourishing of state and society in Israel. We believe Israeli society has great strength and resilience, with a robust sense of the justice of its being and of its achievements. These, too, were expressed during the war in Lebanon and after it. At the same time, we must not underrate deep failures among us.
>
> This conception of our role affected the way we operated. No-one underestimates the need to study what happened in the past, including the imposition of personal responsibility. The past is the key for learning lessons for the future. Nonetheless, learning these lessons and actually implementing them are the most serious implication of the conclusions of the Commission.[37]

This eloquent preamble to a scathing critique of the highest officials of the Israeli administration reveals crisis coexisting with aspirations toward betterment. Due to extreme scrutiny from within and outside, and her willingness to be exposed, Israel's difficulties are often transparent. While transparency makes Israel an easy target, Israel's performance needs to be evaluated not only in terms of theoretical standards, but in relation to other nations and comparable situations. No nation or institution fulfills the highest human ethical standards, regardless of rhetoric. As we should behave with a dear friend, our critique ought to engage with difficulties while upholding our commitment, to seek out responsible ways to relieve distress, and to genuinely contribute to improvement. Thousands of NGOs and social entrepreneurs operate in Israel, criticizing, addressing social and economic gaps, and working to improve society. Rather than affirming ourselves as we are, engaging

---

37. www.mfa.gov.il/MFA/Government/Communiques/2007/Winograd+Inquiry+Commission+submits+Interim+Report+30-Apr-2007.htm.

difficult texts and the complexities of Israel suggests potential routes to personal and social betterment. Like passionate lovers, our relationship with Israel and her difficulties prompts us toward fulfillment even as we bare ourselves and take risks.

Since Maccabean times, Judaism has not been a defining feature of a full-fledged society. Jewish law and practice have had scant occasion to tangle with the businesses of government, military, and economy. During sixty years of statehood, Israel has been striving to create and live out a complex identity as a modern democratic society that is also a *Jewish* homeland in a meaningful sense. The relevance of Judaism to the Jewish state is a matter of dissent with a wide variety of strongly held views. In different sectors, Israeli citizens feel completely alienated from Judaism while others burn with religious fundamentalism. Many campaign virulently against religious coercion by state and constituent parties. Public Shabbat observance, marriage, divorce, and burial are among the contested issues. These are a source of discontent particularly among secular Jews who long for alternatives. Precisely how Judaism(s) are to be expressed in the formal and informal structures of Israeli society: in language, the national calendar and public rituals, the legislature and court systems, institutions of education, finance, health care, the army, immigration, public ritual – all of these areas are the subject of vibrant contention among people who hold incompatible commitments, to the nation, to humanity, and to the divine. These issues are subject to debate – at home, in community centers, in educational institutions, in the media, in the Knesset, and the Supreme Court.

Israel renegotiates Jewish iconoclasm. When democratic, religious or ethical convictions contradict one another, sometimes all of the mechanisms legitimized by democracy are exhausted. Civil disobedience is only appropriate within a framework that supports the institutions of civil society and takes responsibility for the ongoing health and vitality of Israel. The public campaign and resistance to the government policy of withdrawal from the Gush Katif settlements in the Gaza Strip during the summer of 2005 tested boundaries of dissent. The settlers expressed their passion and religious fervor through confrontation with and violation of one of the major institutions of Israeli society – calling upon soldiers to disobey orders to evict the settlers. This example highlights the intensity and complexity of homeland and territory for the Jewish People. The daily struggles of Israeli society explore multiple dimensions of Jewish destiny, a trajectory forward from the biblical period into the twenty-first century.

The "March of the Living"

Israel is an effective mechanism for Jewish identity-building – particularly for non-Israelis. One of the reasons that Israel "works" in the Jewish identity-construction project is that Israel has the potential to arouse fresh, intense, positive emotions, something that the post-Holocaust guilt methods of "Never Forget" do not usually accomplish. The "March of the Living" culminates at the Israeli airport.

> The March of the Living is an international, educational program that brings Jewish teens from all over the world to Poland on Yom Hashoah, Holocaust Memorial Day, to march from Auschwitz to Birkenau, the largest concentration camp complex built during World War II, and then to Israel to observe Yom HaZikaron, Israel Memorial Day, and Yom Ha'Atzmaut, Israel Independence Day.
>
> The goal of the March of the Living is for these young people to learn the lessons of the Holocaust and to lead the Jewish people into the future vowing "Never Again."[38]

Against the dark void of the death camps, the multi-dimensionality of a functioning Jewish society – with Hebrew its living language – is vibrant, colorful, and compelling. As Simone de Beauvoir poignantly observes, "[T]he most ardent recollections are cold in comparison with an actual, present sensation."[39]

Israel programmers tend to idealize and over-simplify Zionism. Delighting in the presence of the Jewish People in the land, many shirk the earthly challenges of this stage of nation-building. This generation deserves rich and meaningful encounters with Israel. Sharing the struggles openly is more real than pretending that all is well. The difficult texts of Israel invite commitment and responsibility. Israel is not a fantasy escape from the trials of human coexistence. Israel is not a Jewish Disney Land.

---

38. March of the Living website. www.motl.org/.
39. *The Second Sex,* H. M. Parshley, trans., New York: Knopf 1952/1993), 172.

Worlds (A)Part

Leaders, policy-makers, and educators of the organized Jewish community underwrite the journeys of young Jewish adults to Israel. Many of their post-high school Israeli counterparts are also taking a "gap year." For the Israelis, the next stage is army service; for the rest of Jewry, it is often four years of college education, or work and play.

Jewish young people come to Israel on various short-term and one-year programs. Youth movements, non-profit organizations, post-secondary colleges and universities, kibbutzim, and *yeshivot* run programs proffering various ideologies, skills, and opportunities – traditional Zionism, outdoor skills, religious study and observance, and more. According to guidelines devised by the Jewish Agency for Israel, the programs combine Hebrew, Jewish/Israel study with travel and volunteering. In addition to subsidies from the program benefactors, including philanthropic foundations and Israeli agencies, parents are funding their children's expenses. Many of the participants defer their acceptance into college or university to attend. For these young people, a program in Israel is a welcome departure from home, the first taste of independence. The programs focus on personal growth and encounter with Israel – a living museum of the Jewish People. Beyond the requirement of attendance, the students have few obligations. The gap year is a transit point en route to higher education, career, and family-life.

For Israelis at the same stage, army service looms large. Some of the Israeli programs, *mechinot*, involve academic study to complete or improve high school matriculation exams, social service, and/or yeshiva learning. Like the programs for young people from abroad, some Israelis explore their relationship with Israel, land and institutions, focusing on the group process among young citizens. Some involve rigorous physical training to prepare future soldiers for combat units. Religious young women have the option of national service in place of army service, taking direct full-time responsibility for the lives of needy students in youth villages, for example. More of these frameworks are also evolving for Israeli young men. There are also development town initiatives, education and social action projects of many varieties. While participating, some young Israeli wo/men are periodically negotiating various selection trials for special units in preparation for enlistment the following year, including the air force pilot course, intelligence, paratroops, anti-terror, and "seals." Along with the camaraderie among peers, there is an atmosphere of seriousness, heavy-headedness, responsibility, and fear that they share as Jews who incur responsibility for the security of their nation.

Israeli and Diaspora Jews of the same age, in the same place, inhabit utterly different realities. Diaspora Jews experience a feeling of the world as an open playground, thrilling-adventure-under-control, life brimming with the potential to study, to earn, to socialize, to consume, to own, and to enjoy.

Israelis experience the obligation to give, to serve, to contribute, and to sacrifice. Some will soon encounter mortal danger, testing themselves at the limit of their strength and endurance, their faithfulness to principles, and their obedience. They will be expected to fulfill demands to defend and protect family, state, and People. In the army, some are called upon to enforce policies that might disturb their conscience. They submit life and limb to a massive and powerful institution that controls and determines every motion. Israelis experience two, three, or more years with scant opportunity to escape the commander's eye.

Beta Yisrael

The case of Ethiopian immigrants to Israel highlights the extreme acculturation process that culminates in army service. When they arrive, many are assigned names by absorption officials; Addis and Mangisto, Asneka and Almaz become David and Rachel. At the same time as their friends continue to call them by the names they held from their infancy, schools and institutions refer to them by the new Jewish/Israeli names. One young man, Noam, arrived from a remote village when he was twelve. During his childhood and young adulthood, his parents had hidden his Jewish identity from him so that he could get along with the non-Jewish villagers and attend the local school. They secretly lit candles on Friday night without explanation, their only Jewish observance (like some Conversos in Spain during the fourteenth and fifteenth century). Noam's father served six years in the Ethiopian army. Having had his Jewishness suddenly revealed to him, Noam was airlifted to Israel with his large family. He says that they would be murdered if they tried to return to their village in Ethiopia – all their property and land had been confiscated. After a grueling basic training – he won an award for excellence for his performance – he serves with the Border Police, posted in a Palestinian village between Beit Lechem and Ramallah. There, in addition to guard duty at the base that is the constant target of stone-throwing and Molotov cocktails, Noam performs house search-and-arrest operations against suspected terrorists. His conviction to defend the safety of his People drives him to fulfill his responsibilities beyond the expectations of his officers. With his head hung low, he acknowledges that he also experiences racism in the system that affects his prospects for promotion, promotion that he dearly seeks.

Convergence?

After the army, many Israeli young people flee from the weighty demands on their lives. Israelis roam the globe in search of freedom, space, and meaning. Many return to undertake early the commitments of marriage and childbearing, also to begin post-secondary study.[40] Meanwhile, most of their overseas counterparts have completed their baccalaureate, are beginning graduate or professional studies, or are launching their careers and families.

The mutual alienation of Israel and the Jewish community throughout the world does not suit the contemporary predicament of the Jewish People. How, or ought the separate realities of Diaspora and Israeli Jews to be reconciled? These disparate worlds of Jewish young adulthood converge at a troubling connection point. Young Israelis defending the Jewish state make possible the Disney Land Israel that their Diaspora peers enjoy and consume carefree. These roles are particularly apparent during a crisis. During the summer of 2006, while the Second Lebanon War was raging in the north and Israeli young people were called up to fight Hezbollah forces, Diaspora programs were withdrawing their participants from the north and even recalling them *home* to safety.

---

40. Leif Danziger, Shoshana Neuman, "On the age at marriage: Theory and evidence from Jews and Moslems in Israel," *Journal of Economic Behavior & Organization*, 40(2), 1999, 179–193.

Beyond the army service that Israelis discharge to protect Diaspora Jews when they visit Israel and to rescue Jews outside of Israel when they are in danger, the dignity and well-being of Jews throughout the world depends upon the fate of Israel. After the Six-Day War in June 1967, Diaspora Jews stood tall, bearing the signs of their Jewish identity outwardly. Being a Jew became *cool* because being Israeli was cool. As the OPEC oil embargo and the First *Intifada* – Palestinian Uprising heated up, being Israeli became less cool. The burden to defend Jewry grew even weightier as civilian targets of terror increased. After the 2006 Lebanon War, world Jewish leaders gathered in Israel during a rash of anti-Semitic incidents to strategize about what they considered to be a deteriorating security situation in their regions. Rabbi Israel Singer, chairman of the World Jewish Congress Policy Council, was quoted as saying that "the situation in the Middle East is not just Israel's problem, but it reflects on small Jewish communities all around the world."[41] This candid acknowledgment of inter-dependence calls for us to re-evaluate the distribution of responsibilities and opportunities among world Jewry.

Military Land

At the same time as critiquing the *Disney Land* of Jews visiting Israel, we peel back the glorification of Israeli army experience – *Military Land*. While arising from a legitimate need to defend civilians from proven threats, Military Land perpetuates a culture in which force is an instrument of identity and power, even meaning. Military Land supports hierarchy, privileges maleness, demands conformity, subsumes individuality, prepares for combat, seeks victory. Military Land normalizes the possibility and the actuality of life sacrifice. The military claims priority and, derivatively, trivializes the daily practices of service in society, of caring for young and old. The values and behaviors of the army impose a gendered hierarchy that pervades society. In Military Land, women are often as marginal as their power.[42] The structure and methods of military command seep into many domains

---

41. Vita Bekker, "Wave of Bias Attacks Sweeps Diaspora" *Forward*, Sept. 2, 2006, www.forward.com/articles/wave-of-bias-attacks-sweeps-diaspora/.

42. See H. Patricia Hynes, "On the battlefield of women's bodies: An overview of the harm of war to women," *Women's Studies International Forum*, 2004, 27(5/6), 431.

of Israeli civilian life. Many prominent political positions including the office of Prime Minister have been dominated by retired high-ranking and elite soldiers.[43]

The competence of Jews to defend our own lives has overtaken the stereotype of the pale, spindly Jewish weakling, often the object of caricature, mockery, and persecution. Military Land figures the Israeli body as a courageous soldier, muscular, weapon-bearing, in short, invincible. For some, joy at the reversal from powerlessness to power distorts human priorities. The Israeli military is not a goal in itself but an unavoidable instrument whose only purpose ought is to ensure Israel's survival and defend the Jewish People. Despite accusations to the contrary, the IDF operates according to the highest standards of military ethics.[44]

Jewish National Service

While dealing with war, terrorism, unresolved borders, absorbing complex populations, and disputed territories, Zionism has progressed very far toward fulfilling its initial purposes – to create and consolidate the infrastructure of the Jewish homeland. Yet, Jewish homecoming in the land of Israel is only partially a material pursuit. Secure and lasting peace, a flourishing culture that integrates and celebrates the diversity of the Jewish People and the minority populations, and nurtures a dynamic and developing Jewish society require much more than military competence and economic viability. Many visitors come to Israel to "see" the land as voyeurs, as if it is an object to be beheld with the

---

43. For an academic analysis, see Udi Lebel, "'Communicating Security': Civil–Military Relations in Israel," *Israel Affairs*, Jul. 2006, Vol. 12 Issue 3, 361–364; Amir Bar-Or, "Political–Military Relations in Israel, 1996–2003," *Israel Affairs*, Jul. 2006, Vol. 12 Issue 3, 365–37," *Israel Affairs*, Jul. 2006, Vol. 12, Issue 3, 430–438.

In the popular press, Hillel Halkin, "Israel's Army of Politics," *New York Sun*, January 23, 2007, www.nysun.com/article/47180.

44. The IDF basic statement of ethics, "Spirit of the IDF." Retrieved Feb 15, 2012, http://dover.idf.il/IDF/English/about/doctrine/ethics.htm. See Avi Sagi, "The Spirit of the IDF Ethics Code and the Investigation of Operation Cast Lead, Shalom Hartman Institute, 23.11.2009. Retrieved, Feb 16, 2012, http://www.hartman.org.il/Blogs_View.asp?Article_Id=401&Cat_Id=275&Cat_Type=Blogs. Asa Kasher, "Operation Cast Lead and the Ethics of Just War," Azure no. 37, Summer 5769/2009, 16pp.

eyes. This was the fatal error of the biblical scouts whose superficial vision, fear, and criticism plunged the Israelites into pointless wandering in the desert until a new generation came forth with the desire and readiness to commit to living in the land.[45] Even studying history, language, nature, and national accomplishments – worthy pursuits in themselves – do not guarantee a meaningful relationship with Israel and her people.

Conceiving the destiny of world Jewry as a joint endeavor, we can begin to collaboratively distribute responsibilities for the security and thriving of the Jewish People in the land of Israel and throughout the world in the coming generations. The vision of Masa: Israel Journey is to bring massive numbers of young people to Israel for long-term programs.[46] Beyond *viewing*, a year-long commitment might initiate a shared venture for Israelis and Jews from around the world – a Jewish National Service Corps. Every Jew could serve the Jewish People for one to three years, in different capacities and communities – in arms, in social services, education, agriculture, ecology, arts, health, *et cetera*.

Jews who arrive in Israel from the West bring with them the experience of religious pluralism as a minority in democratic civil society. One American young woman visiting Israel explains how going to the Kotel, the Western Wall, alienates her from Israeli Judaism. She feels that the women's side of the partition is lonely, quiet, and weepy, not a joyous celebration of Jewish homecoming. Being in Israel, she needs to bracket her connection with Jewish tradition in order to survive often harsh Israeli intolerance and delegitimizing of her Jewish faith, practice, and sensibilities. Conservative, egalitarian, liberal, Reform, humanitarian, Reconstructionist, and renewal Jews – the vast majority of the Jewish People – find scant affirmation of their egalitarian progressive Judaism in Israel. Often they experience denigration. Israeli religious Orthodoxy blatantly offends against Israeli ideals and law that illegalize discrimination on the basis of sex. In spite of the fact that the vast majority of Israelis do not identify as *religious* or practice according to Orthodox interpretations, they acquiesce to the dominion of an ultra-Orthodox chief rabbinate over their personal status. Israel has made major strides in the realms of education, leadership, and spiritual

---

45. Num. 13–14.
46. http://www.masaisrael.org/masa/english/.

office, yet the participation of women in Israeli public functions and responsibilities of Jewish society has yet to achieve full expression.

A Jewish National Service Corps has potential to renew Zionist visions with better reciprocity and cross-fertilization among the Jewish People. Such a framework proposes to grapple with the "difficult texts" of the Jewish People in a culture of productive controversy.

Israeli Torah

One of the long-standing features of Jewish life is *machloket*: dispute. The rabbinic texts record ongoing, dynamic debates among sages. The Oral Torah is layered with generations of argument, revisiting difficult questions and exploring new ones, anchoring opinions in biblical proofs whose meaning shifts with new and unanticipated contexts. The most popular and authoritative text of the Oral Torah is the Talmud compiled and redacted in Babylon during the four centuries following the destruction of the Second Jerusalem. Much of the content pertains to the defunct Temple rituals. There are no Babylonian tractates interpreting the Mishnaic Order *Zeraim-Seeds* that deal with inhabiting the land of Israel.[47] This omission is not coincidental. In exile away from the land, the questions that arise from Israel lay fallow for two thousand years. With the modern return to Israel, the need to interpret the meaning and practical expression of sacred service in the Jewish state arises afresh. The complex and difficult *texts* of the State of Israel pose a momentous project of study and practice. The Jewish literatures can yield meaning and depth to Zionism. This book begins to turn over some earth in the Jewish-Israeli garden of text and society, and calls to activate a neglected process of interpreting Jewish sources in relation to contemporary Israel.

Spiritual-Material Process

This book proposes "spiritual materialism," a process of embodying textual, spiritual and social practice. It invites world Jewry to collaboratively offer our gifts toward Zionism. The historical attainment of

---

47. The one Babylonian tractate from the Order *Zeraim* – *Brakhot* – sets out a theology of blessing.

our destination, the national sovereignty of the Jewish People, does not fulfill our destiny. It restores materiality to the national longing of the Jewish People for sacredness. Consider a contemporary Tibetan rumination on the struggle for statehood.

> "Our ultimate goal," Samdhong Rinpoche told me, "is not just political freedom but the preservation of Tibetan culture. What will we gain if we win political freedom but lose what gives value to our lives? It is why we reject the option of violence. For respect for life is an inseparable aspect of the Tibetan culture we are fighting for."[48]

Tibetans grapple with their nationalism, reevaluating their history, religious roots, texts and practices, strategizing for the present and future. They strive to constitute the meaning of an ancient and refined culture in the post-modern world, burdened by greater powers. Zionism must similarly face spiritual-material challenges. Like unfolding Tibetan nationalism, the quest for the meaning of Zionism transpires in the homeland and among dispersed communities whose identity and fate are inextricable from one another. Unlike the brutal Chinese occupation of Tibet, the State of Israel affords the opportunity for the Jewish People to freely enact Zionism. Nonetheless, we mostly hover at the cusp, at the boundary of dream and the possible. Some hesitate, some resist, some deny, some grope, some plead, some strive, some complain, as did the Israelites in the desert. In the land, the achievements of six decades of statehood have barely begun to actualize the accumulated capability of the Jewish People during thousands of years of exile.

A Palace in Space

Israel builds Abraham Joshua Heschel's amorphous "palace in time" – in space.[49] During the later period of his life, Heschel himself had a profound apprehension of modern Israel. Visiting the united city of Jerusalem in 1967, Heschel records his testimony,

48. Pankaj Mishra, "The Restless Children of the Dalai Lama," *New York Times*, Dec. 18, 2005.

49. See Chap. 2, "A Palace in Time" section.

At first I fainted. Then I saw: a wall of frozen tears, a cloud of sighs.

The Wall. Palimpsests hiding books, secret names. The stones are seals.

The Wall. The old mother crying for all of us. Stubborn, loving, waiting for redemption. The ground on which I stand is Amen. My words become echoes. All of our history is waiting here.

The Wall. No comeliness to be acclaimed, no beauty to be relished. But a heart and an ear. Its very being is compassion. You stand still and hear; stones of sorrow, acquaintance with grief. We all hide our faces from agony, shun the afflicted. The Wall is compassion, its face is open only to those smitten with grief.

When Jerusalem was destroyed, we were driven out; like sheep we have gone astray; we have turned, each one to his own way. The Wall alone stayed on.

What is the Wall? The unceasing marvel. Expectation. The Wall will not perish. The redeemer will come.

Silence. I embrace the stones. I pray: "O Rock of Israel, make our faith strong and your words luminous in our hearts and minds. No image. Pour holiness into our moments."

Once you have lived a moment at the Wall, you never go away.[50]

Standing before the Kotel, the Western Wall, Heschel senses the *eternity* of space, the embodiment of spiritual connection. He poetically melds the fiery lightness of word with the unbearable heaviness of stone. Yet, he claims, it is available only to those "smitten with grief," those who know the agony of the path which the remnant of the Jewish People has trod to that remnant of our sacred place. "Pour holiness into our moments" he implores, for he recognizes the precariousness of our mortal position in space, the newness of a sacred moment in sacred territory. Heschel's declarations of the impact of Israel on his own experience are profound, his articulations fresh.

What is the meaning of the State of Israel? Its sheer being is the message. . . . Israel is a personal challenge, a personal religious issue. It

---

50. Abraham Joshua Heschel, Susannah Heschel, ed., *Moral Grandeur and Spiritual Audacity. Essays.* (New York: Farrar, Straus, Giroux, 1996), 283–5.

is a call to every one of us as an individual, a call which one cannot answer vicariously.[51]

Unlike the "palace in time" retreating from or transcending the material world, Heschel achieves an insight of the "sheer being" of Israel while he is *in* space. The existence of Israel is a binding imperative. Israel addresses "every one of us," he contends. We cannot fulfill our connection to Israel through proxies, nor through material gifts. Israel invokes a personal embodied obligation.

In her sixties, the State of Israel does not yet fulfill the covenant of the Jewish People and our longing for home. This book demonstrates how Zionisms are an ongoing and subtle process. Though Heschel once dismissed space as a less worthy pursuit – a finite domain of ownership – the land exceeds our mortal possession. There are no certain outcomes. If we continue to offer our creativity and perseverance, the Zion Cycle will spiral on.

The teachings and traditions that have borne us to this moment are valuable input into the Zionist process. Study, however, is insufficient. Rabbi Yitzchak HaCohen Kook, one of the masters of religious Zionism, perceives the need for critical, embodied engagement.

> From the well of kindness, your love for humanity must burst forth – not as an unreasoned commandment, for then it would lose the most clear aspect of its brilliance, but as a powerful movement of the spirit within you.
>
> This love must withstand very difficult challenges. It must overcome many contradictions, which are scattered like boulders upon which you may stumble. These are found in isolated Torah statements, in the superficial aspect of some Torah laws, and in a multitude of points of view that stem from the constriction within the revealed aspect of the Torah and the national ethical sense.[52]

Rav Kook points critically to the narrowness of the interpretation of Torah and commandments. In his day and in ours, Torah study can act as an obstacle to the development of Zionism. Each generation must revision, reformulate, reconstruct; each of us can apply mind, body,

---

51. Abraham Joshua Heschel, *Israel: An Echo of Eternity*, (New York: Farrar, Straus and Giroux, 1967, 1969 edition), 224–5.

52. *Orot Ha-Kodesh*, 3, 318.

and spirit toward next steps, and new leaps. According to Rav Kook, love for humanity must guide the study and meaning of Torah. It must be an inner process as well as a public conversation. Kook imagines Zionism as the project that binds the Jewish nation, religious and secular. Recent decades call into question the success of Kook's conception.

The Road Ahead

Returning to the theme of liberation, the biblical Exodus enacts an inspiring narrative that sustains the Jewish People throughout thousands of years of journeying. While Pharaoh presents a violent threat to an inchoate nation, later generations of the Jewish People face this, as well as more subtle and complex challenges – cultural seductions and crises of meaning and identity. The Exodus sets out from persecution toward liberation with the goal to arrive in the land. Previous generations did not have the capability to envision Zionism far beyond survival and building the material infrastructure of Israel. With the attainment of the material goal, we recognize that Exodus is an ongoing narrative – it is up to us to write the sequels.

ReReading Israel focuses on the next chapters of Jewish experience, on deepening the Zionist process. Engaging faith, commitment, and political action, Exodus aspires to continuously, critically renew liberation. Now that we are more the authors of our destiny than ever before, how can Israel embody sacred processes for working out Jewish destiny while embracing peaceful coexistence and ever-refining ethical conduct? Are we committed enough to the sanctity of space without capitulating to the machismo of territorial possessiveness that fuels conquest, conflict, and draws blood? How will the Jewish People subdue our ethnocentrism, while honoring our uniqueness? These questions arise for Jews and Israelis as the West reevaluates national identity. There is "a new frankness" emerging in Europe about how to protect national culture along with open-mindedness.[53]

------

53. In Germany, Chancellor Angela Merkel has now expressed concern about supposed violent tendencies of fundamentalist Muslim youth ("We can talk about it without suspicion of being anti-foreigner"). And she has said that "severity" is an important factor in dealing with those immigrants who resist integration – an attitude she described as far away from the previous emphasis on multiculturalism. John Vinocur, "A New Shift in Candor on Immigrants," *New York Times*, 20/09/2010,

The Winograd Interim Report continues,

> [The] emphasis on learning lessons does not only follow from our
> conception of the role of a public Commission. It also follows from
> our belief that one of Israeli society's greatest sources of strength is
> its being free, open and creative. Together with great achievements,
> the challenges facing it are existential. To cope with them, Israel must
> be a learning society – a society which examines its achievements
> and, in particular, its failures, in order to improve its ability to face
> the future.[54]

The authors of the report emphasize, "Israel must be a learning
society." Beyond the search for personal fulfillment, each member of
the Jewish People is called upon to take part in the learning process
that is Zionism. Together, both in concert and contradiction of one
another, we can strive to enact our ever more inspired humanity. Loving compassion – with each other, our partners and opponents, and
with creation – are vital elements in the program for improvement. We
must continuously demonstrate our worthiness to inhabit the land.

For thousands of years, the text enterprise inspired the Jewish mind
and spirit. In exile, Jews built visions, theories, and prepared longingly
to traverse the unfathomable distance that separated us from our sacred
home – a distance not measurable only geographically, but emotionally, spiritually, and politically. In terms of survival and legitimacy, the
bold experiment that Zionism pursues reaches far beyond survival,
assimilation, beyond self-denial and fear. Israel beckons diverse and
far-flung Jewry toward extraordinary challenge and fulfillment.

There is no conclusion to these chapters, for the purpose is to travel
ahead on the Zion Cycle, humble, grateful, and willing to offer our
unique contributions. This is an historic moment for our generation
to step forward with desire for Zion aroused. The destiny of Israel – a
precious, shared, and unfinished sacred project – is, ultimately, our
responsibility.

---

retrieved Sept. 21, 2010, www.nytimes.com/2010/09/21/world/europe/21iht-
politicus.html?ref=europe.

54. Winograd Report, May 2006, www.mfa.gov.il/MFA/Government/
Communiques/2007/Winograd+Inquiry+Commission+submits+Interim+Rep
ort+30-Apr-2007.htm.

About the Author

BONNA DEVORA HABERMAN has taught at the Hebrew University, at Harvard University and at Brandeis University, where she founded and directed the Mistabra Institute for Textual Activism, addressing difficult social problems with creative strategies and performance arts. Having grown up in Canada, Bonna studied in the US and England, earning her doctorate in Ethics and Education at the University of London. Dr. Haberman's work in and out of the academy fuses critical interpretation of texts and culture with passion for social betterment. She moved to Israel in 1986, where she helped initiate a movement for women's public participation and leadership in Judaism and religious pluralism, "Women of the Wall." She has published widely in scholarly and popular venues. Among her endeavors, Bonna co-directs YTheater, an Israeli-Palestinian community theater project. Bonna, her spouse, and five children live in Israel.